Gods, Emperors, Philosophers, and a New Movement

Gods, Emperors, Philosophers, and a New Movement

Discovering the Movement of God in the Archaeological Record of Asia Minor

MICHAEL T. COOPER

Foreword by MICHAEL FROST

WIPF & STOCK · Eugene, Oregon

GODS, EMPERORS, PHILOSOPHERS, AND A NEW MOVEMENT
Discovering the Movement of God in the Archaeological Record of Asia Minor

Wipf & Stock
An Imprint of Wipf and Stock Publishers
199 W. 8th Ave., Suite 3
Eugene, OR 97401

www.wipfandstock.com

PAPERBACK ISBN: 979-8-3852-3578-0
HARDCOVER ISBN: 979-8-3852-3579-7
EBOOK ISBN: 979-8-3852-3580-3

To James Michael and Timothy Kaylor

The world feels pretty perfect at the moment, although I know it's not true. Complete might be more theologically accurate. Now that you both are here, there will be so many things I want to show you. We'll dig in the dirt and go on adventures. We'll discover new things and be super excited when we do. We'll think deeply about missiological theology and be amazed at how God reaches people with good news. I want to show you planets and stars and take you to places few have seen. We'll be curious together and explore. We'll wonder and marvel about all we learn. So, perhaps the world isn't perfect, but it is certainly more complete now that you are here. I love you boys!

Contents

Timelines

PRE-ROMAN ERA (BEFORE 27 BC)

- Tenth century BC: Smyrna boasts a long history dating from this period
- Seventh century BC: Smyrna is occupied by the Ionians
- Seventh century BC: the Lydian Empire, with Sardis as its capital, flourishes
- Sixth century BC: the philosopher Heraclitus articulates his *logos* philosophy in Ephesos
- Sixth century BC: Smyrna is destroyed by the Lydians; its inhabitants live in villages for approximately four hundred years
- Fourth century BC: the city of Smyrna is "resurrected" in a dream where the twin goddesses Nemeseis visit Alexander the Great
- Third century BC: the *prytaneion* in Ephesos is constructed during reign of Lysimachos
- 263–241 BC: Eumenes I of Pergamon receives divine honors after defeating Antiochus I
- 260 BC: Laodicea is constructed by Seleucid ruler Antiochus II, built upon an earlier settlement known as Diospolis (city of Zeus)
- 241–197 BC: Attalos I of Pergamon accepts titles of "king" and "savior" after defeating the Gauls
- Second century BC: Laodicea becomes part of the Roman Empire
- 197–159 BC: Eumenes II of Pergamon accepts titles "savior" and "divine benefactor"; the Great Altar of Zeus is built during his reign

- Second century BC: Philadelphia is founded during the Attalid dynasty, named after the brotherly love between Eumenes II and Attalos II
- Second century BC: Crates, a Stoic philosopher, becomes the head of the Pergamene library and school, emphasizing Aristotelian and Stoic philosophy; Judaism experiences rapid expansion in the Hellenistic world due to proselytizing
- Second Century BC (later): Jews are well-established in Ephesos
- 167 BC: Antiochus IV, the Seleucid king, desecrates the Jewish Temple in Jerusalem
- 178th Year (likely second century BC, specific date unclear): an inscription at Triglia in Bithynia depicts an honorific sacrifice to Cybele and Apollo at a *synagōgē* (gathering place)
- First century BC (early): Dionysos *Kathegemon* is associated with Pergamon.
- First century BC (mid): John Hyrcanus II, ethnarch of the Jews under Julius Caesar, secures concessions for Jews in the Roman Republic; Jews in Ephesos, including Roman citizens, are granted rights to religious ceremonies and military exemption
- 29 BC: Augustus commissions a temple in Pergamon, solidifying Roman control in Asia Minor

EARLY IMPERIAL ROMAN PERIOD (FIRST CENTURY AD)

- ca. 10s AD: Theophilos is born in Ephesos; his grandfather, Memnon, is the *grammateus* (town clerk) and includes Theophilos's name on coins, indicating his prominence
- AD 14–37 (Tiberius' reign): Theophilos becomes a Kouretes in Ephesos, serving in ritual processions for Artemis
- AD 17: catastrophic earthquake devastates Philadelphia and Sardis; Philadelphia is briefly renamed Neocaesarea in honor of Tiberius
- AD 23: Tiberius commissions a temple in Smyrna, granting it *neokoros* status; an earthquake causes changes in Ephesos, shifting the focus of Artemis celebration to the prytaneion.

- AD 38–54 (Claudius' reign): Theophilos in Ephesos, possibly having acquired Roman citizenship as "Claudius Theophilos," becomes a *neopoi* (temple administrator) or *hiereus* (priest) of Artemis
- AD 40: Gaius Caligula commissions a temple in Miletos, granting it *neokoros* status (later revoked in AD 41)
- AD 49: Claudius disperses Jews from Rome, leading to various trials for Christians
- Late 40s AD: Paul and his associates begin missionary endeavors in Galatia
- AD 51: Paul visits Corinth and resides there for nearly two years, engaging with trade guilds and philosophers
- AD 52: Paul departs Corinth, leaving a community of Christ followers; Priscilla and Aquila travel with him to Ephesos; Paul dialogues with Jews and Greeks in a *synagōgē* in Ephesos
- AD 50s–60s: Luke's Gospel and Acts are composed, addressed to Theophilos
- AD 54–68 (Nero's reign): Paul stands before Nero; Theophilos in Ephesos, now 40s–50s, becomes *patrogeron* (patriarch) and likely converts to Christianity
- AD 60: earthquake devastates Laodicea, Hierapolis, and Colossae; Laodicea refuses Roman aid and reconstructs independently; Colossae does not recover until the second century AD
- AD 66–73: Jewish–Roman wars and destruction of temple in AD 70
- AD 70–90 (late first century): 1 Clement, a Christian text from Rome, references God as "Almighty" (*pantokratoros*)
- AD 81–96 (Domitian's reign): Ephesos receives its second *neokoros* status; Domitian issues a controversial decree ordering the destruction of half the vineyards in Asia Minor; Philadelphians resist.
- Late first to early second century AD: the Didache, an early Christian text, uses "Master Almighty" in eucharistic prayer
- End of first century AD: Christianity is well-established in Smyrna

SECOND CENTURY AD

- Early second century AD: migration from Asia Minor to Gaul is not uncommon
- AD 110: Ignatius of Antioch, on his way to martyrdom in Rome, writes letters to the churches in Smyrna and Magnesia, equating *logos* with Christ.
- AD 117–138 (Hadrian's reign): Ephesos receives its third *neokoros* status; persecution of Christians occurs in Bithynia and likely extends to Pergamon, a judicial center; Emperor Hadrian is declared god and savior in Pergamon
- AD 125: Roger Bagnall dates the Smyrna logos word squares to this year
- AD 138–161 (Antoninus Pius's reign): the temple of Artemis in Philadelphia is depicted as dipteral and tripteral on coins
- AD 150–220: Clement of Alexandria writes *Paedagogus*, hinting at Christians "going to church"
- AD 152: Theodotus, a bishop of Pergamon, allegedly deposes the heresy of the Colarbasians at an undocumented synod (unreliable tradition)
- ca. AD 156: martyrdom of Polycarp in Smyrna
- AD 160–181: the Epistle to Diognetus, a Christian text, uses "Almighty and All-Creator" for God
- Mid-second century AD: Montanism (New Prophecy) emerges in Phrygia/Lydia, around Philadelphia, espousing new revelations and ecstatic experiences
- Mid-second century AD: Galen, a physician and philosopher from Pergamon, critiques Christians for their lack of arguments
- Late second century AD: Irenaeus suggests John appointed Polycarp as bishop of Smyrna
- ca. AD 177 (Marcus Aurelius's reign): persecution breaks out in Lyon and Vienne, Gaul, leading to the martyrdom of Attalos from Pergamon
- AD 177–192 (Commodus's reign): Laodicea achieves *neokoros* status

- AD 178: earthquake destroys the Smyrna agora, which is later reconstructed by Marcus Aurelius
- Late second to early third century AD: Tertullian suggests that John appointed Polycarp as bishop of Smyrna

THIRD CENTURY AD

- Early third century AD: the Chester Beatty collection (𝔓45) papyrus codex, containing the Gospels and Acts, dates to the first half of the third century.
- ca. AD 200: the Talmud suggests 394 Judean synagogues in Jerusalem before the temple's destruction
- AD 205 (March 7): Saturus, Saturninus, Revocatus, Secundulus, Felicitas, and Perpetua are martyred in Carthage
- AD 218–222 (Elagabalus's reign): Laodicea is identified as *neokoros* in the numismatic record
- AD 249–251 (Decius's reign): martyrdom of Karpos (bishop from Lydia) and Papylos (deacon from Thyatira) in Pergamon; Agathonike, converted by their work, also chooses martyrdom; Dionysos appears on Philadelphia coins no fewer than fourteen times until this reign
- AD 250: Nemeseion in Smyrna is the scene of a struggle between magistrates and Christians over sacrificing to Emperor Decius
- AD 253–268 (Gallienus's reign): images of Cybele appear in the numismatic record of Smyrna
- Third to fourth century AD: the Sardis "synagogue" (later repurposed for Christian use) is dated to this period
- Third century AD: Neoplatonism rises, offering an alternative spiritual worldview; the Library of Pergamon is less dominant but still a significant intellectual hub
- Third century AD: the Sardis synagogue undergoes its second stage renovation

FOURTH CENTURY AD

- AD 300–900: Christian symbols acquire apotropaic properties and are used to ward off evil
- Early fourth century AD: an inscription honors Gennadeios, a "shepherd of sheep" who died for holy Scriptures, possibly a Montanist
- AD 324: church of St. John Lateran founded in Rome
- AD 330: Constantine moves the capital to Byzantium, gradually leading to the Byzantine Empire
- ca. AD 340: Dracontius, a bishop of Pergamon, is allegedly deposed at a Synod of Gangra (details unreliable)
- Mid-fourth century AD: the Sardis Synagogue becomes a site of Christian gathering and undergoes its final stage renovation
- Late fourth century AD (last quarter): the Regina inscription in the Sardis Synagogue is dated to no earlier than this period; destruction of paganism advances "apace" at the hands of missionary bishops, monks, and pious individuals
- Fourth century AD: Aedesius of Pergamon carries on the peripatetic tradition; streams of Montanism shift toward modalistic theology

FIFTH CENTURY AD

- AD 431: third ecumenical council held at Ephesos, condemning Nestorius and affirming Mary as Theotokos; most likely held at the temple-church once the site of the worship of Serapis
- AD 474: Church of St. Mary built in Ephesos within the Olympeion temenos

SIXTH CENTURY AD

- Sixth century AD: Montanism endures until this century

- AD 507–588: John of Ephesos, a Miaphysite missionary and historian, travels to Pergamon to destroy the Altar of Zeus

SEVENTH CENTURY AD

- AD 602–628: climactic Byzantine–Sasanian War
- AD 614: Persian sack of Jerusalem, Church of the Holy Sepulcher razed
- AD 615: Persians invade Sardis, burning buildings and causing the disappearance of the numismatic record; the Sardis synagogue, likely repurposed as a Christian church, is destroyed

ROMAN EMPERORS

The following timelines represent the emperors mentioned in the book.

Augustus (27 BC–AD 14)

- Commissioned a temple in Pergamon in 29 BC
- Theophilos was born during his reign, likely in the 10s AD
- Coins minted during his reign reveal the legend "grammateus Memnon, of the Ephesians, Theophilos"
- Later coins conferred divine status on him as "Caesar Augustus god"

Tiberius (AD 14–37)

- Commissioned a temple in Smyrna in AD 23
- During his reign, Theophilos, the grandson of Memnon, was in his twenties and a member of the Kouretes.
- The numismatic record from his reign testifies to the deification of living emperors
- After the catastrophic earthquake of AD 17, Philadelphia was briefly renamed Neocaesarea in his honor

Gaius Caligula (AD 37–41)

- Commissioned a temple in Miletos in AD 40, though its *neokoros* status was revoked by the Roman senate in AD 41

Claudius (AD 41–54)

- Christians dispersed from Rome experienced trials during his reign, around AD 49
- During his reign, one of the Theophiloses acquired the praenomen Claudius, potentially becoming a *neopoi* (temple administrator) or *hiereus* (priest)
- Images of Cybele appear in the numismatic record beginning in his reign
- The Roman emperor Claudius held no consideration for vocational associations as they could be a political threat

Nero (AD 54–68)

- The apostle Paul ultimately stood before him by the end of Luke's account in Acts
- Paul wrote to Timothy during his reign, urging Christians to pray for kings
- Theophilos became a *patrogeron* (patriarch) around the 60s AD during his reign
- Laodicea famously refused his offer of help to reconstruct after the earthquake of AD 60

Vespasian (AD 69–79)

- Philadelphia briefly bore the name Flavia under him
- He was honored in Laodicea with a sports stadium

Domitian (AD 81–96)

- Ephesos's second neokoros status was granted during his reign
- Issued a controversial decree ordering the destruction of half the vineyards in Asia Minor, which the Philadelphians resisted

- Honored in Laodicea with a dedicatory inscription on the Syrian and Ephesian gates

Nerva (AD 96–98)

- An inscription dedicated to him and Trajan reads "son of the divine Nerva"
- T. Statilius Kriton served as procurator for Emperor Nerva Trajan Caesar Augustus

Trajan (AD 98–117)

- Conferred divine status in Pergamon while alive
- Celebrated across Asia Minor with monikers like *germanikon* and *dakiko* for his military victories
- Pliny the Younger's letter (10.96) to Trajan described persecution in Bithynia
- The rise of Zeus Philios in Pergamon occurred under his reign
- Dionysos appeared on Philadelphia's coins from his reign to Decius's
- Honored in Laodicea with a fountain.

Hadrian (AD 117–138)

- Ephesos's third neokoros status was established by him
- A marble base in Smyrna proclaims him as Caesar Augustus, an Olympian god, and savior
- His adoptive father, Trajan, was declared "divine"
- Persecution likely extended to Pergamon during his reign
- He was honored in Laodicea with a bath–gymnasium complex
- A group of Greek-speaking Christians from Asia Minor, including Attalos from Pergamon, were martyred in Gaul during the reign of Marcus Aurelius, possibly influenced by Hadrian's era of persecution

Antoninus Pius (AD 138–161)

- The temple of Artemis in Philadelphia was depicted as dipteral on coins during his reign

Marcus Aurelius (AD 161–180)

- The Smyrna agora was reconstructed by him following its destruction by an earthquake in AD 178
- Christians from Gaul, including Attalos from Pergamon, were martyred around 177 AD during his reign
- The temple of Artemis in Philadelphia was depicted as dipteral on coins during his reign

Lucius Verus (AD 161–169)

- Co-emperor with Marcus Aurelius

Commodus (AD 177–192)

- Laodicea eventually achieved *neokoros* status under his rule

Caracalla (AD 198–217)

- Philadelphia was granted neokoros status under him
- Honored in Laodicea with the cult of the sebastos

Geta (AD 209–211)

- Co-emperor with Septimius Severus and Caracalla

Severus Alexander (AD 222–235)

- The temple of Aphrodite in Philadelphia is depicted as dipteral during his reign

Decius (AD 249–251)

- Bishop Karpos from Lydia and Papylos from Thyatira stood before the proconsul in Pergamon during his reign and were martyred

- Dionysos appeared on coins from Trajan's reign up to Decius's reign

Gallienus (AD 253–268)

- Images of Cybele appear in the numismatic record through his reign

Diocletian (late 3rd–early 4th century)

- He was honored in Laodicea with two columns celebrating the twentieth year of his reign

Constantine the Great (early fourth century; reign begins AD 306)

- Christianity was legalized during his time
- The Church of St. John Lateran in Rome was founded in AD 324
- He moved the capital to Byzantium in AD 330
- The Laodicea Church was built at the time of Constantine the Great
- Montanist presence was still visible in inscriptions as late as the Constantinian period

Julian (the Apostate) (AD 361–363)

- Constantine the Great's nephew, he renounced Christianity and attempted to restore traditional Greco-Roman religions
- Pergamon's continued importance as a philosophical and religious stronghold factored into Julian's efforts

List of Tables

List of Maps

List of Photographs

Foreword

I'm neither an archaeologist nor an ancient historian, but I've come to value the enormous contribution both disciplines make to my field of missiology. Certainly, without the anchoring in history that those disciplines offer, missiology can become untethered and inclined toward mere pragmatics. Indeed, Michael Cooper makes this very point in the volume you're now reading. In his meticulous reconstruction of the sociopolitical and religious dynamics of life in early centuries AD Asia Minor, Cooper reveals the care taken by the earliest Christians to communicate the message of Jesus Christ to all levels of society with both clarity and integrity. And he commends mission practitioners to be equally careful today.

Some years ago, together with my colleague Dr. Darrell Jackson, I led a student field trip looking at both ancient and contemporary expressions of Christian missions in Europe. Our itinerary included a visit to the ruins of Pompeii. Taking seriously the old Mortimer Wheeler quote about archaeology being a science that must be lived ("dead archaeology is the driest dust that blows"), we figured a walk through the cobbled streets of the abandoned ancient city would allow our students to imagine what life might have been like for the earliest Christians. Of course, it's a contested point as to whether there was a Christian community in Pompeii. In his book *The Crosses of Pompeii*, Baylor professor Bruce Longenecker analyzes over twenty examples of *Christianos graffito* found among the ruins—crosses, slogans, and symbols—and concludes that they must point to the existence of a small but recognizable Christian presence prior to the eruption of Mount Vesuvius. But our reason for taking students there was so that the site could stand in for *any* ancient Roman town. The catastrophe of AD 79 had frozen the city in time, creating a remarkably intact snapshot of Roman life. Walking through it stimulates your imagination like nothing else.

Not being ancient historians, we invited Jim Memory, a lecturer in European missions at All Nations Christian College (UK), to lead this leg of our tour, exploring the well-preserved buildings, streets, and public spaces like the forum and amphitheater, in order to help us imagine how early Christians would have lived, where they might have met, and how they might have lived out their faith. He took us to a housing complex and got us to imagine if a Christian family had lived in one of the small apartments. He explained how that family might have hosted a weekly Christian love feast in the common garden area. He took us to a take-out food servery that had recently been excavated, its counter dotted with holes in which vats of food would bubble away over open fires. Here, he fantasized, Christians could have purchased food to bring to the common table we imagined earlier.

As we passed by the one remaining triumphal arch of the grand Temple of Jupiter, it occurred to us how warm and rustic these love feasts must have been by comparison with pagan temple worship. We read aloud from 1 Cor 14:26—"When you come together, each of you has a hymn, or a word of instruction, a revelation, a tongue or an interpretation. Everything must be done so that the church may be built up"—and Col 3:11—"Here there is no Gentile or Jew, circumcised or uncircumcised, barbarian, Scythian, slave or free, but Christ is all, and is in all." This conjured images of a multiethnic, intergenerational community of women and men worshiping and learning together, each contributing to the liturgy. As Stanley Hauerwas observes, quoting John Yoder,

> It was a society that, counter to all precedent, was mixed in its composition. It was mixed racially, with both Jews and Gentiles. It was mixed religiously, with fanatical keepers of the law and advocates of liberty from all forms; with both radical monotheists and others just in the process of disentangling their minds from idolatry. It was mixed economically with members both rich and poor.[1]

Jim Memory compared these love feasts with the more common guild meetings that happened routinely in ancient Roman cities. At guild dinners, only men from the same trade or profession were welcome.

1. Hauerwas, *Matthew*, 67.

Prayers and incantations were offered to the pagan gods that patronized their industry in hope of continued success and prosperity. Burnt offerings were made, the smoke rising to the heavens in the vain hope of tickling the nostrils of their patron deities. Outsiders—women, the enslaved, immigrants, the poor—were not only uninvited, they were ignored.

But Christian love feasts were expressions of audacious hospitality. In fact, there was nothing else like it in the ancient world. Outsiders were welcomed to the table. They were invited to share the Christians' meat and wine. Prayers were offered, not skyward, but in the sure hope that whenever two or three gathered Christ was right there in their midst. Indeed, in the strange ritual of breaking bread and drinking wine, the earliest Christians proclaimed their Lord's presence even as they anticipated his return. It's been said that the early Christians didn't conquer the Roman Empire with swords and spears, but with tables. All this came to beautiful light for me as the late afternoon sun was making long shadows over the cobbled streets of one of the world's most famous archaeological sites.

Michael Cooper's research, captured in this book, goes even further than my memorable time in Pompeii. Through his studies in archaeology, he proves that the earliest Christians were a radical, loving, united community focused not only on the practice of hospitality, but also on the well-being of the people in a city. They sought out influential patrons as well as serving the lowest of the low. Whether they met in a courtyard in Pompeii, or a lecture hall in Ephesos, or a trade guild in Sardis, or a theater in Laodicea, they were learning how to shift their allegiance from cruel and capricious gods and goddesses to the king of kings, Jesus Christ. And they were committed to alerting their neighbors to his good and beautiful kingdom of liberation, healing, justice, and joy.

As Cooper points out, there are a lot of anachronistic things said about the growth of the early church. Sadly, some missional writers simply observe what's happening in various parts of the world today and read those patterns back into the biblical text. That's why we need ancient historians to draw from both archaeology and Scripture to help us better understand the world of the New Testament, which in turn instructs us on how to live missionally in our complex, pluralistic world. Ultimately, I think what we all want is a clearer, truer vision of Jesus, and discovering how ancient Christians were shaped by their belief in him as well as how they presented him to a brutal polytheistic empire is absolutely essential to our current missional task.

Dr. Michael Frost
Morling College, Sydney

Acknowledgments

ONE OF THE HIGHLIGHTS of my academic career was teaching a class on cultural engagement with Michael (Mike) Card, Scott Roley, and Charles Robinson. We met Mike and Scott on the evening of my wife Loré's birthday in 2010. Mike had been invited to lead a couple chapel services at Trinity International University and consequently invited to a faculty dinner one evening. I noticed him standing in the midst of some of the administrators and I asked Loré if she wanted to meet him. So, we approached Mike and I introduced Loré.

I had never met him but Loré and I both enjoyed Mike's music tremendously. He is one of the few theologically conscientious Christian music artists, which bears prominently in his music. During the course of the conversation, we were introduced to Scott Roley, Mike's longtime friend and pastor. We struck up quite a conversation that extended over dinner, into the next day after chapel, and ultimately resulted in a graduate course.

He might actually be one of the primary people responsible for my archaeological research. He graciously interviewed me for his podcast when *Ephesiology: A Study of the Ephesian Movement* was published in 2020. I don't think the podcast ever aired, or if it did I missed it. Nevertheless, his question regarding whether my research included a visit to Ephesos challenged me, and, frankly, embarrassed me as I had not visited the city. I'm grateful for his challenge.

Several other people have contributed to my interest in archaeology over the years. First, Dr. James Hoffmeier introduced me to the Old Testament world of archaeology during my doctoral studies at Trinity Evangelical Divinity School. His influence is seen throughout this volume in my use of the Christian era dating convention of BC–AD.

During the course of my research, several students traveled with me on research trips as their insatiable curiosity about the early church continued to spark my imagination. Those students included Dr. Michelle Wegner, David Brunelle, Wade Mantlo, Praveen Emmanuel, Matthew Harbour, Kevin Mast, and Aki Gibson. This group epitomizes what it means to do theology in community. These research trips would not have been possible without the invaluable help of Sonat Fisek, Levent Oral, and the team at Tutku Educational Tours.

Colleagues working in the region often referred to as MENA merit mention as well, although their names cannot be included in print. Even so, they know who they are and their passion for movements inspired many of the conclusions in this book. Additionally, I'm grateful for a learning community of missiologists, missionary trainers, and missionaries who met during the months of June and July 2025, to discuss the book in the course Archaeology and Early Christian Missiology. They helped sharpen and clarify some of my thinking. Their insights, observations, and thoughts regarding application in their missions contexts were extremely helpful.

Our family plays a formative role in what I do. Two of our newest members have already received attention. Yet all of them form in me an insatiable appetite and curiosity for discovery. They are the reason I do what I do, but please do not blame them for my idiosyncrasies.

Chapter 1

Filling a Missiological Gap

Years ago, Mark Noll alluded to the idea that who better to dive into the complexities of history than a missiologist.[1] The missiologist holds the skill set to navigate cultural issues and sort through particularities and nuance while being comfortable with tensions that such issues present. In many ways, I believe the same might be said for the missiologist's engagement in the field of archaeology. As a discipline, archaeology naturally addresses the layers of human existence: religion, politics, economics, philosophy, language, and symbols—areas of culture where the missiologist probes deeply. Naturally, it would seem that the intersection of archaeology and missiology holds the potential for a promising field of research in the areas of material culture and the history of the Christian movement. Such an intersection might offer insights into the relationship between architecture, ritual development, cultural studies, biblical studies, and indigenous civilizations. It could not only bridge disciplines but also unearth a treasure trove of knowledge that enriches and illuminates our understanding of culture, religious practices, and the human experience.[2] This is the scope of *Gods, Emperors, Philosophers, and a New Movement: Discovering the Movement of God in the Archaeological Record of Asia Minor.*

At its core, I will propose that the relationship between missiology and archaeology serves to unveil God's movement in the material context in which Christianity emerged and allow us to see evidence for the mission of God in the early centuries. Archaeological excavations uncover

1. Noll, "Challenge," 61.

2. Graham, "Mission Archaeology"; Ross, "Archaeology of Mission."

artifacts, monuments, and inscriptions that provide tangible links to the past as they elucidate the societal, cultural, and religious landscapes in which Christian missions advanced. In a very real sense, archaeology can "fill the gap left in the historical record"[3] as well as the missiological one. This historical and material context is essential for comprehending the challenges that shaped the course of Christian engagement with diverse ethnic groups. When illuminated by archaeology, the study of early Christian missiology enhances our ability to interpret the biblical texts and historical narratives related to the growth of Christianity in its early centuries. The interdisciplinary collaboration fosters a more comprehensive story of Christianity's adaptation to various cultural realities.

Beyond the academic inquiry, the interaction between missiology and archaeology holds practical implications for contemporary missions work. Insights gleaned from past missionary efforts inform strategic approaches, cultural sensitivity, and contextual engagement in contemporary contexts. By learning from the successes and challenges of early missionaries, contemporary practitioners can navigate complex cultural landscapes with greater wisdom, empathy, and effectiveness. In essence, the intersection of missiology and archaeology opens doors to a holistic exploration of history, faith, and culture that models a missiological exegesis of ancient sites in order to illustrate early missionary activity. It invites us to embark on a journey of curiosity, discovery, and wonder that transcends disciplinary boundaries whereby we deepen our appreciation for the rich tapestry of ancient human experience woven through the ages as it challenges us to answer the question of why it is important for today.

Gods, Emperors, Philosophers, and a New Movement delves into this fascinating interdisciplinary intersection by considering the archaeological excavations of Asia Minor and their implications for our understanding of the early mission and church. But why Asia Minor? Most of the New Testament (NT) connects directly with the region. We often think of Ephesians, Colossians, Philemon, 1 and 2 Timothy, Revelation, as well as two chapters in Acts as the most relevant NT documents associated with Asia Minor. In and of themselves, that is a significant corpus of sources. However, NT scholars identify the provenance of 1 Corinthians, as well as 1, 2, and 3 John as Ephesos, not to mention that the destination of 1 and 2 Peter includes Asia Minor. Most scholars also agree that the Gospel of John was written from Ephesos. However, few hold to the significance

3. King and McGranaghan, "Archaeology and Materiality," 629

that the Ephesian context played on John's stories about Jesus. Instead, some commentators on the Fourth Gospel argue that the letter applies as much to Ephesos as any metropolitan city in the Roman Empire, something I argued as an overstatement.[4] Ignoring the cultural context of Ephesos impedes our understanding of the uniqueness of John compared to the Synoptics. Outside of these letters, I suggest both Hebrews and the two volume set, Luke-Acts, were addressed to those in Ephesos. As we'll see in chapter 3, Theophilos, Luke's addressee, resided in Ephesos as one of the civic and religious elite. So, if my count is correct, sixteen of the twenty-seven books of the NT are directly tied to Asia Minor and we should safely assume that Asia Minor influenced them in ways that we can observe in the archaeological record. Additionally, just as much as the cultures of Asia Minor provide the background for our understanding of the NT, so they also provide the fertile soil in which we might cultivate the field of early Christian missiology. I trust this will become increasingly clear throughout the book.

As we journey through the material evidence of Asia Minor, we'll observe a rich mosaic of cultural, religious, and archaeological significance that offers a unique lens through which we understand the NT and early Christian missions as well as their impact on a region. Indeed, as David deSilva recognizes, "The fruits of archaeology, visible for us in well-curated sites and museums, provide us with a great deal of raw material for such reflection."[5] The present book seeks to unravel the threads of history and faith intertwined in Asia Minor's material past by exploring how archaeological discoveries shed light as much on the theological formation of the church as on the missiological application out of which the church's theology emerged. The contextual challenges faced by early Christian communities will become progressively apparent in our investigation. By digging into the excavations and discoveries in Asia Minor, we uncover not just the physical remnants of an ancient civilization, but also the spiritual and cultural dynamics that shaped the region; a task we might rightly call archaeological exegesis. From ancient *graffito* and *spolia* to architectural marvels, artifacts, and structures unearthed in Asia Minor, we'll hear the stories of religious zeal, community resilience, and the adaptive nature of *ekklēsia* in a dynamic missiology of the NT. Through this exploration, we aim to bridge the gap between missiological theory and archaeological discovery, offering insights into how past missions

4. Cooper, *Ephesiology*, 83.

5. deSilva, *Archaeology*, xii.

navigated cultural contexts and contributed to the spread of Christianity across Asia Minor. Ultimately, we want to know how archaeological exploration might inform our contemporary missiological practices so we conclude each chapter with some observations for application.

A MISSIOLOGICALLY UNDERUTILIZED TOOL

There is little doubt that archaeology has been an underutilized tool in missiology. A few scholars studying the colonial era have suggested that the discipline is important in understanding the development of missions.[6] As might be expected, archaeology of the colonial era reveals the impact of the missionary's material culture on the material culture of indigenous people whether in Africa, Asia, or the Americas. Not completely unexpected, what the intersection of missiology and archaeology of the first Christian centuries reveal diverges significantly with the "mission archaeology" of the colonial era. For example, Elizabeth Graham rightly notes that archaeology unearths a colonialism inherent in missionary activities among the ethnic groups of North and South America. The material culture often exposes structures and religious artifacts foreign to the indigenous people. She states, "The overwhelming impression derived from mission archaeology is that Christianity is both monolithic and genetically European."[7]

That is not to say that European Christianity was immune to the indigenous culture. Christianity certainly changed in the New World just as it had changed when it first arrived in Europe.[8] The archaeological record indicates that missionary culture, along with aspects of its ecclesiology, was influenced by—and at times syncretized with—indigenous culture. Nevertheless, archaeological discoveries of current missionary practices also reveal the monolithic nature of the missionary's ecclesiology. Few, however, consider the implications of what archaeological data from the first centuries of Christianity might hold for our understanding of God's mission in Asia Minor as well as for our understanding of contemporary missiology. By considering these implications, I suggest, we increase the likelihood of avoiding a repetition of our colonial past.

6. Graham, "Mission Archaeology"; Ross, "Archaeology of Mission."

7. Graham, "Mission Archaeology," 29; See also King and McGranaghan, "Archaeology and Materiality."

8. Graham, "Mission Archaeology," 30.

The study of the first centuries AD archaeology is eminently important for missiology. It provides a deeply rich understanding of the material culture of ancient people. By weaving the disciplines of missiology and archaeology together, we recognize that first-century Christianity, devoid of pomp and circumstance, required allegiance while fourth-century Christianity, evolving in ritual and tradition, required membership. Indeed, early Christianity testifies to the fact that there was no identifiable architectural type for the *ekklēsia*. Instead, space was adapted and that space most often resided in places of peace (chapter 6) as well as in the private homes of wealthy saints.[9] Certainly this is not to be considered normative but rather adaptive as we observe the evolution of architectural spaces for Christian gathering.

HISTORY AND ARCHAEOLOGY

Alongside of archaeology, history might also be an underutilized tool of the missiologist. At least Noll seemed to be alluding to this when he called for missiologists to examine history. He writes, "Who in the tribe of Christian historians is in the best position to work simultaneously with aspects of the pre-modern, the modern, and the post-modern? The answer certainly must be missiologists."[10] However, history is largely an interpretive science. It is often colored by a reflexivity—the idea that the interpreter of history influences the interpretation with her own bias. For that matter, archaeology might also suffer from reflexivity. Indeed, Daniel Schowalter warns,

> As use and abuse of archaeological material becomes more common in New Testament studies, scholars must consider how to make such a comparison without allowing what we "know" from the text to overshadow what we can learn from either new archaeological evidence or a fresh reading of the archaeological record.[11]

Let me suggest five reasons why studying archaeology alongside history is crucial for missiologists:

9. White, *Building God's House*, 18–19.
10. Noll, "Challenge," 61.
11. Schowalter, "Seeking Shelter," 327.

1. Contextual understanding. History provides the background and context for archaeological findings. It helps archaeologists interpret artifacts, structures, and sites by placing them within a historical framework. Without historical knowledge, interpretations of archaeological evidence can be incomplete or inaccurate. Missiologists live in the world of contextual understanding. When exegeting the literary record of early Christian missiology, the missiologist avoids anachronisms when taking an interdisciplinary approach by incorporating archaeology and history in the exegetical act.

2. Chronological perspective. History offers a chronological perspective, allowing archaeologists to understand the development, evolution, and interactions of societies over time. This perspective is essential for tracing cultural changes, technological advancements, and societal shifts revealed through archaeological discoveries. In the study of culture, missiologists trace cultural trends over time and observe how such trends impact theological development. Including archaeology and history as research tools for early Christian missiology, missiologists illuminate the trajectory of theology.

3. Cultural insights. History provides insights into the political, religious, social, and economic aspects of past societies. These insights help archaeologists interpret artifacts in terms of their cultural significance, religious practices, social structures, and economic activities, leading to a deeper understanding of ancient civilizations. The missiologist benefits from such insights by entering dialogically with ancient culture for a better-informed understanding of early Christian missiology.

4. Validation and corroboration. Historical records often complement archaeological findings. They can validate or corroborate interpretations made based on archaeological evidence. For example, written records may mention events, people, or customs that align with archaeological discoveries, reinforcing the accuracy of archaeological interpretations. From a missiological perspective, the archaeological and historical records validate the tremendous growth of Christianity observed in the biblical record.

5. Interdisciplinary collaboration. The collaboration between historians and archaeologists fosters interdisciplinary approaches to studying the past. This collaboration allows for a more comprehensive

analysis of historical and archaeological data leading to richer narratives about human history. Including missiologists in such conversations moves discussions from interpretation to application. The eyes of the missiologist are keenly trained to observe evidence for Christian expansion and to utilize that evidence in developing strategic principles for contemporary missions.

Overall, combining history and archaeology in our missiological studies enhances our understanding of the past, enriches interpretations of archaeological findings, and contributes to a more holistic view of human societies and their cultural heritage as well as God's movement in those early centuries. Such an interdisciplinary approach adds to a greater depth of understanding and appreciation for the efforts of our ancestors. This approach promises to resolve contemporary anachronisms in church-planting movements (CPM) and disciple-making movements (DMM), as well as traditional church planting (chapter 10), and affirm innovatively adaptive methods for contemporary missions as God continues to make the missional move to people around the world.

ARCHAEOLOGY AND MISSIOLOGY

Archaeological evidence reveals the manner in which Christianity adapted to its material context. Missiologically speaking, this is significant for any contemporary application of early Christian missiology. However, we must keep at the front of our minds that archaeologists have only scratched the surface in Asia Minor. In spite of the magnificence of Ephesos, Pergamon, and Laodicea, for instance, only a fraction of those cities have been unearthed. Excavation of Colossae only began to uncover two thousand years of dirt in May of 2025. Even so, what we are learning from the archaeology of Asia Minor is that early Christianity arises from within ethnically diverse and religiously pluralistic cultures. In this context, it did not impose monolithic forms—which had not yet developed—on culture as we see in later colonial missions and even today in contemporary church planting.

Combined with the historiographic record, the picture that emerges from first centuries AD archaeology is a Christianity comfortable in its cultural context—architecture, language, clothing, customs, etc.—while sufficiently countercultural in order to present itself as a unique tradition or school of thought (*hairesis*). Indeed, as we will iterate repeatedly,

Christianity presents a missiological parallel to religion, politics, and philosophy that situates Jesus Christ, not in competition with but better than the current cultural expressions attempting to form ancient life.[12] More often than not, this juxtaposing of Jesus as *theos*, *logos*, *kyrios*, and *soter* for all people constitutes an implicit revelation of God's missional activity in preparation for the explicit revelation of the eternal gospel by faithful witnesses. Apart from missiology, such information remains confined to lecture halls and textbooks. They are intriguing, perhaps, but ultimately unengaged with the church's mission. Missiology brings such juxtapositions into clear view as intentional ways in which early missionaries engaged culture.

When we encounter the historiographic record of the New Testament, breathing the air of the geography and architecture, the text enlivens places where the early disciples walked and God moved. The knowledge and insights discovered in the material record of Asia Minor enrich the corpus of more than half of the NT. For example, once we understand the archaeological record of the Lycus Valley, we become aware that the first chapter of Colossians—intended as much for that city as for Laodicea and Hierapolis—reveals how culturally in tune Paul was with his audience. For Paul, cognizant of the sundry statues of gods, goddesses, and emperors imbued with powers, proposes a missiological parallel where Christ is the statue (*eikon*) of the invisible God (Col 1:15). Additionally, he states that in Christ dwells fullness (*pleroma*), obviously alluding to the Platonic and Neoplatonic ideas of completeness and totality of existence that transcends the material world (Col 1:19). In this case, the parallelism serves as a clarification of what had been expressed in Greek philosophy now fulfilled in Christ—an idea Justin Martyr will reiterate in the second century. Paul is also apparently aware of the geological area's susceptibility to earthquakes as he reminds the saints to "continue in faith, stable and steadfast, not shifting from the hope of the gospel" (Col 1:23).

What will be emerging in an interdisciplinary approach to the study of the early centuries of Christianity is a picture that will inform our understanding of early missiology and transform our contemporary missiology; at least I will attempt a compelling argument for this case. If I'm successful, we will begin to see how those first missionaries joined with God who had long been moving and orchestrating events in preparation

12. Amberg and Cooper, "Revisiting Contextualization."

for the announcement of good news. We will observe the adaptive nature of their work as they identified how he worked to bridge gaps in language, spaces, and worldviews so that Jesus Christ might be seen with unveiled eyes.

OUTLINE OF THE BOOK

Having established the significance of archaeology for shaping our understanding of missiology, this book explores how material culture—inscriptions, architecture, and artifacts—complements the biblical and historical record to illuminate the dynamics of early Christian mission. Each chapter examines a key archaeological discovery or historical context that informs our interpretation of the churches addressed in Revelation and offers insights into contemporary mission practice. However, do not take this volume as a rehearsing of William Ramsay's or Colin Hemer's magnificent treatments of the seven churches.[13] While I certainly draw from their excellent scholarship, I am primarily concerned for what we can learn about the missiological practices which contributed to the transformation of the people in those cities. From the obstacles faced by the churches in Asia Minor to the strategic engagement of cultural elites, marketplace influence, communal worship, and resilience amid opposition, the following chapters provide a blueprint for faithful and effective church planting today. By bridging the gap between past and present, this book aims to equip missionaries, church planters, and missiologists with a deeper, historically and archaeologically grounded understanding of the early Christian movement and its implications for global mission strategy.

Church	Commendation	Admonition	Warning	Reward
Ephesos	Patient endurance; stand against false apostles; hates the works of those who exploit women	Repent from abandoning the work of their first love	Removal of lampstand	Eat of the tree of life in paradise

13. Ramsay, *Seven Churches of Asia*; and Hemer, *Seven Churches of Asia*.

Church	Commendation	Admonition	Warning	Reward
Smyrna	Not to fear suffering; be faithful until death			Crown of life; not hurt by the second death
Pergamon	Did not deny faith	Some who continue to practice magic; eating food sacrificed to idols; sexual immorality; exploitation of women	Jesus will come and war against those who do not repent	Hidden manna; white stone with a new name
Thyatira	Faith, service, endurance, greater works; hold fast the faith	Tolerance of sexual immorality; eating food sacrificed to idols; learning the deep things of Satan	Throw practitioners into a great tribulation; children struck dead	Authority over nations; morning star
Sardis	A few who continue to walk with Christ	Dead works	Jesus will come against them like a thief	Clothed in white garment; never blot from book of life
Philadelphia	Kept the word; not denied Christ; hold fast			Keep them from the hour of trial; make a pillar in God's temple; write the name of God and his city on him; Jesus' new name

Church	Commendation	Admonition	Warning	Reward
Laodicea		Complacency; not recognizing true state; be zealous and repent	Jesus disciplines those he loves	Christ will dine with those who repent; sit with Christ on his throne

Table 1.1: Jesus and the seven churches[14]

To that end, chapter 2 examines the cultural context of Asia Minor and the various challenges early Christian missions faced. This historical and archaeological investigation of culture teaches us something about the missiology of those faithful witnesses. I hope we will see how much our study parallels contemporary missions challenges and opportunities. It highlights how missiological exegesis of culture demands a far deeper probing than sloppy evangelistic efforts informed by a once-saved-always-saved theology. Early missionary efforts purposefully engaged culture in order to see where God worked, and then joined with his work to bring to light what had remained in the shadow.

As our investigation continues, chapter 3 investigates epigraphic evidence for Theophilos as a key figure among the elite of Ephesos. By exploring his role in the city, the investigation reveals how contemporary missions must connect with prominent community members as a part of an effective missionary strategy. Chapter 4 delves into the inscriptions and graffiti found in the agora of ancient Smyrna, several of which help us understand the early Christian community there. By interpreting these graffiti, the chapter provides insights into the ways in which Christ followers communicated the Christian message with others as it offers contemporary lessons for navigating opposition in today's missions.

Chapter 5 explores the intricate relationship between religion, politics, philosophy, and Christian witness in ancient Pergamon, a city known for its imperial cult and diverse religious practices. By examining the historical and material context as well as the steadfast faith of the early Christians, it draws parallels to modern-day challenges (particularly places where persecution is prevalent), offering strategies for maintaining a vibrant Christian witness amidst political, intellectual, and religious pluralism in spiritually dark places.

14. Cooper, *Ephesiology*.

Chapter 6 investigates the historical and cultural background of guilds in the social, economic, and religious life of Asia Minor, highlighting how their pervasive influence created both opportunities and challenges for early Christians. By exploring the guilds' connections to idolatry, civic identity, and economic networks it offers insights into how the early church navigated cultural pressures while remaining faithful to the gospel. Chapter 7 examines the archaeological and historical evidence of early Christian worship practices in relationship to a vibrant Jewish community in Sardis as well as the sundry pagan temples throughout the empire. Focusing on the "synagogue" of Sardis, the chapter provides insights into the use of communal space, adaptation of *spolia* for Christian purposes, and offers practical application for creating indigenous worship experiences in modern church-planting efforts.

Chapter 8 examines Philadelphia as a religiously diverse "gateway city" whose cultural and economic setting made it fertile ground for the rise of the Montanist movement—a prophetic, ascetic, and over-contextualized form of Christianity that blended local ecstatic traditions with Christian themes. Drawing lessons from archaeology and history, it warns that shallow theological grounding and uncritical accommodation to culture can lead to syncretism and distortions of the gospel. Chapter 9 dives into the spiritual complacency of the first-century Laodicean church. It examines the factors that led to their lukewarm faith and Jesus' admonishment. By studying the material culture of the city, it demonstrates how the Laodiceans repented of their complacency and became a vibrant church in the Lycus Valley. Such an example offers contemporary church plants a blueprint to avoid spiritual mediocrity in their mission.

The concluding chapter examines how missiologists and missionaries often overlook the important contribution archaeology makes for our understanding of the early Christian movement. The gap between the literary record and material culture that archaeology fills reveals a richness and depth to understanding the dynamics of communication and architectural space, and how they intersect with the interpretation of the NT movement. This chapter hopes to inspire missiologists to consider the importance of an interdisciplinary approach that includes history and archaeology in their examination of the early Christian movement in order to avoid anachronistic assumptions sometimes evident in contemporary CPM and DMM methodologies as well as traditional church planting models.

*

Perhaps more than anything, my hope is that this book will not only fill a gap in our missiology but inspire others to deeper exploration into the depths of God's movement in the world today. Walking on the paths of the early disciples, seeing the architecture and landscape they would have seen, and breathing the air they breathed has illuminated God's mission in ways that I could not have imagined after a decades-long career as a missionary and missiologist. In a very real sense, the God who moved in the ancient world continues to move today. The things he did then, the manner in which he revealed himself to our ancestors, may not look the same, but be assured that he continues to make himself known. The material culture of the first centuries of Christianity give us a glimpse into how he did that if only we can see it. I hope this book will help bring our eyes into sharper focus. After all, the history we'll explore is our history. We are in this story because it is his story.

As is my custom in the age of technology, you have free access to a study guide called "Gods, Emperors, Philosophers, and a New Movement" at Ephesiology Master Classes. The study guide includes, not only discussion questions and chapter summaries but also the pictures documented in the book. I decided this would be the best option to illustrate the archaeological record; otherwise, the book would have been twice as long and twice as expensive. I have photographed thousands of pieces of the archaeological record and include more than one hundred of the best high-resolution pictures from the various archaeological sites at Ephesiology Master Classes. Simply scan the QR code to learn more about the resources and use the code "anewmovement" for free access. Also, be sure to keep watch for our next trip to Asia Minor. I'd love to have you come along and walk the ancient roadways with me. There is still so much to learn.

Chapter 2

Asia Minor and the Context of Ancient Missions

Missionaries learn early in their careers that effectiveness in different cultures correlates directly to their observation and dialogue with those cultures. The degree to which they immerse themselves in language acquisition, cultural understanding, and conversation with people impacts their ability to relate the eternal gospel of Jesus Christ in language that is meaningful. This is the essence of missiological theology,[1] and it can be applied as much to modern missions as to ancient missions. In this way, the missiologist plays a vital role in interpreting the New Testament through the missionary milieu in which it was written. So, the missiologist must be conversant with the language, culture, and people of the ancient world for a proper understanding of early Christian missiology.

In this chapter, we'll examine six topics which help us orient to the complexity of the first-century milieu and the challenges confronting ancient missionary efforts. In subsequent chapters, these themes will be recapitulated in more detail as we study important evidence in the material culture. In spite of N. T. Wright's insistence that there are few

1. A hermeneutic that observes the divine mission and movement of God in human history—both the past and present histories—and interprets those actions in dialogue with biblical, systematic, and historical theology and through the lens of God's meaningful communication with his object of love. By meaningful communication I mean how God is making himself known. Yet, this revelation is often distorted by human fallibility or demonic influence. I suggest, as did C. S. Lewis, that God was working as much through the pagan religions and philosophies as through the Hebrews and the Old Testament (OT). For, if we truly believe that God's mission reveals his movement, then we must also believe that he is *omni-operatio*.

"archaeological finds which come to our aid"[2] in understanding the New Testament, I'll suggest that without a proper examination of extant archaeological evidence, we risk anachronisms, historical amnesia, and all sorts of other interpretive missteps that obscure the sociohistorical realities of the New Testament world. Granted, Wright might have changed his perspective now, thirty years after *The New Testament and the People of God*, as the archaeology of Asia Minor has picked up productivity only since the 2000s, especially in Laodicea and Colossae. Nevertheless, I contend that archaeology provides critical material context that complements textual analysis, helping us avoid imposing modern assumptions onto ancient narratives. This is especially true for missionaries reading the NT through the lens of contemporary missions practices. There is an inherent danger when they see their strategies in the strategies of Peter, Paul, James, Timothy, and others.

So, we begin with the Jewish context of Asia Minor and move our way to understanding the various gods and goddesses, emperor worship, philosophical schools, women, and finally households. These will paint an interesting mosaic in which early missionaries dipped their brushes to color the work of God hidden in plain sight.

JEWS IN ASIA MINOR

Jewish presence in Asia Minor is well-attested in the literature. The archaeological record, on the other hand, sheds light on the fact that their population was not as extensive as once believed. Michael Toch argues, "The archaeological evidence, though considerable, in no way supports the widely-held opinion of a vast Jewish population in the Roman Empire, a notion that has lately been subjected to well-deserved criticism."[3] Nevertheless, to begin to understand the challenges early Christianity faced in the first to third centuries AD, we must understand provincial Judaism from ca. 1 BC to ca. AD 1. In general, during the intertestamental period, roughly between 420 BC to AD 50, Judaism experienced an evolution that transformed it from a strictly monotheistic religiopolitical system to an accommodating, Jewish-Hellenistic-Roman, syncretistic religiophilosophical system. The combined proselytism conducted by Jewish missionaries and the religiosocial context of evolving Roman

2. Wright, *New Testament*, 341.

3. Toch, "Jewish Demographics and Economics," 326–27.

paganism presented new opportunities for Judaism to express itself in culturally dynamic ways. Indeed, Scot McKnight points out that the Hebrew and Hellenistic context of Philo "expands what we have grown to see as Judaism."[4] Related specifically to Asia Minor, Clinton Arnold recognizes,

> Therefore, in spite of the fact that the primary impetus for the Colossian "philosophy" may have been "folk Judaism," this Judaism had already assimilated certain beliefs and practices from the surrounding environment and, now, the teachers of "the philosophy" were combining a still greater variety of practices.[5]

The depiction of Judaism as an innocent and faithful monotheism dominates conversations regarding diaspora Judaism.[6] Such a perspective, however, is overstated.[7] The Greco-Roman civic system that intertwined religion, culture, and politics is far more complex. The fluidity of ideas flowing between Jews, Christians, and pagans demonstrates an environment which freely borrowed from the other. In this sense, we can rightly infer various folk practices which easily found their expressions among all religious adherents (magical invocations, charms and amulets, apotropaic graffiti, and more). McKnight notes, albeit acknowledging the rarity, that "there is no doubt that participation, through education and intermarriage, eventually led to deeper assimilation and apostasy, but integration shows quite clearly that Judaism was permeated with Hellenism and that Jews were an integral part of the fabric of culture."[8]

Nevertheless, Louis Feldman paints a monolithic picture of Judaism along with its proselytizing efforts. In so doing, he insists that the so-called "Godfearer" (a mistranslation of *theosebes*) was a sympathizer of the Jewish YHWH. He writes,

4. McKnight, *Light Among the Gentiles*, 18.

5. Arnold, *Colossian Syncretism*, 227.

6. It is important to make the distinction between Judaism in what becomes Palestine after the destruction of the temple in AD 70 and diaspora Judaism (See McKnight, *Light Among the Gentiles*, 21–29). We tend to think of the diaspora as an ethnically identifiable people who migrated from Israel to other parts of the Roman Empire. Instead, it is more accurate to think of diaspora Judaism as comprising both Gentile converts to Judaism, Hellenized Jews, as well as the remnant of Jews populating North Africa and Asia Minor as a result of captivities under the Egyptians, Persians, and Babylonians.

7. Harland, "Honoring the Emperor," 100.

8. McKnight, *Light Among the Gentiles*, 27.

> The term G-d-fearers or sympathizers apparently refers to an "umbrella group," embracing many different levels of interest in and commitment to Judaism, ranging from people who supported synagogues financially (perhaps to get the political support of the Jews) to people who accepted the Jewish view of G-d in pure or modified form to people who observed certain distinctively Jewish practices, notably the Sabbath.[9]

While there certainly exists indications of such an understanding for *theosebes* in Philo and Josephus, Feldman seems to ignore the writings of Herodotus, Strabo, and Diogenes who use *theosebes* in reference to Egyptian, Thracian, and Stoics' religious conduct respectively. Additionally, Julian, the so-called last pagan emperor (r. AD 355–360), uses *theosebes* eight times throughout his fourth-century *Letters* to refer to anyone who reveres the gods indifferent of who the gods were. *Theosebes* simply cannot be viewed as an exclusive technical term for those sympathetic with the God of Israel.[10] For a millennium, the word *theosebes* clearly referred to a person's piety and devoutness to the gods so highly valued in Greco-Roman society. Indeed, we might go as far to say that the word implies a tolerance that society expected among those who acknowledged the existence of the gods.[11] If I am correct, then NT scholars must revisit the stele at Aphrodisias which dates to AD 210. The fifty Greek and Roman names in a list of *theosebeis* cannot be conflated with the Lukan idea of "Godfearer" and must be taken in light of: 1) Jewish accommodation and integration in Asia Minor; and 2) the Greco-Roman value of piety and devotion to the gods.

Jewish Sacrifice and the Temple

There is little question that the temple and the sacrificial system stand as a central motif in Jewish history, embodying the very heart of Israel's worship and national identity. Its origins trace back to the tabernacle—a portable sanctuary during the Israelites' wilderness journey, described

9. Feldman, *Jew and Gentile*, 344.

10. Trebilco, *Jewish Communities*, 146. The NT does not shine any light on the term as it is a hapax legomenon only used in John 9:31. Unfortunately, NT scholars have conflated *theosebes* with Luke's "devout man who feared God" (Acts 10:2, 22) and "you who fear God" (Acts 13:16, 26) to give us the technical idea of "God-fearing" Gentiles *Phoboumenos ton theon* is not synonymous with *theosebes* (cf. McKnight, *Light Among the Gentiles*, 112 where he conflates *theosebes* and *phoboumenos/sebomenos ton theon*).

11. Fox, *Pagans and Christians*, 77.

in Exod 25–31. This precursor to the temple symbolized God's presence among his people and set the stage for a more permanent structure. Ultimately, the wedding of a monarchial political system and a religious sacrificial system manifested in the construction of the temple in Jerusalem. King David envisioned a grand temple to house the ark of the covenant. Although Solomon brought this vision to fruition (1 Kgs 7), the splendor of the First Temple met a tragic end in 587 BC when Nebuchadnezzar's army destroyed it, leaving Jerusalem in ruins and its treasures carried off to Babylon (2 Kgs 25).

Under Persian rule, the Second Temple rose from these ashes in 515 BC, though it lacked the grandeur of its predecessor. Over the centuries it endured desecration by the Seleucid king Antiochus IV Epiphanes (168 BC), was cleansed by Judas Maccabeus, and later robbed by Roman general Marcus Crassus (54 BC). Herod the Great sought to restore its magnificence in 20 BC, initiating an ambitious remodeling project that transformed the temple precincts. Much to the delight of Philo decades later, Caesar Augustus provided daily sacrifices to YHWH in the temple.[12] Later in AD 39, Augustus's great grandson (by adoption) Gaius Caligula determined to erect a bronze statue of himself in the temple. Met with vigorous protest by the Jews, the plan was thwarted by his untimely death. Even so, while the temple in Jerusalem continued to factor prominently in Jewish sacrifices, we begin to see sacrificial offerings conducted on behalf of Roman emperors. Perhaps such practices provide the context for Jesus' confrontation with money lenders in the temple (Matt 21:12–13).

Ultimately, by AD 70, as predicted by Jesus (Luke 21:5–6), the monumental edifice was reduced to rubble by Roman forces forever changing the religious landscape of Judaism. Where once the sacrificial system consisted of the high priests offering sacrifices for the people, after AD 70 it consisted of a rabbinic adaptation focused on prayer and reading the Torah.[13]

Jewish Accommodation

As we've seen in Philo, just as the Jews had no problem honoring Emperor Caligula with a hecatomb of sacrifices, so the pagans had no issue with

12. Philo, *Embassy to Gaius* 36.291:147.

13. Weddle, *Sacrifice*, 47–99.

Augustus offering daily sacrifices to YHWH in the temple in Jerusalem.[14] While Jewish sacrifice could only occur at the temple (Deut 12:13–14), it is quite surprising to read about sacrifices on behalf of a Roman emperor. Indeed, Philo readily admits to participating in such accommodating offerings.[15] During the anti-Jewish riots in Alexandria in the early first century, Philo, the great Jewish philosopher, travels on an ambassadorial mission to Emperor Gaius Caligula (r. AD 37–41). Appealing to Caligula based on his grandfather Augustus's worship of God,[16] the Jews had been accused of not honoring the emperor. In their defense, Philo writes,

> Lord Gaius, we are slandered; we did sacrifice and we sacrifice hecatombs too, and we did not just pour the blood upon the altar and then take the flesh home to feast and regale ourselves with it as some do, but we gave the victims to the sacred fire to be entirely consumed, and we have done this not once but thrice already, the first time at your accession to the sovereignty, the second when you escaped the severe sickness which all the habitable world suffered with you, the third as a prayer of hope for victory in Germany.[17]

This astonishing confession of Jewish accommodation to a living emperor is accentuated by the extravagance of the sacrifice. Philo remarks that they offered a hecatomb in sacrifice. A "hecatomb" refers to an ancient Greek and Roman religious practice involving a grand sacrifice. The term derives from the Greek *hekatombe*, meaning "a sacrifice of one hundred oxen." Historically, it symbolized an offering to the gods in times of great need or thanksgiving, often associated with communal gatherings or significant public ceremonies. Additionally, the significance of oxen sacrifice indicates the prominence of the honorand. In Philo's case, Caligula was worthy of such a grand offering exclusively reserved for the gods. Indeed, in the biography of Josephus, Norman Bentwich tells us that Caligula imagined himself as the supreme deity,[18] and the Roman populace seemed to agree when they offered, according to Suetonius, 160,000 "victims" in his honor, although the Roman senate never conferred upon him deification.[19] Even so, that did not prohibit Caligula

14. Philo, *Embassy to Gaius* 36.291:147; cf. John 19:15–17.

15. Price, "Between Man and God," 30.

16. Philo, *Embassy to Gaius* 40.317:159.

17. Philo, *Embassy to Gaius* 45.356:179.

18. Bentwich, "Biography," 9632.

19. Suetonius, *Lives of Caesars* 1:4.15.

from dedicating a temple to himself, as we'll see. Regarding sacrifices in the Roman Empire, Ittai Gradel explains what they entailed:

> In Roman sacrifice, the sex and nature of the victim usually corresponded to those of the gods who received them. Thus gods received male victims, and goddesses female ones; celestial gods received fertile victims, such as bulls, whereas the gods of the infertile underworld received castrated animals, such as steer. Jupiter was the odd exception to these rules, since his victims were castrated animals such as steers. According to these rules, we would expect the proper bovine victim, that is, the costliest and most honorific type of animal, to have been a bull to the living emperor.[20]

Similarly, epigraphic and archaeological evidence also testifies to this Jewish-Roman accommodation. For instance, Steven Fine notes the third-century imperial dedicatory inscription in Latin at a synagogue in Ostia: "For the well-being of the Emperor."[21] In the material record of the Jewish synagogue in Sardis, we observe *spolia* from a local Phrygian temple as well as the Roman Empire's symbol of Zeus or perhaps Theos Hypsistos (Figure 2.1), demonstrating the ease with which the Jew traversed the social realities of the day. It is not difficult to imagine that the Jews were just as involved in the imperial cult and various other pagan celebrations as any other citizen.[22] Thus, the presence of Jews at the theater in Ephesos when all the citizens joined in one voice chanting "Great is Artemis of the Ephesians" should be read as Jewish accommodation (Acts 19:33–34). To further understand Jewish accommodation, we look at the theater in Miletos.

Accommodation and Theosebes

Noticeably obvious on seats in the theater at Miletos are inscriptions identifying the spaces secured for particular people and guilds. Whether they were benefactors of the spectacular theater or those who somehow secured the right to claim the seat, such inscriptions were common in many theaters in Asia Minor (Figure 2.2). Even seats in the theater of Dionysos in Athens were inscribed with the names of those who claimed

20. Gradel, *Emperor Worship*, 79.
21. Fine, "Synagogues," 118.
22. Harland, "Honoring the Emperor," 110–111.

their place. In this case, the names included the priests of Dionysos (Figure 2.3). In Magnesia, we have examples in the stadium which designated places for the athletic teams from different cities to sit (Figure 2.4).

According to Cassius Dio, Miletos featured as the third imperial cult in Asia Minor during the reign of Gaius Caligula. However, the numismatic record only chronicles Miletos as a *neokoros* during the brief reign of Balbinus (AD 238). Suetonius tells us that Caligula took responsibility to complete the temple of Apollo in Didyma, so it seems likely such a feat accompanied the identification of the temple with the *sebastoi* cult (Figure 2.5).[23] Indeed, Cassius Dio writes,

> Gaius ordered that a sacred precinct should be set apart for his worship at Miletus in the province of Asia. The reason he gave for choosing this city was that [Artemis] had pre-empted Ephesus, Augustus Pergamum, and Tiberius Smyrna; but the truth of the matter was that he desired to appropriate to his own use the large and exceedingly beautiful temple which the Milesians were building to Apollo.[24]

Clearly, Caligula fashioned himself as a god worthy of worship. In fact, he ultimately criticizes Philo for simply offering sacrifices for the benefit of rather than in worship of himself. "Grant," said he to Philo, "that all this is true, and that you did sacrifice; nevertheless you sacrificed to another god and not for my sake; and then what good did you do me? Moreover you did not sacrifice to me."[25] Philo clearly believed that Caligula was deranged as he made jest of his comparison with other gods and goddesses acknowledging what might be best described as a Jewish henotheism. While diaspora Judaism focused its worship toward YHWH, they also recognized the existence of other deities as might be expected if Gentiles converted.

Still, an inscription at the fifteen-thousand-seat, Greco-Roman theater in Miletos reveals ΤΟΠΟC ΕΙΟΥΔΕΩΝ ΤΩΝ ΚΑΙ ΘΕΟCΕΒΙΟΝ ("Place of Jews who were also God-reverers," Figure 2.7). The inscription raises the question about a presumed redundancy. If *eioudeon* is taken as synonymous with that ethnic group who worshiped YHWH, then why describe them as also *theosebion*? Considering the apotropaic invocation to guardian angels at the western entrance to the Miletos theater (Figure

23. Suetonius, *Lives of the Caesars* 1:4.21.

24. Cassius Dio, *Roman History* 7:59.28.1–2.

25. Philo, *Embassy to Gaius*, 45.357:179.

2.8), which is certainly of a Jewish folk religious provenance, then we can easily imagine a Jewish population which comfortably incorporated indigenous magical practices into their own. Indeed, Arnold sees as much in the Lycus Valley. He notes, "Jewish involvement in magical practices is well-attested for the Roman era in Palestine and throughout the Mediterranean world. Jews living in Asia Minor, Phyrgia, and the Lycus Valley also embraced many of these practices."[26] Arnold continues to enumerate the Jewish use of amulets to invoke angelic power to ward off demons and magical texts like *The Testament of Solomon*, among others.[27]

Indeed, David Pao agrees: "Few would argue against a syncretism in the Judaism of first-century Asia Minor, and it is also possible that the Jewish angelology was influenced by the Hellenistic demonology."[28] That being said, ΘEOCEBION on the theater seat at Miletos might rightly be understood as a unique class of Jews who held some notable civic status as demonstrated by their accommodation to Roman deities and folk traditions. In this sense, they remained dedicated to YHWH while adjusting to civic expectations of those who merited reserved seating at the theater.

We see this accommodation to Roman deities clearly in Philo's *On the Embassy to Gaius*. The renowned Jewish philosopher highlights the characteristics of the gods and goddesses creating an impression that Judaism was henotheistic. Philo even argues that it is Gaius Caligula who maintains the Jewish insistence that there is only one God who is Father and creator of all, and for this reason the emperor was justified in his position against the strict monotheistic Jews.[29] In contrast, Philo surprisingly affirms the existence of Roman deities and pokes fun at Caligula's vain attempt to play himself off as Mercury and Apollo.[30]

Jesus and Jewish Accommodation

Far away from Alexandria, yet closer ideologically than we might expect, Judaism in Asia Minor clearly accommodated to Roman society. Indeed, we see hints of it in Ephesos as the Jews participated in the celebration of Artemis (Acts 19:33–34). So, it comes as no surprise when Jesus says

26. Arnold, *Colossians*, 132.
27. Arnold, *Colossians*, 132–44.
28. Pao, *Colossians and Philemon*, 299.
29. Philo, *Embassy to Gaius* 16.115:57.
30. Philo, *Embassy to Gaius* 13.93–95:47–49.

that there are those in Smyrna and Philadelphia who say they are Jews but are not. No doubt, this sort of accommodation must be in his mind as there could be no place where Israel could identify with any other god but YHWH (Rev 2:9; 3:14). Even so, the depth of Jewish accommodation in Roman provinces is understandable at some level. Far away from Israel and the temple rituals, many first-century-provincial Jews were converts from their ancestral religions.[31] Shlomo Sand notes that during the Roman expansion, "The word 'Jew' ceased to denote the people of Judea, and now included the masses of proselytes and their descendants."[32] It should be expected that certain folk religious practices would be maintained and indeed Jesus refers to this tendency among the Israelites. His letter to the church in Pergamom references the OT story of King Balak of the Moabites as well as Balaam (Rev 2:14). While the narrative in Num 23–25 seems innocuous if not favorable to the Israelite identity as the people of God, the passage reveals that they had in fact been persuaded to worship the deities of Moab: "So Israel yoked himself to Baal of Peor. And the anger of the Lord was kindled against Israel" (Num 25:3). Thus, we observe the ongoing Jewish penchant to worship other deities in Asia Minor.

Additionally, Israelites, being situated between Egypt and Mesopotamia, were no doubt aware of ruler cults. Perhaps in part, their motivation for their own king alludes to their desire to be like other people who had powerful leaders acting as mediators seeking divine favor (1 Sam 8:19–20). In fact, the disciples' insistence on Jesus establishing the kingdom is consistent with the ruler cult ideology where the political ruler was also god, lord, and savior (Acts 1:6). These accommodating tendencies continued to express themselves among the Israelites in a desire to be like the people around them and subsequently creating an ideal environment for the Jews and even Christians to wed beliefs systems together through a process of socialization. The end result we see in Jesus' letters to the churches in Pergamon and Thyatira: participation in eating food sacrificed to idols and sexual immorality (Rev 2:14, 21).

Instead of accommodation, Jesus' Revelation to John and message to the seven churches demanded what Colin Hemer described as polemical parallelism: "The claims of Caesar are viewed by John as a Satanic parody of those of Christ."[33] That polemical parallelism can be

31. Cassius Dio, *Roman History*, 37.17.

32. Sand, *Invention*, 166.

33. Hemer, *Seven Churches of Asia*, 87.

extended to the juxtaposition of Christ and the sundry gods and goddesses, not to mention proper apostolic teaching versus false teachers.[34] To the churches, there is no room for accommodation to Rome nor to the various false teachings leading Christians astray (Rev 2:2, 14–15, 20). The consequence of such actions would be the removal of the churches' witness in the cities. The remedy is faithfulness to Jesus Christ, the King of kings and the Lord of lords (Rev 19:16).

GODS AND GODDESSES

Throughout the volume, we'll look at many gods and goddesses presenting opportunities and challenges to Christianity. They will no doubt be familiar to many readers. They include the traditional pantheon of Olympians like Zeus, Hera, Demeter, Athena, Artemis, Apollo, Dionysos, and Aphrodite. Their images, names, and temples appear frequently throughout Asia Minor. However, there were other local gods like Cybele and her consort Attis, Hecate as well as others who were syncretized with the Greeks. As Mitchell recognizes, "The gods of pagan Anatolia were not abstract and remote. At Lystra they could walk among their people and make themselves seen or heard."[35] He continues,

> Men prayed to the gods because they were there. It was always prudent to acknowledge demonstrations of the gods' power, for to neglect them was to invite their anger. This is surely the chief reason why so many inscribed monuments were dedicated to them. Men were obliged to make a public demonstration of their respect and honour for the gods. If there was an overriding motive that caused men to pray, it was not gratitude for services rendered, but awe and fear of what the gods might do if their cult was overlooked.[36]

While we fully expect to see local deities mingling with the Greek, the appearance of Egyptian deities reveals just how cosmopolitan some cities of Asia Minor became. Ephesos's Temple of Serapis and Pergamon's Temple of Isis (Red Basilica) are two prime examples of religious interchange between the Egyptian and the Roman worlds. Yet, such interchange came also from the south with reference to the Nabatean god

34. Amberg and Cooper, "Revisiting Contextualization."
35. Mitchell, *Rise of the Church*, 11.
36. Mitchell, *Rise of the Church*, 12.

Zeus-Dushara in Miletos[37] as well as the funerary rituals in Lycia clearly influenced by the monumental stone tombs of Petra and Hegra.[38] Still, another god appears on the scene and stood much better attested than any other: *Theos Hypsistos*.

Theos Hypsistos: Between Paganism, Judaism, and Christianity

Among the sundry gods who merited the prayers of people in the Roman Empire, one emerges in prominence unlike the others. By the second and third centuries AD, *Theos Hypsistos* becomes one of the most widely attested divine designations in the Eastern Mediterranean, bridging religious worlds, provoking theological debate, and, as Stephen Mitchell notes, functioning as "the seed-bed into which Jewish and Christian theology could readily be planted."[39] So, we'll give some attention to this deity as context for the emerging Christian movement.

The Greek term *hypsistos*—"highest" or "most exalted"—is not unusual in Judeo-Christian literature. In the NT, we see it used primarily for God, appearing 13 times, most often in the Gospels and Acts (Luke 1:32; Acts 16:17). In the Septuagint, the moniker occurs no fewer than 110 times in various instances including Melchizedek's interaction with Abram and Balaam's oracle emanating from "the knowledge of the Most High."[40] Yet, the linguistic simplicity of the term contradicts its complex religious meaning in the Hellenistic and Roman periods.

The worship of *Theos Hypsistos* presents a curious blend of aniconism, absence of animal sacrifice, and veneration of a transcendent deity associated with light, fire, and the sun.[41] The Oenoanda inscription famously declares this god "born of itself, untaught, without a mother, unshakeable, not contained in a name, known by many names."[42] Such language situates the cult within a philosophical-religious trajectory that increasingly valued the abstraction of the divine over anthropomorphic

37. Petrantoni, *Nabataean Aramaic-Greek Inscriptions*, 133.
38. Al-Salameen, "New Dedicatory Nabataean Inscription."
39. Mitchell, "Cult of Theos Hypsistos," 128.
40. Mitchell, "Cult of Theos Hypsistos," 110.
41. Mitchell, "Cult of Theos Hypsistos," 187.
42. Mitchell, "Cult of Theos Hypsistos," 86.

representation—an impulse visible both in Middle Platonic theology and in certain strands of Jewish thought.[43]

Epigraphic evidence—about two hundred surviving inscriptions—shows remarkable uniformity across geographic contexts, from Athens to the Bosporan kingdom.[44] While some dedications explicitly name Zeus Hypsistos, others simply say *Theos Hypsistos*, leaving room for both pagan and Judaic interpretations. This ambiguity is at the heart of Robert Parker's debate over whether we are dealing with a distinct non-sacrificial cult or merely a "megatheistic" epithet applicable to any local high god.[45]

Christian sources such as Epiphanius, Gregory of Nazianzus, and Cyril of Alexandria often present the Hypsistarians (worshipers of Theos Hypsistos) as quasi-Jews—observing Sabbath, dietary restrictions, and honoring the *Pantokrator*—yet without circumcision.[46] The use of terms like *proseuchai* and *pantokrator* suggests close contact with Jewish traditions, and in some cases, as in the Pydna inscription, the overlap extends to synagogue titles (*archisynagogos, proselytos*) within a Zeus *Hypsistos* context.[47]

Mitchell argues for a strong correlation between *theosebeis* ("god-reverers") and *Hypsistos* worshipers, seeing them as Gentiles drawn to the Jewish God yet unwilling to fully convert.[48] Collar nuances this by suggesting that many Gentile Godfearers (a mistranslation of *theosebeis* as we discussed above), cut off from synagogue life, found in the *Hypsistos* cult a space to express monotheistic tendencies without ethnic or legal obligations.[49] While Mitchell's and Collar's readings privilege Judaism as the primary formative influence, I am less persuaded that borrowing was so deliberate of a factor for not converting. The broader Greco-Roman philosophical climate—especially Stoic and Platonic notions of a supreme, immaterial principle—offers an equally compelling background. The convergence between Jewish monolatry and pagan philosophical monotheism was perhaps more an instance of parallel development than one-way influence; even a divine orchestration ahead of Christian missionary efforts.

43. See *Wisdom of Solomon* 13–15.
44. Mitchell, "Cult of Theos Hypsistos," 100–101; Collar, *Religious Networks*, 259.
45. Parker, *Religion in Roman Phrygia*, 136–37.
46. Mitchell, "Cult of Theos Hypsistos," 94–96.
47. Collar, *Religious Networks*, 260.
48. Mitchell, "Cult of Theos Hypsistos," 119–20.
49. Collar, *Religious Networks*, 244.

From a missiological perspective, the *Hypsistos* phenomenon illustrates the permeability of religious boundaries in the first centuries AD. As I have argued elsewhere, early Christian missions thrived, not in religious vacuums but in contexts where philosophical, ritual, and communal patterns prepared audiences to hear the gospel.[50] Paul's encounters with *sebomenoi ton theon* in Acts (e.g., Acts 16:14–17) may well have included *Hypsistos* adherents.[51] The conceptual overlap—one supreme God, mediated by messengers, approached through prayer rather than sacrifice—meant that Christianity could be presented as the clarification and fulfillment rather than the negation of their deepest convictions. In this sense, the *Hypsistos* network functioned like what Collar describes as a "religious network," lacking ethnic cohesion but bound together by a shared divine title and devotional posture.[52] Christianity's ability to graft itself into such a network—offering a named Savior and a more fully articulated theological narrative—partly explains its rapid spread in these regions.

The religious nature of Asia Minor and the penchant of people to find solutions to their everyday struggles provided opportunities for Christians to connect the pagan objects of worship with the one true God. In this milieu, the worship of *Theos Hypsistos*—the "Most High God"—provided theological flexibility. As such, *Theos Hypsistos* bore resemblance to the "unknown god" of the Athenian Areopagus (Acts 17:23): transcendent, uncontainable, and accessible only through the proper invocation. In the rural interior, where temples were sparse and folk beliefs widespread, this conception of deity allowed Christians to coexist within a broader religious ecosystem without direct confrontation and perhaps provided the fuel for movements such as the Montanists (see chapter 8).

Whatever the case, Christianity's challenges were more than simply religious; they were also political. In fact, the two were so intertwined in the lives of the ancient world that it is difficult to separate the one from the other. Nevertheless, our modern minds easily if not wrongly separate them as we tend to impose an ideal that religion and politics should never mix. For the ancients, the cult of the ruler included not only the benefaction of the people but divine favor of the gods secured by imperial edict and occasionally conveyed by the people.

50. Cooper, *Ephesiology*.

51. Mitchell, "Cult of Theos Hypsistos," 110–22.

52. Collar, *Religious Networks*, 241.

EMPEROR WORSHIP

In the first century AD, the Roman Empire was not merely a political powerhouse, it was also a stage for a deeply intertwined system of civic loyalty and religious devotion. Roman emperors were not only militarily ambitious but also politically masterminds. They walked the line between retaining power and appeasing people. In so doing, they assumed divinity and, becoming gods, they bestowed favor on their citizens to retain their loyalty. One striking example of this is what appears to be the pedestal of a statue in the upper gymnasium of Priene, an ancient Ionian city on the west coast of Asia Minor. This pedestal, originally inscribed with praises to an emperor as ΘΕΟΝ ΑΝΙΚΗΤΟΝ ("God Invincible") and ΚΤΙΣΤΗΣ ΤΗΣ ΠΟΛΕΩΣ ("Founder of the City"), reveals how emperor worship permeated daily life and posed a profound challenge for early Christians (Figure 2.9).

The pedestal's dedication likely originated during the reign of Gaius Caligula (AD 37–41), the third in line of Roman emperors after August and Tiberius. A ruler infamous for his self-deification as we've noted above, he attempted to win favor and to secure his own power and divinity by funding monumental projects such as the completion of the Temple of Apollo at Didyma intending it to be a *sebasteion* (a temple dedicated to emperor worship). He also granted nearby Miletos the prestigious title of *neokoros*, marking the city as a custodian of the imperial cult. Priene's proximity to these sites and its cultural ties to Miletos suggest that this pedestal was part of a regional network promoting emperor worship.

While we do not know much about early Christianity in Priene, we do know of its presence through the numerous graffiti and at least two, maybe three, early churches.[53] One such church appears to have been a *proseuche* and later adapted for Christian use presumably as the Jews of Priene came to understand Jesus as their Savior (Figure 2.10).[54] For early Christians, pedestals like this one symbolized more than political allegiance—they embodied a direct confrontation with their faith; a polemical parallel that we'll often observe all throughout Asia Minor.[55] The

53. Two of the churches are dedicated structures and one an example of an *oikia ekklēsia* (see chapter 10).

54. *Proseuche* is the more common word for the place where Jews gathered. The telltale signs that this *proseuche* became a church are the Christian graffiti, namely the eight-spoked wheel, and the inclusion of peacocks in a relief (see chapter 7's discussion of the peacock).

55. Amberg and Cooper, "Revisiting Contextualization."

imperial cult demanded acts of devotion, including sacrifices and public declarations of loyalty, that elevated the emperor among the Olympian gods. To Christians, whose allegiance was to Christ alone, such practices were idolatrous and non-negotiable. This refusal to participate in emperor worship often brought severe consequences. Christians were labeled as subversive, risking social ostracism, economic hardship, and even martyrdom. In cities like Priene, where civic and religious life were deeply intertwined, standing apart from these rituals might have been both conspicuous and perilous.

The pedestal in Priene serves as a tangible reminder of the cultural and religious dynamics of the first century. While it reflects the widespread veneration of emperors as divine, its inscription also tells a story of shifting power and contested memory. For early Christians, it represents a symbol of the profound challenges they faced in navigating a world where civic loyalty often clashed with their exclusive devotion to Christ. As we explore the archaeological remnants of such pedestals and inscriptions, among other pieces of the material culture, we'll gain a deeper appreciation for the courage and conviction of early Christians who, in the face of immense pressure, held fast to their faith and proclaimed, "Jesus is the Savior and Lord"—a declaration that stood not only in stark defiance of the emperor's claims to divinity but as a missiological parallel demanding that he is better and more benevolent than any Roman emperor.

PHILOSOPHICAL SCHOOLS

Roman emperors, sundry gods and goddesses, and diaspora Judaism were not the only challenges confronting the early mission. Asia Minor was renowned for its philosophical innovations dating well before Athens' rise to prominence with Socrates. Notable among those early philosophers were Thales of Miletos (624–546 BC), the ostensible first philosopher, and Heraclitus of Ephesos (540–480 BC), whose *logos* philosophy factored prominently in all subsequent philosophical development as well as Christian theological development. Together, their thought shaped Western philosophy no matter if other philosophers agreed with them or not. Their shift away from myth to reason as well as a worldview which perceived the cosmos not as static but dynamic, paved the way for further reflections that—in the *logos spermatikos* of Justin Martyr—would recognize God's activity. Justin writes, "For not only among Greeks through Socrates were these things revealed by reason [*logos*], but also among Barbarians were they revealed by *logos* personally, when He had taken shape, and become man, and was called Jesus Christ."[56]

There is little doubt that the most influential philosophical school in Asia Minor was the Pergamene School (see chapter 5). While other cities might boast of being the home of philosophers—Ephesos the home of Heraclitus; Miletos the home of Thales; Smyrna the home of Homer—the Pergamene School stands far above as an intellectual center comparable to Athens and Alexandria of the day. Of the various philosophers, Aedesius stands out for his focus on the character of his students:

> And [Aedesius] used to instill in his pupils a feeling of harmony and of responsibility toward humanity, when he observed that they were headstrong and arrogant because of their overconfidence in their own opinions (their wings bigger and softer than those of Icarus), he would force them back down, not into the sea, but to earth and to human life.[57]

There is also evidence of women's participation in philosophy, which is noteworthy given the modern misunderstanding of the cultural position of ancient women. One passage from Eunapius's *Lives of Philosophers* describes how Aedesius of Pergamon deeply respected Sosipatra. After the death of her husband, he took it upon himself to care for and educate her. Eunapius writes,

> After Eustathius had passed away, Sosipatra returned to her own estate, and lived in Asia in the ancient city of Pergamon; and the great Aedesius loved and cared for her and educated her sons. Sosipatra set up a chair, teaching philosophy in her own home opposite to his, and after attending the lectures of Aedesius, the students would go to hear hers; and there was not one person who greatly appreciated and admired the accurate learning of Aedesius, who did not also adore and revere the woman's inspired teaching.[58]

This suggests that, in some circles, Pergamene philosophy promoted an intellectual equality between men and women, which is particularly striking since modern Christianity is quick to communicate how it raised

56. Justin Martyr, *First Apology* 5.

57. Philostratus, *Lives of the Philosophers and Sophists*, 8.6.

58. Philostratus, *Lives of the Philosophers and Sophists*, 33.80–81.

the dignity of women. The role of women in Asia Minor is of no small importance. From their participation in philosophical schools—whether as a philosopher or *hetaira*—to their prominence in the marketplace—as we see in the NT with Lydia and Priscilla—their mark on every aspect of society factors significantly in the story of early Christianity.

It is precisely this intellectual climate that Christians in Pergamon and across Asia Minor would have had to traverse, and it is no wonder that it presented such a challenge. The convergence of social, intellectual, political, and religious currents presented opportunities for early missionary efforts to juxtapose a message that was demonstrably better than culture could offer.

WOMEN IN THE EMPIRE

In spite of the female involvement in philosophical schools, and Sosipatra was not unique, the women of antiquity are frequently portrayed in light of Western perceptions informed by a long tradition of misinterpreting the NT. While there were certainly social expectations on the role of women—for example, their silence in the political process (cf. 1 Cor 14:34)—their importance can be observed simply in the significance and prominence of goddess worship. The Temple of Demeter, located at the upper agora of Pergamon about a fifteen-minute walk from the Altar of Zeus, remarkably testifies to the role of women in the religious and civic life of the city. Symbolizing agriculture, fertility, and the natural cycles of the seasons, Demeter's distinction in Pergamon is observed in the large complex dedicated to her worship. On an inscription located in the temple complex (Figure 2.11), Julia is identified as an obvious religious and civic leader. Her high status in imperial and religious life of the "twice neokoros" testifies to the status of women. Not only was she a priestess and member of the *prytanis*, she was also a leader (*gymnasiarch*) of both athletic and educational competitions at the gymnasium adjacent to the temple (Figure 2.12).

In Ephesos, while we are most familiar with Artemis, inscriptions in Dwelling Unit 6 of Terrace House 2 point to the importance of Aphrodite in Ephesian life and highlight the challenges faced by the early Christian church as it sought to navigate and engage the cultural paradigms of its day. By examining these inscriptions in their context, we begin to see how archaeology, history, and missiology intersect to illuminate the world of the NT; especially Paul's concern for the dignity of the women of Ephesos expressed in 1 Tim 2:8–15. While Artemis reigned as the primary deity of Ephesos, Aphrodite's presence reflects the city's religious diversity and its embrace of sensuality and love. As the patron goddess of courtesans (*hetaera*), Aphrodite was revered, not only for her divine beauty but also for her association with the art of social refinement and influence.

There is no denying acts of sexual service associated with courtesans. However, it's important to dispel the common misconception of Aphrodite as merely a "whore goddess" or a deity of prostitution. While she was certainly connected to sensuality and love, her domain extended far beyond physical desire. Aphrodite embodied ideals of beauty, attraction, fertility, and even political harmony, as seen in her role as a unifying figure in marriage and civic relationships. Her patronage of courtesans did not glorify immorality but rather it aligned with the Greco-Roman admiration for elegance, social influence, and the cultivation of relationships. Indeed, Plutarch describes a courtesan, Aspasia from Ephesos, who was admired as much for her beauty as her intellect:

> And so Aspasia, as some say, was held in high favour by Pericles [the Athenian military leader and statesman] because of her rare political wisdom. Socrates sometimes came to see her with his disciples, and his intimate friends brought their wives to her to hear her discourse.[59]

We'll stitch together a dynamic tapestry of the role of women in the ancient world (see appendix 2), but a more in depth study of the archaeological record is equally demanded. For now, we move to the final topic informing early Christian missiology.

SOCIOECONOMIC SYSTEM AND THE HOUSEHOLD

The socioeconomic system of Asia Minor might be best described as patronage. The multiple references to households (whether of Caesar or a patron) and the agrarian nature of the economy tells us that the economic system of the period was in the form of the institution of the *clientela*. This system of market distribution of goods and services was based on reciprocity where the patron provided protection and the client provided

59. Plutarch, *Pericles*, 24.

legitimacy and power; the greater the number of clients, the greater the influence of the patron.[60]

Indeed, many parts of the Roman Empire shared the same system, and we find as much in the NT. The Gospels tell us of people who sold their goods at the temple, but nothing in regards to how they were organized (Matt 21:12–13). There are clear references to land ownership and cultivation that seem to indicate some larger production of produce rather than subsistence farming (Matt 20:1–16). Wealthy households are referenced occasionally and we learn that they were made up of servants and slaves as well as family members who held particular responsibilities (Luke 15:11–32). This seems to be the situation with James and John and their fishing business which included multiple boats and employees (i.e. hired servants; Mark 1:19–20). Tax collection is often mentioned, indicating that people did generate revenue, and that such revenue taxation supported the government (Mark 2:13–17; Luke 19:1–9, 20:19–26).

Outside of the Gospels we learn of various types of business people, from lawyers and physicians to those in the clothing and leather industries. Paul certainly gives attention to households and the treatment of slaves, which seems to indicate that, in some instances, people willingly sold themselves into slavery, hoping for a better quality of life (Rom 6:15–22). One persistent question emerging from the Pauline corpus is of the role of the slave. While on the one hand some theologians and sociologists have argued that Paul was on a trajectory of manumission or at least emancipation for the slave due to his insistence that all were free, others saw the lack of a first-century slave revolt as indicating contentment of those enslaved.[61] Whatever the case, slaves were certainly a part of an economic system that made up the household in first-century Roman society.

The notion of household (*oikos*) is of importance in the New Testament. Wayne Meeks argued that the household "was the basic unit in the establishment of Christianity in the city, as it was, indeed, the basic unit of the city itself."[62] Churches often met in the houses (*oikia*) of prominent members—as seen in Laodicea and Tralles—up until the first

60. Stambaugh and Balch, *New Testament*, 63–64; Stegemann and Stegemann, *Jesus Movement*, 34.

61. Stambaugh and Balch, *New Testament*, 124. See also Osiek and Balch, *Families*, 192. For another example, see Byron, "Background of Slavery" for an overview of the theological literature on slavery.

62. Meeks, *First Urban Christians*, 29.

archaeological evidence of a dedicated church building in Dura-Europos. Those households (*oikos*) were made up of family members, hired servants, and slaves and were led by the head of the family who might have been a woman, as in the case of Lydia (Acts 16:14–15), Mary (Acts 12:12), and perhaps Phoebe (Rom 16:1–2) and Nympha (Col. 4:15), or a man, as in the case of Cornelius (Acts 10) and Philemon. Such households constituted social units that served economic, political, and religious purposes. One might naturally assume that a similar household system was existent with Priscilla and Aquila (Acts 18:1–4). The fact that Paul knew he could find employment with them might indicate that others had done similarly. Priscilla and Aquila were also invested in the religious life of people as we see with Apollos (Acts 18:24–28) and, eventually, a church meeting in their house, first in Ephesos (1 Cor 16:19) and then in Rome (Rom 16:3–5).

The *oikos* unit is important in understanding the development of the early church. The Greek word meant a body of people who were related by blood or marriage and included servants and servants' families as well as slaves which constituted a socioeconomic unit.[63] The household functioned as a small business enterprise first and foremost, but certainly not in the modern sense of such an enterprise. The head of the household was responsible for the well-being of all in his care and this provided a natural connection between business and ministry. It is highly likely that when Paul greets the churches meeting in the *oikia* of various friends, he is greeting people associated with a particular socioeconomic unit that made up the household business operation (Rom 16:5; 1 Cor 1:16; Phlm 1).

Ekkehard Stegemann and Wolfgang Stegemann noted that "the home, the fundamental socioeconomic unit of ancient societies, is of eminent importance both in the social context of early Christian communities and in the New Testament linguistic usage."[64] The implications of the *oikos* as a socioeconomic unit which became a focal point of the early churches' gatherings are significant. First, the *oikos* had a natural leader in the head of the family. This seems to be Paul's indication when giving instructions to Timothy in 1 Tim 3:4—the leader of the *ekklēsia* must demonstrate that he can also manage his *oikos* well. Second, someone who leads a socioeconomic system is in fact a businessperson in every

63. See also Meeks, *First Urban Christians*, 30.

64. Stegemann and Stegemann, *Jesus Movement*, 277.

modern sense of the understanding and the household was a business enterprise. Third, the businessperson had a natural responsibility to care for those under his employ, and such care would lead to a spiritual role. Fourth, wealth creation was for good works rather than riches, which cannot be stored in heaven. We'll explore this further as we consider the *oikos* and *oikia* as places of worship in chapter 7.

FROM ARCHAEOLOGY TO APPLICATION

From inscriptions on a pedestal at Priene to those at the apsidal hall in Dwelling Unit 6, from diaspora Judaism and its accommodating posture to the myriad of gods and goddess, the value of archaeology for understanding the cultural context of the NT seems obvious. Inscriptions, artifacts, and architectural features provide tangible evidence of the pressures faced by early Christians as they navigated their pluralistic and often morally complex world. For example, the devotion to Aphrodite and the prominence of courtesans in Ephesos help set Paul's exhortations in 1 Tim 2:11–15 in its *Sitz im Leben*.[65] He was not propagating some first-century notion of complementarianism. Instead, he upheld the dignity and respect of women while condemning their exploitation by men frequenting places like Gaius's apsidal hall in Ephesos (see appendix 2).

The early church's response to cultural pressures offers a model for modern missionary efforts. Similarly, modern believers can draw on a model for navigating cultural challenges while remaining faithful to biblical truth. The church of Asia Minor resoundingly rejected any association with Artemis, Dionysos, Aphrodite, or even emperor worship as it worshiped the one, true God who saves both men and women. Archaeology, combined with the biblical text, helps us better understand the NT world, bringing its teachings into sharper focus. By studying the cultural and historical background of Scripture, we gain not only a richer understanding of its message but also valuable lessons for living faithfully in a complex and often pluralistic world. A proper understanding of the world of the NT reduces the chance of anachronistic theological tripe that so often divides the body of Christ.

65. See Bird, "Challenging Mike Winger."

*

So, we are off on our archaeological exploration. Throughout, our focus will be on uncovering the missiology of early Christianity. For the most part, this is an interpretative task of the missiologist. With an understanding of culture combined with both the historical and material records, I contend that we will discover what has been in plain sight for two millennia. It hasn't always been apparent to biblical theology, but that is what makes missiological theology distinct. Those of us who view history as revealing God's redemptive plan see things in history as his divine orchestration to make the missional move to people. The early Christians understood this as they lived in a world imbued with signs and symbols of God's working. To them, as Paul exclaims, the gospel was present. It simply needed clarification:

> And even if our gospel is veiled, it is veiled to those who are perishing. In their case the god of this world has blinded the minds of the unbelievers, keeping them from seeing the light of the gospel of the glory of Christ, who is the image of God. For what we proclaim is not ourselves, but Jesus Christ as Lord, with ourselves as your servants for Jesus' sake. For God, who said, "Let light shine out of darkness," has shone in our hearts to give the light of the knowledge of the glory of God in the face of Jesus Christ. (2 Cor 4:3–6)

Chapter 3

Luke's Theophilos: Ephesos

My foray into a world where Christianity and government were at odds came in the late 1980s. The summer after the catastrophe at Chernobyl, I co-led a team with Loré which spent the summer in Sopot, Poland evangelizing on the beach. We were young without a care in the world and emboldened by James Bond movies as well as the adventurous Indian Jones. We were impervious to risk. That daring spirit and disregard took me to Pakistan in 1988 where we openly shared the *Jesus Film* in villages without fear, mostly due to our ignorance but always with the permission of the village leaders. Eventually I learned that a dose of alarm is healthy, especially when crossing borders into communist countries as I frequently did. The first real sense of alarm I felt came on a trip to Romania during the summer of 1989, followed by a different fear when crossing into the Soviet Union with a box of Bibles later that year. Thanks to Brother Andrew and others, I had heard the stories about persecution in the communist world which helped create, not only an awe for those faithful disciples living in precarious times but also the necessary fear I lacked as a university student. Today, I regularly cross borders into countries where Christianity is unwelcome, and I often wonder if my sense of right and wrong, good versus evil, however ill-informed by spy movies, creates an unwarranted anxiety about the legality of Christian witness in places with anti-conversion laws.

The apostle Paul seemed to have no such anxiety. Mistakenly called the Apostle to the Gentiles, Paul's mandate from Christ included his witnesses "before Gentiles and kings and the children of Israel" (Acts 9:15). This mandate was never relinquished, for he did "open their eyes, so that they may turn from darkness to light and from the power of Satan to God, that they may receive forgiveness of sins and a place among those who are sanctified by faith in [Jesus]" (Acts 26:18). Throughout his ministry, Paul indeed stood before kings and rulers (see Table 3.1). Ultimately, by the end of Luke's address to Theophilos in Acts, Paul would stand before Nero Claudius Caesar Augustus Germanicus better known simply as Nero (Acts 23:11). Although we do not have the account of his appeal, for two years Paul declared the kingdom of God in the heart of the kingdom of Rome—and during the reign of the notoriously narcissistic Nero no doubt. He displayed no fear or concern for his own well-being as he knew the mission given to him came from the rightful King himself.

In this chapter, we will explore the implications of a movement focused in a place of opposition to the message by looking at the archaeological record. Such opposition seemed to always be religious, but as we know, rarely were the lives of first-century people bifurcated between the social, economic, religious, and political. Indeed, isn't this what Jesus' Revelation to John addresses? As Scot McKnight puts it, "The book of Revelation, when read well, forms us into dissident disciples who discern corruptions in the world and church. Conformity to the world is the problem. Discipleship requires dissidence when one lives in Babylon."[1]

So, we'll begin with a bit of background on Ephesos and move to a fascinating possibility for the identity of Theophilos as a potential member of the elite in the beautiful first-century city located at the mouth of the Cayster River on the Aegean Sea. Along the way, we'll see that political pressure never deterred Luke's bold witness about Jesus just as it never deterred Paul's. In fact, Luke certainly fits McKnight's call to be a dissident disciple, and I think Theophilos just might have imitated his example. But, I'm giving away the chapter before getting started. Nevertheless, what we will learn will provide an important lesson for church planting today.

BACKGROUND

The city of Ephesos was impressive even before the dominant edifice of the second-century Celsus Library containing twelve thousand scrolls and parchments. In Asia Minor, only the library of Pergamon, the

1. McKnight and Matchett, *Revelation*, 13.

birthplace of parchment,[2] could compete while the Alexandrian library eclipsed them both. The city's *bouleuterion* and upper agora on the east side, along with the *prytaneion* and terrace houses as you walk west on Embolos Street, not to mention the great theater that dominants the view when approaching the city from the harbor, all testify not only to the economic and political significance of the city but also the wealth of its citizens. No doubt Paul saw an opportunity in this magnificent first-century metropolis (1 Cor 16:9). Indeed, Julien Ogereau concludes, "As a vibrant city located at the junction between East and West, Ephesos itself represented a wide-open door to the rest of the world."[3] Such a city would expectantly rise to the status of thrice *neokoros* (temple guardian or keeper) and claim to be "the most illustrious metropolis."[4]

Holding the coveted status of *neokoros* was competitive and resulted in the establishment of a cult of the *sebastoi* (emperor worship) in the city. Among other things, the emperor became the mediator of divine grace and favor duly bestowed upon the cities of his cult. Some emperors claimed the title of *kyrios* (lord) of earth and sea whereas others claimed to be *sotera* (saviors) and sons of god. To solidify Roman control of Asia Minor, the title of *neokoros* grew in prominence when Augustus commissioned a temple in Pergamon in 29 BC. Afterwards, his adopted son Tiberius commissioned one in Smyrna in AD 23, then Gaius Caligula in Miletos in AD 40. Miletos's status as *neokoros* would be revoked by the Roman senate in AD 41 due to common political posturing. The cult of *sebastoi* provided certain assurances for cities with the coveted moniker, which Steven Friesen enumerates: "The benefits of imperial authority, gratitude toward and dependence upon the emperors, the ordering of the cities of the province, and the role of the elite in the mediation of imperial influence."[5] Ephesos assumed the status of *neokoros* almost by default as it was home to the Temple of Artemis (Acts 19:35; Figure 3.1). While not an imperial *neokoros*, Ephesos prided itself as the guardian of the goddess whose worship dominated Asia Minor. Even though the city competed with other cities in the region for Tiberius's favor, its second *neokoros* would not be granted until Domitian (AD 81–96)[6] and its third established by Hadrian (AD 117–138).

2. Ramsay, *Seven Churches of Asia*, 290.
3. Ogereau, "Methodological Considerations," 267.
4. Friesen, *Twice Neokoros*, 188.
5. Friesen, *Twice Neokoros*, 164.
6. It should not escape notice that Ephesos's emperor worship grew significantly at

In this milieu of goddess worship and competition for imperial favor, Luke tells the story of Paul and his missionary band of more than twenty co-laborers engaging Jews and the many ethnicities in Ephesos, as well as trade guilds, philosophers, and politicians in his account recorded in Acts 18:18—19:41. Indeed, the story features prominently in the Acts of the Apostles as the city plays an important role in early missionary efforts if not also in the composition of the entire NT.[7] Mark Fairchild does not exaggerate the city's importance when he notes, "No other location provides us with the opportunity to examine the development of a church in such detail."[8]

In this context, Paul and Peter both would still require Christians to be good citizens of the empire. However, both would do so with qualifications. Paul, on the one hand, reassured the Ephesians that there was only one mediator between God and humanity; not the emperor nor the goddess Artemis or the sundry other gods and goddesses proliferating Ephesos. Rather, through Jesus Christ, God not only reconciles humanity's relationship to him but Jesus was also the mediator of this divine favor and grace (1 Tim 2:4–5; 2 Cor 5:18–19; Eph 2:9–10). Peter, on the other hand, insists that all Christians submit to authorities, even emperors (1 Pet 2:13–17). Yet, still, God is the purveyor of mercy (1 Pet 2:10). Both writing in a climate where Christians were experiencing increasing pressures, they could continue as good citizens in submission to human institutions as they were assured that God was instrumental in giving those very institutions authority. Writing during the reign of Claudius, those dispersed from Rome in AD 49 no doubt experienced various trials, and Peter insists that Christians honor the emperor (1 Pet 2:17).[9] Paul, writing to Timothy during the reign of Nero, insists that Christians pray for kings so that there would be peace as the message about Jesus continued to spread (1 Tim 2:1–2). So, let's turn to Luke for more information about the various authorities he identified to Theophilos.

---

the time of John's apocalyptic vision from Jesus.

7. Cooper, *Ephesiology*.

8. Fairchild, *Christian Origins in Ephesus*, 28.

9. I date 1 and 2 Peter to the 40s, following Thomas Oden who posits Peter's departure from Jerusalem to Cairo Babylon in Acts 12 (Oden, *African Memory of Mark*, 38).

LUKE AND ROMAN OFFICIALS

Luke, a coworker of Paul and most likely a part of his mission in Ephesos, demonstrated a remarkable skill as a historian. His two-volume biography focused on Jesus in the Gospel, and Peter and Paul in Acts of the Apostles. They recount the stories of early Christianity with an unprecedented precision. Indeed, it was Luke's Acts that compelled William Ramsay to write,

> Luke's narrative was trustworthy, it was for me exceptionally valuable, as giving evidence on a larger scale. There was nothing else like it. No other ancient traveler has left an account of the journeys which he made across Asia Minor [Xenophon gives little more than names and distances]; and if the narratives of Paul's travels rests on first-class authority, it placed in my hands a document of unique and exceptional value to guide my investigations. To determine the value of this narrative was a fundamental condition for my future work.[10]

Since the second century AD, scholarly consensus affirms Luke as the author of both the Gospel and Acts (Acts 16:6, 11; Col 4:14; 2 Tim 4:11). While he is never named in his writings, Paul identifies Luke as the beloved physician in his letter to the saints in the Lycus Valley (Col 4:14). Interestingly, Strabo notes that a school of medicine was founded in the Lycus Valley with a special attention on the anatomy based on the work of Herophilus.[11] Originally established by Zeuxis, the school continued its function under Alexander Philalethes. Among his students was Demosthenes, who specialized in the field of eye diseases.[12] In this context, Paul's reference to Luke as a physician makes sense. He most likely attended to the physical well-being of Paul as some maintain that Paul's encounter with Christ on the road to Damascus left him with permanent eye damage (Acts 9:18). Paul, himself, seems to indicate that he does in fact have some sort of problem with his sight (Gal 4:13–15, 6:11).[13] Luke, then, plausibly studied at the medical school in the Lycus Valley, specializing in eye diseases.

10. Ramsay, *Bearing of Recent Discovery*, 81–82.

11. Strabo, *Geography* 12.8.20.

12 Smith, *Dictionary*, 991; cf. Galen, *Hygiene* 12. In fact, Jesus alludes to eye diseases in his letter to the church in Laodicea (Rev 3:18).

13. See Stott, *Message of Galatians*, 113–14, 176.

Luke's travel with Paul would have created opportunities to encounter many officials, from jailers in Philippi to magistrates in Corinth, to the Asiarchs in Asia Minor, even the various authorities in Judea. Indeed, he mentions the names of several officials of the Roman Empire (Table 3.1).

Theophilos, Acts 1:1	Asiarchs, Acts 19:31
Sergius Paulus Proconsul, Acts 13:7	Alexander, Acts 19:33
Rulers/Magistrates, Acts 16:19, 22	Town Clerk, Acts 19:35
Jailer, Acts 16:23	Claudius Lysias, Tribune, Acts 21:33, 37; 22:26, 29; 23:10, 17, 19–30
City authorities, Acts 17:6	Centurion, Acts 22:25; Acts 23:17, 23
Epicurean and Stoic philosophers, Acts 17:18	Felix, Governor, Acts 23:26; 24:2
Aeropagus, Acts 17:19	Herod's praetorium, Acts 23:35
Dionysius the Areopagite, Acts 17:34	Porcius Festus, governor, Acts 24:27
Titius Justus, Acts 18:7	Nero, Caesar, Acts 24:11–12, Acts 29:19
Gallio, proconsul of Achaia, Acts 18:12	Agrippa (II), King, Acts 24:13
Tyrannos, Acts 19:9 (see appendix 1)	Julius, centurion of the Augustan cohort, Acts 27:1, 3
Demetrius, silversmith, Acts 19:24	Publius, chief man of the island, Acts 28:7

Table 3.1: Luke's officials in Paul's ministry

Theophilos, the recipient of Luke's two volumes (Luke 1:3; Acts 1:1), is often identified by scholars in a range from a fictitious character aiding Luke's agenda, to a symbolic reference for anyone who claims to be a "lover/friend of god,"[14] and finally a real person.[15] While the majority of scholars hold the view that Theophilos is a real person, his identity remains a mystery. Some suggest the mystery is deliberate as Luke wanted to conceal Theophilos's real identity out of concern for his safety. This seems far-fetched yet anachronistically appeals to a modern sense of secrecy that simply wasn't a concern in the first century. In the Gospel, Luke identifies Theophilos as "most excellent" (*kratiste*), a title no doubt reflecting something of his social standing as Luke uses it for other

14. Levine and Witherington, *Gospel of Luke*, 8–9.

15. Creamer et al., "Who Is Theophilus?," 1.

prominent figures in Acts (Felix in Acts 23:26; 24:3; Festus in Acts 26:25). Outside of this moniker, Luke does not provide any clues to his identity unless his unique stories are considered evidences.[16]

Nevertheless, we can rightly conclude that Theophilos held a prominent position in Greco-Roman society, perhaps a political or even a religious position. Such a social role would situate him with wealth, leading some to suggest that he contributed financially as a patron for Luke's research.[17] Depending on the interpretation, Theophilos could be Luke's patron, disciple, or apologetic interlocutor.[18] N. T. Wright and Michael Bird summarize the views: "The books are dedicated to 'Theophilus,' whose name means 'friend of God,' which could be symbolic for everyone who seeks such friendship. Yet it is more likely that Theophilus is actually Luke's patron, sponsoring his literary enterprise, or maybe even a disciple of Luke to whom the teacher writes."[19]

But what has Luke's Theophilos to do with Ephesos? I wondered the same. If in fact Luke was a medical student in the Lycus Valley as I suggested, it seems most plausible that someone bearing the moniker "most excellent" would reside in Asia Minor and less likely that Theophilos would reside in Macedonia, Achaia, or Judea. If Asia Minor is his region as the archaeological record might suggest, then Ephesos, along with Laodicea, Pergamon, and Smyrna would be the most likely cities with Ephesos being preferred. So, let's consider the archaeological record.

THEOPHILOS AT THE PRYTANEION

Bart Ehrman maintains that Theophilos is a common name in Greek antiquity.[20] According to the Packard Humanities Institute's 210,000 searchable Greek inscriptions, we have at least 414 references to Theophiloses around the Greco-Roman world giving us a 0.2 percent frequency for the name. The dating of these Theophiloses ranges from the third century BC to the third century AD. Contrary to Ehrman, this suggests that the name

16. The four-document hypothesis in source criticism asserts that Luke not only used Mark as a source but also "Q," or *quelle* (source) and "L." "Q" is also used by Matthew who also uses his unique source "M." "L" is unique material to Luke (see Jones, *Matthean and Lukan*). I suggest that "L" holds a clue to Theophilos's identity.

17. Kuecker, "Luke,"104.

18. Powell, *Fortress Introduction*, 141–42.

19. Wright and Bird, *New Testament*, 1719.

20. Ehrman, *New Testament* 126.

was relatively uncommon.[21] Moreover, only 37 of the 414 inscriptions fit the first-century time frame for the NT. Of the 37 inscriptions, 29 are from cities with a documented Christian presence in the first century and 9 are from cities believed to have been visited by Luke. Among those 9 are 5 from Ephesos. Three of the 5 occur in the historical period covered in Luke-Acts.[22] These 3 instances appear in the *prytaneion*: 2 times on the repositioned left Doric column (once in the genitive form [ΕΥΜΕΝΗΣ ΘΕΟΦΙΛΟΥ] and once in the nominative [ΘΕΟΦΙΛΟΣ ΟΛΥΜΠΟΥ ΤΟΥ ΜΕΜΝΟΝΟΣ]; see Table 3.2) and once on the lintel block resting on the two Doric columns partially restored by anastylosis (ΘΕΟΦΙΛΟΣ ΜΕΝΑΝΔΡΟΥ).[23]

At first glance, these appear to be three different people all indicating their families' position as religious and civic leaders (Figure 3.2). Most prominent of the three, the name on the lintel block above the Doric columns (Figure. 3.3)[24]—"Theophilos son of Meandros"—is quite compelling. Dieter Knibbe dates the lintel block inscriptions to the first half of the first century AD while the column inscriptions date to the early first century AD.[25] The columns and lintel block served as archives for the names of *prytanai*, *Kouretes*, and other religious cult attendants. Constructed in the sixth century BC, the *prytaneion* functioned as the seat of the *prytanis*, the president of civic and religious affairs in the city.[26] Located in the upper part of Ephesos adjacent to the *bouleuterion* and across from the state agora, the *prytaneion* held special significance as it also became the new location for activities of the *Kouretes* of Artemis during Augustus's reign. Among the activities associated with the Artemis cult, religious officials sang liturgical hymns, poured libations, and

21. See Packard Humanities Institute, "Searchable Greek Inscriptions." Most occurrences are in Attica (196 inscriptions) and Asia Minor (68 inscriptions).

22. Ehrman dates Luke to 80–85 (*New Testament*, 57). Witherington dates Luke to the 70s–80s and Levine to the end of the first century (Levine and Witherington, *Gospel of Luke*, 9). Leon Morris dates Luke to the early 60s (*Luke*, 28). Morris seems the most reasonable given that Luke leaves Paul in Rome at the end of Acts. If so, Theophilos must be a prominent citizen in the 50s–60s.

23. See Table 3.2 for relevant inscriptions.

24. Inschrift Nr. B10 in Knibbe, *Der Staatsmarkt*, 200.

25. Knibbe, *Der Staatsmarkt*, 162.

26. Wilson, *Biblical Turkey*, 208. Those affairs included maintaining the eternal flame in honor of Hestia, the Greek goddess of hearth, home, and family. The flame symbolized unity, stability and continuity of the community (see Wilson, *Biblical Turkey*, 207).

performed rituals of celebration related to the Ephesian patron goddess, especially those associated with her mythological nativity.[27]

Just as intriguing as "Theophilos son of Meandros," Guy Rogers also dates the ΘΕΟΦΙΛΟΣ ΟΛΥΜΠΟΥ ΤΟΥ ΜΕΜΝΟΝΟΣ inscription on the left Doric column to the first century AD during the late reign of Augustus or early reign of Tiberius (Figure 3.4). He ties this Theophilos to the numismatic record.[28] Two first-century-BC to first-century-AD coins minted during the reign of Augustus (27 BC–AD 14) reveal the legend "*grammateus* Memnon, of the Ephesians, Theophilos" (Figure 3.5). One possible interpretation of the legend would be to consider *theophilos* literally as an epithet for lover/friend of god which would suggests that the town clerk (*grammateus*) might have served in some religious capacity. However, we have many examples of a *grammateus*, including someone's name in the legend on the reverse of a coin. Indeed, the same Memnon includes Theudas and Nikolaos on similar coins around the same date. All this to say that it does seem plausible to assert the name Theophilos as inscribed on the coin's legend as the same one who appears on the Doric column in the *prytaneion* (B2; Figure. 3.6). So, if Theophilos were a *Kouretes*, he would have been young as only young men served in that capacity. Assuming a *terminus ad quo* based on the Augustan period coins, Theophilos was born at the beginning of the imperial age in the first century AD. During the reign of Tiberius (AD 14–37), he would have been in his twenties and a member of the *Kouretes* as recorded on the column archive. This Theophilos, grandson of Memnon the town clerk, also appears to be a plausible candidate for Luke's addressee as he would have been in his forties or fifties at the time of Luke–Acts' composition.[29]

27. Rogers, *Mysteries of Artemis*, 10, 131. Mark Powell points out that Luke 1–2 are unique to the Gospel, not only in style and the use of Greek, but also in the fact that they record four liturgical hymns (1:46–56; 1:67–79; 2:14; 2:29–32; see Powell, *Fortress Introduction*, 134). Luke's inclusion of these hymns further connects the *Kouretes* Theophilos as Luke's addressee.

28. Rogers, *Mysteries of Artemis*, 134.

29. Whether or not a connection can be made to Theophilos son of Meandros as the grandson of Memnon is suspect although the naming convention during the Roman period would permit the use of different *praenomen* and *cognomen* as well as *signum*. In this case, Olympos might function as *signum* or *cognomen* of Meandros (see Douglas, "Roman *Cognomina*"). If so, we might hypothetically assert that Theophilos, son of Meandros the Olympian and grandson of Memnon, became *Kouretes* during the reign of Tiberius, then *hiereus* during the reign of Claudius. At the time, Theophilos was granted Roman citizenship and took on the *praenomen* Claudius. After which, he advanced to *neopoi* or *hiereus* of Artemis during the time of Paul's ministry in Ephesos.

Date	Emperor	Position	Evidence (current location)
27 BC–AD 14	Augustus	"Grandson" of Memnon, the town clerk of Ephesos	Silver and Bronze Coin (RPC I 2583)
AD 14–37	Tiberius	Theophilos, *Kouretes*, son of Olympos, grandson of Memnon (town clerk of Ephesos)	*Kouretes* Doric column (B2; Ephesos 448 [IEph 1002])
AD 14–37	Tiberius	Theophilos, father of Eumenes	*Kouretes* Doric column (B1)
ca. AD 23	Tiberius	Theophilos, son of Theophilos, *grammateus* (?)	Marble slab found at the Bath of Varius (Inscription Gallery)
AD 38–54	Claudius	Theophilos, *Kouretes*, Son of Meandros	*Kouretes* Lintel Block Inscription (B10; Ephesos 453)
AD 38–54	Claudius	Claudius Theophilos, *neopoi* or patriarch and priest (?)	*Neopoioi* list; Inscription Ephesos 513 (IEph 1573)
AD 92–93	Domitian	Theophilos, *Kouretes*, Son of Demetrios Markos	*Kouretes* Doric column (B12; Ephesos 457 [IEph 1012])
n.d.		The gymnasiarch	Inscription Ephesos 3741 (IEph 1944)

Table 3.2 Theophilos in Ephesos
(most probable Theophilos of Luke's volumes shaded)

Undoubtedly, whoever the Theophiloses of the *prytaneion* were, they must have been prominent figures in Ephesian society. For instance, regarding Memnon's grandson, Rogers notes, "Theophilos, in other words, belonged, if not to the socioeconomic class in the city that could qualify for and afford membership in the Boule, then certainly to the group of families that could sponsor these comparatively inexpensive acts of euergetism."[30] Thus, the mention of a name on the *prytaneion* column and lintel block suggests that a civic/religious function such as *prytanis* or *Kouretes* reflected prominently on those citizens of Ephesos. Additionally as plausible, during the reign of Claudius, one of our two Theophiloses acquired the *praenomen* Claudius as an expression of his new Roman citizenship (see Table 3.3).[31] At this point, he most likely became a *neopoi* (temple administrator), or *hiereus* (priest), taking on more

30. Rogers, *Mysteries of Artemis*, 134.

31. Hildebrandt, *Emperor Claudius*, 223.

responsibility for the cult of Artemis and earning him Luke's moniker of "most excellent." Indeed, Joel Green leaves open the possibility that the title is honorary, rather than a Roman official, indicating an individual with social status.[32] However, before moving further, let's explore the role of a *Kouretes* as it possibly intersects with Jesus' unique nativity story in Luke, leaving us more certain that Theophilos was from Ephesos.

Kouretes of Ephesos

In the mythological birth account of Artemis and Apollo, *Kouretes* were the young men serving as guardians of Leto who became impregnated by Zeus with the twin gods. In an attempt to conceal her pregnancy from Hera, Leto fled to a mountainous forest location known as Ortygia. By the first century AD, the role of the *Kouretes* focused primarily on Artemis rather than Leto. Each year on the sixth of Thargelion (late April/ early May) the *Kouretes* took responsibility during the goddess's birth festival to create noise by clanging their spears against their shields in a reenactment of scaring Hera away from Leto as she gave birth to the twin gods. The myth of Artemis's nativity evolved over the centuries. Beginning initially with an account occurring in the woods of Ortygia on the island of Delos, by the time of Strabo (d. AD 24), Ephesos took center stage in the Artemis myth:

> On the same coast [of Ephesos, Asia Minor], slightly above the sea, is also Ortygia [an island which in rivalry with Delos, claimed to be the birth place of Apollon and Artemis], which is a magnificent grove of all kinds of trees, of the cypress most of all. It is traversed by the Kenchrios River, where Leto is said to have bathed herself after her travail. For here is the mythical scene of the birth [of Apollon and Artemis], and of the nurse Ortygia, and of the holy place where the birth took place, and of the olive tree near by, where the goddess is said first to have taken a rest after she was relieved from her travail. Above the grove lies Mt. Solmissos, where, it is said, the Kouretes stationed themselves, and with the din of their arms frightened Hera out of her wits when she was jealously spying on Leto, and when they helped Leto to conceal from Hera the birth of her children [Apollon and Artemis].[33]

32. Green, *Gospel of Luke*, 119.
33. Strabo, *Geography* 14.1.20.

Of no coincidence, Mount Solmissos is the location of the so-called house of the Mother Mary (*Meryemana Evi*, Figure 3.7). The site of the house was revealed in a vision to the Blessed Anne Catherine Emmerich in the nineteenth century. For twenty-two years, Emmerich took part in an order of Augustinian nuns. She was known to be devout for her entire life and from childhood she had many visionary encounters with the child Jesus. Considered a mystic, her life was documented by the German poet Clemens Brentano. In 1818, Brentano began visiting the bedridden Emmerich and recorded her many visions over the following years. Included among the visions was a visitation from the Virgin Mary directing her to a small stone house in Turkey. After reading Brentano's biography of Emmerich, a French priest from Izmir embarked on a journey to find the house, which he did in 1881.[34]

The story of Artemis's birth and Mary's house provide an interesting example of Christianity's displacement, or perhaps conflation, of the goddess cult for the virgin cult. Indeed, Ephesos factors prominently in the cult of the virgin Mary. The third ecumenical council held at Ephesos in 431, convened to condemn Nestorius's assertion that Mary was *Christotokos* rather than *Theotokos*. The consensus of the two hundred bishops from Asia Minor, Italy, and North Africa favored Mary as the mother of God. Consequently, the veneration of Mary became more prominent in Christianity. Prudence Jones and Nigel Pennick note, "The procession celebrating the beatification of Mary used smoking censers and flaring torches, as were once used in the procession of [Artemis]."[35] Rogers comments are apropos:

> Five hundred years after Strabo recounted the sacred story of the Kouretes scaring Hera away from Leto during the birth of Artemis, the Ephesians connected themselves once again to the divine through the story of a mother who gave birth to a deity and were just as ready to riot on her behalf as they had been in support of the "daimon" Artemis when the Apostle Paul visited the city in the middle of the first century.[36]

34. Wilson, *Biblical Turkey*, 235.

35. Jones and Pennick, *History of Pagan Europe*, 75; cf Laing, *Survivals of Roman Religion*, 93. The council also adamantly condemned creature-worship—"whether of the Perfect Man, Jesus, the Virgin Mary, and apostle, prophet, or saint" (Rushdoony, *Foundations of Social Order*, 41).

36. Rogers, *Mysteries of Artemis*, 185.

As we tie the mythical nativity account of Artemis to Theophilos, a *Kouretes* of Ephesos, Luke's unique nativity account of Jesus resounds as a striking polemical if not a missiological parallelism.[37] Juxtaposing the birth of Artemis to the birth of Jesus would weigh heavy in a message of certitude necessary for religious switching. Artemis's birth was hidden in the forest near Ephesos. As a young man, Theophilos would have participated in the annual celebration by re-enacting the actions of the first guardians of the goddess. He would have, no doubt, joined with the cult attendants singing hymns in praise Artemis. Jesus' birth, on the other hand, was on full display by the heavenly beings announcing good news and singing, "Glory to God in the highest" (Luke 2:14).

Interestingly, when Ignatius of Antioch recounts Jesus' birth story to the Ephesians in AD 110, we sense the significance of the message to those living among the *Kouretes* and *hierius* of Artemis. The similarities between the nativities seem apparent:

> Now the virginity of Mary was hidden from the prince of this world, as was also her giving birth and the death of the Lord—three mysteries of a scream which were accomplished in silence by God. How, then, was he revealed to the world? A star shined out in heaven brighter than all the other stars, the light of which was inexpressible, while its novelty struck people with astonishment. And all the rest of the stars, with the sun and moon, formed a chorus to this star, and its light was exceedingly greater than them all. And there was a disturbance felt as to where this new spectacle came since it was so unlike anything else.
>
> Consequently, every kind of magic was destroyed, and every bond of wickedness disappeared. Ignorance was removed and the old kingdom abolished as God himself was revealed in human form for the restoration of eternal life. And now, that which has been prepared by God takes effect. Namely, from that time on, all things were in a state of turmoil because the destruction of death was being carried out.[38]

37. Polemical parallelism is a literary or rhetorical device in which a writer intentionally presents a narrative, idea, or image that mirrors another but does so to critique, challenge, or subvert the original. The parallelism highlights contrasts or conflicts between the two, often to elevate one view while diminishing the other. For example, in biblical studies, polemical parallelism might involve presenting a story or hymn in a way that parallels a known cultural or religious narrative but reinterprets or re-centers it around a biblical informed worldview or message.

38. Ignatius of Antioch, *Letter to the Ephesians*, 19 (author's translation).

Just as Leto's birth was hidden from Hera, Mary's birth was hidden from the "prince of this world." (cf. Rev 12:6) Yet, Jesus did not remain hidden. Indeed, the announcement of his birth was nothing short of extraordinary. In fact, we observe interesting parallels of archetypal motifs in the birth accounts of Jesus and Artemis. Themes such as maternal struggle, sacred settings, wilderness, and hymns of praise reflect storytelling themes that connect Luke's Jesus to Theophilos in a way that he could understand.[39]

THEOPHILOS OF EPHESOS

Perhaps the lists of *Kouretes* in the *prytaneion* have helped us solve the mystery of the enigmatic Theophilos. If so, what we have in the lintel block and Doric column inscriptions (Figure 3.2–5) is a name of a previously unidentified person who potentially played a significant role in early Christianity. Theophilos, the most excellent addressee of Luke's two volumes, was a high-standing citizen of Ephesos. Feasibly during the reign of Claudius after serving as a Kouretes in his youth, he became a *neopoi* responsible for the care of the Temple of Artemis. We should not be surprised if he might also have achieved a position as patriarch and priest in the *prytaneion* (Table 3.3). Luke's careful treatment of the Jesus story would hold noteworthy importance for someone of Theophilos's status. He must have certainty of Jesus' claims of divinity and authority if he were to switch allegiances (see Table 3.4).[40] This hypothesis is buttressed by the fact that Luke continues his story with the development of Christianity. Primarily focusing on Paul's work in the empire, Luke portrays Christianity, not as a rival to the *neokorate* metropolis of Ephesos, but as innocent of any accusation of sedition.

In summary of the archaeological and biblical record, the timeline for Luke's addressee would look something like the following: Theophilos was born during Augustus's reign, probably in the AD 10s. His

39. Luke's account of Jesus highlights different stories (Luke's source "L") when compared to the two other synoptic gospels (Matthew and Mark). His unique account of Jesus at the temple marks another occasion that connects with Theophilos who performed religious duties at the temple in celebration of Artemis. In this instance, Luke focuses on Jesus being about his Father's business, a hallmark sign of his maturity and awareness of his mission (Luke 2:41–52). Callimachus recounts Artemis's discussion with her father, Zeus, as also a sign of her maturity and recognition of her mission ("Hymn to Artemis"). Yet another example of a polemical parallelism.

40. Creamer et al., "Who Is Theophilus?"

grandfather, Memnon, was the *grammateus*. Proud of his grandson, he included his name on the legend of coins ensuring his place of prominence among the elite of Ephesos (Figure 3.4). With change to the city brought about by an earthquake in AD 23, the focal point of the Artemis celebration turned attention away from the temple to the *prytaneion* of Ephesos. Now, even more citizens could participate in the procession as they sought the well-being of their city by its protector. In the 30s, during Tiberius' reign, Theophilos became a *Kouretes* and served in ritual processions from the *prytaneion* as a guardian of Artemis.

That procession of *Kouretes* clanging their spears against their shields while the *hiereis* and *neopoiai* sang hymns to Artemis as the *Boule* watched, proceeded each May from the *prytaneion* westward down the marble Embolos Street toward the Tetragonos Agora (see Map 3.1). At the intersection of the *Tridos*—the crossroad of three prominent streets in central Ephesos—others from the city would join the procession after offering sacrifices to Artemis at the monumental altar marking the site of departure to Ortygia. The procession then continued to wind its way to the birthplace of Artemis on Mount Solmissos. First walking northwest and then turning south, they continued for about nine kilometers, singing hymns to the savior of their city.[41]

Less than thirty years after the processional change, Paul would have seen Theophilos among *hiereis*, the *Kouretes*, and the *neopoiai* processing to the site of the mythological nativity. His name stood out prominently on the columns at the *prytaneion* and Paul would have certainly known this conspicuous individual who shared Roman citizenship with him as indicated by his name change to Claudius Theophilos. No doubt, in this context of civic and religious pride, it is easy to imagine the seats of the theater filled with twenty thousand people chanting, "Great is Artemis of the Ephesians" (Acts 19:28). By the 60s, during Nero's reign, Theophilos became *patrogeron* (i.e. patriarch). Around this time, he most likely also became a Christian as he interacted with Luke's unique stories about Jesus and the growth of Christianity in the Roman Empire. If I am correct, then what we have from Luke and the archaeological record is the story of a remarkable person who gave up his social standing to ultimately follow Christ. Theophilos, truly a friend of God, provides a beautiful example of religious switching.

41. Rogers, *Mysteries of Artemis*, 135–40. Before Augustus changed the religious and civic center to the *prytaneion*, the *Kouretes*, *hiereis*, and *neopoiai*, would process past the stadium and theater on their way from the Temple of Artemis to Ortygia.

AD 14–37	AD 37–54	AD 37–54
Ephesos 448 *Kouretes* List	Ephesos 453 *Kouretes* List	Ephesos 513 *Neopoioi* List
ΕΠΙ ΠΡΥΤΑΝΕΩΣ ΑΡΤΕΜΙΔΩΡΟΥ ΤΟΥ ΑΠΟΛΛΩΝΙΟΥ ΤΟΥ ΑΠΟΛΛΩΝΙΟΥ ΤΟΥ ΔΙΟΓΕΝΟΥΣ ΚΟΥΡΗΤΕΣ ΕΥΣΕΒΕΙΣ ΓΑΙΟΣ ΑΓΙΛΗΙΟΣ ΓΑΙΟΥ ΥΙΟΣ ΣΕΒΗΡΟΣ Ο ΚΑΙ ΥΜΝΩΔΟΣ ΔΕΙΦΙΛΟΣ ΔΕΙΦΙΛΟΥ ΤΟΥ ΗΛΙΟΔΩΡΟΥ ΛΕΥΚΙΟΣ ΓΡΑΝΙΟΣ ΚΑΠΙΤΩΝ Ο ΚΑΙ ΙΕΡΟΚΗΡΥΞ ΠΟΠΛΙΟΣ ΡΟΥΤΕΙΛΙΟΣ ΠΡΙΜΙΓΕΝΗΣ ΕΥΜΕΝΗΣ ΘΕΟΦΙΛΟΥ ΘΕΟΦΙΛΟΣ ΟΛΥΜΠΟΥ ΤΟΥ ΜΕΜΝΟΝΟΣ ΑΛΕΞΑΝΔΡΟΣ ΣΠΟΝΔΑΥΛΗΣ	ΕΠΙ ΠΡΥΤΑΝΕΩΣ ΤΙΒΕΡΙΟΥ ΚΛΑΥΔΙΟΥ ΝΥΣΙΟΥ ΥΙΟΥ ΚΥΡΕΙΝΑ ΝΥΣΙΟΥ ΚΟΥΡΗΤΕΣ ΕΥΣΕΒΕΙΣ ΘΕΟΦΙΛΟΣ ΜΕΝΑΝΔΡΟΥ ΜΟΥΝΔΙΚΙΟΣ ΑΓΝΕΑΡΧΗΣ ΔΙΑ ΒΙΟΥ ΜΑΡΚΟΣ ΓΕΡΙΛΛΑΝΟΣ ΑΛΟΦΟΡΟΣ ΜΑΡΚΟΣ ΛΩΡΕΝΤΙΟΣ ΑΓΑΘΟΠΟΥΣ ΛΥΣΙΜΑΧΟΣ ΛΥΣΙΜΑΧΟΥ ΤΟΥ ΛΕΥΚΙΟΥ ΛΕΥΚΙΟΣ ΜΟΥΚΙΟΣ ΜΕΝΕΚΡΑΤΗΣ ΕΙΚΑΤΙΔΑΣ ΗΡΩΔΟΥ ΤΟΥ ΑΡΤΕΜΙΔΩΡΟΥ ΜΑΡΚΟΣ ΙΕΡΟΣΚΟΠΟΣ ΜΗΝΟΔΟΤΟΣ ΙΕΡΟΚΗΡΥΞ ΑΤΤΙΚΟΣ ΕΠΙ ΘΥΜΙΑΤΡΟΥ ΠΑΡΡΑΣΙΟΣ ΣΠΟΝΔΑΥΛΗΣ	[Κ]ΛΑΥΔΙΟΣ ΘΕΟΦΙΛΟΣ [Κ]ΛΑΥΔΙΟΣ ΡΟΥΦΟΣ Μ(ΑΡΚΟΣ) ΑΥΡ(ΗΛΙΟΣ) ΚΑΛΛΙΣΤΟΣ [Ν]ΟΥΜΕΡΙΟΣ ΓΕΡΕΛΛΑΝΟΣ [ΡΟ]ΥΦΕΙΝΟΣ ΚΑΙ ΙΕΡΕΥΣ ΠΑΤΡΟΓΕΡΩΝ Γ(ΑΙΟΣ) ΤΟΥΚΚΙΟΣ ΑΛΕΞΑΝΔΡΟΣ ΚΑΙ ΙΕΡΕΥΣ ΚΑΙ ΙΕΡΕΥΣ [-Σ] ΚΥΡΕΙΝΑ ΣΑΤΟΡΝΕΙΝΟΣ ΦΙΛΟΡΩΜΑΙ<ΟΣ>

Table 3.3: Relevant inscriptions

FROM ARCHAEOLOGY TO APPLICATION

The missiological implications for situating Theophilos in Ephesos are becoming clear. First, Luke's engagement with a prominent social figure cannot escape our notice. While we do not know how their relationship developed over time, it appears from Acts 1:1 that Theophilos is more than a wealthy patron, if a patron at all. The absence of his title "most excellent" and the interjection "O Theophilos" seems to suggest a level of friendship that was not present in his biographical account of Jesus. How that friendship evolved will remain a mystery. At minimum, we can say that it began with respect and we can only hope, with good reason, that Theophilos moved from the worship of Artemis as *soteira* to Jesus as *soter*.

Second, the attention that Luke gives to details in his two volumes also indicate the level of precision required in carefully communicating about the life of Jesus and the early church. There was no room for sloppy evangelism in Luke's exchange with Theophilos. His message focused on the certainty of the accounts he shared. They were not pithy points to force a conversion. Rather, they were pedantically formulated stories—Luke's "L" source especially—that demonstrated the good news in a manner that Theophilos grasped: Jesus is God. If he were to switch allegiances, it would potentially result in social and economic, if not also political and religious, upheaval.

Third, the Gospel of Luke provides another example of the missiological nature of the NT. Luke's deliberate connection of Jesus stories with Theophilos buttresses the importance of connecting the true stories about Jesus with the context of an audience. Rather than contextualization, which focuses on adapting stories, Luke applies what I've called a missiological theology similar to what we observe in John's Gospel.[42] He does not change the stories about Jesus, neither does he use analogies. Instead, he tells the eyewitness accounts of certain stories identified in the four-document hypothesis as "L" that he considered as connecting points in his engagement of Theophilos. Those connecting points were missiological parallels between the deities of Ephesos and the deity of Jesus Christ.

Story of Jesus	**Cultural Connection to Theophilos**	**Missiological Parallel**
Hyperetes of the word (Luke 1:2)	*Kouretes*, *neopoioi*, and *hiereus*	Attendants of the word vs. attendants of Artemis
Nativity Hymns (Luke 1:46–56; 1:67–79; 2:14; 2:29–32)	Hymns sung to Artemis in annual ritual celebration of her birth	Jesus as Savior of the world vs. Artemis as savior of Ephesos

42. Cooper, "John's Missiological Theology."

Story of Jesus	Cultural Connection to Theophilos	Missiological Parallel
Jesus at the Temple (Luke 2:41–52)	Temple practices of young Theophilos in the worship of Artemis	Jesus' missional awareness vs. Theophilos's transactional worship of Artemis
The Good Samaritan (Luke 10:29–37)	Care for those on the margins of society seeking refuge at the Temple of Artemis	Elevating the outsider in a moral framework for caring for the marginalized
The Prodigal Son (Luke 15:11–32)	Artemision as a place of refuge for the marginalized	Refuge in God the Father vs. refuge in Artemis the mother

Table 3.4: Selected examples of polemical parallels in the Gospel of Luke

These three points are, at times, gaps in church-planting movement strategy. Particularly, the rapid expansion of the gospel in church-planting and disciple-making movements does not always permit the careful attention that we see in Luke's message to Theophilos. Nor does rapid expansion always allow for the time it takes to develop relationships with key community officials. What we learn from Luke's example and eyewitness account is that both rapid expansion that accurately communicates the stories about Jesus in culturally meaningful ways as well as the importance of developing relationships with authorities help long-term sustainability including the indigeneity of Christianity. In other words, Luke is far more concerned with telling the depth of the stories than he is with pragmatic strategies.

The figure of Theophilos in Luke's Gospel and Acts emerges as a fascinating nexus of historical, archaeological, and theological, if not also missiological, significance. Positioned within the sociopolitical and religious dynamics of first-century Ephesos, Theophilos represents the type of influential individual for whom Luke crafted his detailed narrative. Whether a *Kouretes*, *neopoi*, or *hiereus*, Theophilos's status underscores the care required to communicate the message of Jesus Christ to those deeply embedded in the civic and religious structures of their communities. Luke's meticulous effort to establish the certainty of the Gospel reflects the precision needed to challenge Theophilos to reconsider changing his allegiances from the worship of Artemis and imperial deities to Jesus

Christ as the true mediator of divine favor; even more, a change to faith in Jesus as Savior of the world rather than Artemis as savior of Ephesos. Truly a missiological parallelism.

This investigation into Theophilos provides, not only a window into the complexities of religious switching in a city like Ephesos but also valuable lessons for contemporary missions strategy. Luke's balance of relational engagement with Theophilos and his precise theological articulation illustrates the importance of deliberate discipleship alongside rapid gospel dissemination. As church-planting movements expand, they would do well to consider Luke's example: developing deep relationships with influential leaders while maintaining an unwavering commitment to communicating the transformative power of Jesus Christ with clarity and integrity.

Chapter 4

The Writing on the Wall: Smyrna

Ancient Smyrna was a pleasant walk from our hotel in Izmir. So, early in the morning, before setting out to Sardis, we strolled the busy streets on our way to the *agora* in the ancient city. Surrounding the ground floor level of the marketplace on three sides is the *basilica* including the main hall and *stoa* extending south on the east and west sides. Today, the word *basilica* is more often associated with a particular style of church architecture that featured a central nave with colonnade aisles on each side. Hagia Eirene is a beautiful example of this style of architecture. Located on the grounds of the Topkapi Palace in Istanbul, this Byzantine church became an example of iconoclastic[1] architecture: it boasts no icons as a protest of images created for veneration if not also as talismans. In Figure 4.1, you can clearly distinguish the apse from the side aisles of the basilica floor plan. The interior nave (Figures 4.2, 4.3) is flanked on either side by columns adjusted in height with the use of capitals from temples (*spolia*). The apse includes the ubiquitous *bouleuterion*-like seating for the church's leaders.

The so-called synagogue in Sardis provides an earlier example of the *basilica* style used in religious architecture (Figure 4.4). The largest

1. The Iconoclast Controversy was a dispute within the Byzantine Empire during the eighth and ninth centuries over the use of religious images (icons) in worship. Iconoclasts, who opposed the veneration of icons, argued that it led to idolatry, while iconodules, who supported it, saw icons as important tools for devotion and teaching. The conflict resulted in several periods of icon destruction and restoration, eventually being resolved in favor of the iconodules at the Second Council of Nicaea in 787.

"synagogue"[2] ever excavated thus far, dates to the third to fourth century, and features a central nave that leads to an altar and *bouleuterion* in the apse. No longer present, the nave was flanked on either side with columns whose bases are clearly marked on the floor. Originally a part of the gymnasium complex, the structure served a public purpose before it acquired a religious one.

Originally, the Greek word derives from *basilias* meaning "king," so a *basilica* referred to the place of royalty. The Smyrna *agora* adopted this style of architecture in the fourth century BC as it was constructed upon a *cryptoporticos* (Figure 4.5). Over the centuries, the *agora* expanded to an upper floor with clerestory windows. As one of the largest *agoras* in Asia Minor, it must have been a remarkable site after its reconstruction by Marcus Aurelius following its destruction by an earthquake in AD 178.[3] Before we dig more deeply into the significance of the *agora* and especially the *cryptoporticos*, let's consider the background of Smyrna.

BACKGROUND

Etymologically, Smyrna is the city of myrrh, or at least this is Mark Wilson's view as he posits a connection between the city and death.[4] David Graves notes that naming a city after a particular product was a common practice in the ancient world even though the product was not manufactured in the region.[5] Smyrna, in Greek, is the same word for myrrh (*smyrna*) found in Matt 2:11—one of the three gifts offered to Jesus at his birth. It is transformed to a verb in Mark 15:23 where Jesus is offered wine mixed with myrrh. Nicodemus used myrrh along with aloes on the dead body of Jesus (John 19:39). Yet, we know that myrrh had many uses besides burial. For example, Hippocrates recommended its medicinal use for the treatment of assorted ailments including ulcers.[6]

---

2. I use quotation marks around "synagogue" for to two reasons: 1) there is question as to whether the structure served multiple purposes, one of which is plausibly a gathering place for Christians—I'll address this in the chapter 7 about Sardis; and 2) "synagogue" is a Greek word meaning gathering or assembly. It is used as much for the place of Jewish gathering as it is a place where members of voluntary associations gathered or pagans gathered to worship their gods and goddesses (see chapter 6).

3. Bagnall, *Everyday Writing*, 29.

4. Wilson, *Biblical Turkey*, 304.

5. Graves, "Local References," 24.

6. Hippocrates, *On Ulcers* 12:350–51.

Richard Ascough suggests the city takes its name from the goddess Myrina.[7] However, no such goddess seems to exist in the Greek pantheon.[8] Contrastingly, William Ramsay identified the tutelary goddess of Smyrna as Cybele (Figure 4.6). Cybele, whom Ovid called the "gods' sacred mother" in the first century BC,[9] factored prominently among the Smyrnaeans. Her images appear in the numismatic record (Figure 4.7) beginning during the reign of Claudius (AD 41–54) through to the reign of Gallienus (AD 253–268). She is most often depicted turreted (wearing a crown) and seated with lions at her feet on either side, acting as sentinels.[10] In her right hand, she holds a *patera* (libation bowl) while leaning on her left arm against a *tympanum* (type of framed drum). The cult of Cybele originated in Phrygia but became one of the most extensively practiced in the Roman Empire, giving Michael Carroll the idea that the Virgin Mary usurped her role as *Theotokos*.[11]

Cybele certainly was not the only goddess worshiped in Smyrna. The twin goddesses Nemeseis flourished from the third century BC to the first century AD.[12] Likewise, Aphrodite's temple provided a place of refuge for the vilest of slaves and criminals as practiced in many temples in Asia Minor.[13] Ascough notes many others goddesses, including "Tyche, Boubrostis, Athena, Here, Hestia, Isis, Persephone, Semele, the Graces, Nymphs, and Muses, and the Fates."[14] Among male deities, we see the usual cohort of Zeus, Asklepios, Dionysos and Apollo.

The city itself boasts of a long history dating from the tenth century BC. Located on the Gulf of Smyrna along the western coast of Asia Minor about eighty kilometers north of Ephesos, the city has always been a strategic location as a major seaport (see map 4.1). Especially as the harbor of Ephesos silted up beginning in the second century, Smyrna's prominence in the region grew as an important trading center. Eventually occupied

7. Ascough, "Interactions Among Religious Groups," 7.

8. Diodorus Siculus (*Library of History* 3.54.2) writes about Myrina as queen of the Amazons.

9. Ovid, *Metamorphoses* 10.104:71.

10. See Murray, "Down the Road," 200.

11. Carroll, *Cult of the Virgin*, 90–99.

12. Cadoux notes, "In 250 A.D. the Nemeseion was the scene of a struggle between the magistrates and a group of Christians over sacrificing to the emperor Decius: the renegade Christian Bishop swore an oath by the emperor's Fortune and Nemeseis." See Cadoux, *Ancient Smyrna*, 222.

13. See Tacitus, *Annals*, 3.60–61:617–21.

14. Ascough, "Interactions Among Religious Groups," 48.

by the Ionians at the end of the seventh century BC, it was destroyed by the Lydians in the sixth.[15] In a very palpable sense, the city died and lived again. Strabo writes, "Its inhabitants continued for about four hundred years to live in villages."[16] Its resurrection, so to speak, appears in the numismatic record depicted in a dream where the twin goddesses Nemeseis visited Alexander the Great with a plan for the city in 334 BC as he slept under a tree (Figure 4.8). Another decade later, Antigonus, a Macedonian general, followed by his successor after his defeat and death at Ipsus in Phyrgia, Lysimachus, rebuilt the city.[17] Strabo writes,

> Then they were reassembled into a city by Antigonus, and afterwards by Lysimachus, and their city is now the most beautiful of all; a part of it is on a mountain and walled, but the greater part of it is in the plain near the harbour and near the Metroeum and near the gymnasium. The division into streets is exceptionally good, in straight lines as far as possible; and the streets are paved with stone; and there are large quadrangular porticoes, with both lower and upper stories. There is also a library; and the Homereium, a quadrangular portico containing a shrine and wooden statue of Homer; for the Smyrnaeans also lay especial claim to the poet; and indeed a bronze coin of theirs is called Homereium. The River Meles flows near the walls; and, in addition to the rest of the city's equipment, there is also a harbour that can be closed.[18]

Smyrna boasted, not only the birthplace of Homer but also the title "First in Asia," although a title contested by Ephesos and Pergamon (Figure 4.9). Coins dating to the second century frequently display CMYPNAIΩN Γ NEΩKOPΩN ΠPΩTΩN ACIAC ("Of the Smyrnaeans three times temple guardian first of Asia," Figure 4.10). Whatever the case, Smyrna became known as one of the most beautiful cities of Asia Minor. Among its attributes of beauty, the acropolis featured a crown-like appearance. Smyrna took great pride in its buildings, especially those lining the acropolis streets of Mt. Pagos.[19] Such pride did not impress the philosopher Apollonius, however. A native of Tyana in Cappadocia, the first century-peripatetic spent his career traveling as far east as India

15. Strabo, *Geography* 14.1.37; Herodotus, *Persian Wars* 1.150:191.
16. Strabo, *Geography* 14.1.37.
17. Ramsay, *Seven Churches of Asia*, 252.
18. Strabo, *Geography* 14.1.37.
19. Ascough, "Interactions Among Religious Groups," 8.

and west as North Africa. Arriving in Smyrna during the Ionian Games, he advised the citizens that it was better for a city to be crowned with good men rather than buildings or gold. His third-century biographer recounts his message:

> Buildings stayed in one place, never seen anywhere except in the part of the world where they were, while good men were seen everywhere and spoken of everywhere, and they made the city of their origin larger in proportion to the number of them that could travel the world.[20]

Of the city brought back to life, Ramsay states, "The later city was intended to be a maritime and trading centre, a good harbor and a convenient starting-point for land-road to the east."[21] Smyrna, so it ostensibly seemed, became the "First of Asia," a sentiment deeply entrenched in the ethos of the Smyrnaeans.[22]

SMYRNA AND THE NEW TESTAMENT

We have no written record of when Christianity first arrives in Smyrna, although by the end of the first century it is well established. In Acts 16, Paul was prohibited from going to Asia. Nevertheless, this did not prevent him from traveling to other regions, namely Phrygia, Galatia, and Mysia on his way to Troas before arriving in Philippi. The *Martyrdom of Polycarp* mentions Quintus from Phrygia, who ultimately betrays the faith and opens a door to a Phrygian mission to Smyrna if not one from the Ephesian church. Still, we have no written account of missionary activity in Ionia. However, it seems plausible that some from Asia Minor who were in Jerusalem on the day of Pentecost might have carried the gospel to Smyrna (Acts 2:9). If so, then perhaps Peter's epistles were also intended for them. Yet, it seems more reasonable to suggest that either a missionary in Paul's cohort assumed that responsibility or someone from Smyrna visiting Ephesos while Paul taught at the hall of Tyrannos was among "all the residents of Asia" who heard about the *logos* of the Lord (Acts 19:10).

20. Philostratus, *Appolonius of Tyana* 4.7:335.

21. Ramsay, *Seven Churches of Asia*, 253.

22. Graves, "Local References," 26.

John's arrival in Asia during the Jewish wars might account for his influence on the city as Polycarp had been called his disciple.[23] In the third century, Tertullian suggests that he was appointed as bishop of Smyrna by John.[24] In late the second century, Irenaeus writes, "I myself saw him in my early years, for he lived a long time and was very old indeed when he laid down his life by a glorious and most splendid martyrdom. At all times he taught the things which he had learnt from the apostles, which the Church transmits, which alone are true."[25] His martyrdom (ca. AD 156) became one of the most remarkable testimonies of early Christianity. Given the opportunity to recant his faith, Polycarp boldly declared, "For eighty and six years have I been his servant, and he has done me no wrong, and how can I blaspheme my King who has saved me."[26]

In spite of the fact that we have no New Testament record of the arrival of Christianity in Smyrna, we do have a remarkable letter from Jesus to the church. In the letter, Smyrna gains the reputation as the city with a synagogue of Satan, a reference that continues to puzzle scholars as a Jewish place of gathering has yet to be excavated. Nevertheless, Jesus begins,

> And to the angel of the church in Smyrna write: "The words of the first and the last, who died and came to life. 'I know your tribulation and your poverty (but you are rich) and the slander of those who say that they are Jews and are not, but are a synagogue of Satan. Do not fear what you are about to suffer. Behold, the devil is about to throw some of you into prison, that you may be tested, and for ten days you will have tribulation. Be faithful unto death, and I will give you the crown of life. He who has an ear, let him hear what the Spirit says to the churches. The one who conquers will not be hurt by the second death.'" (Rev 2:8–11)

Jesus' letters to the churches demonstrate his remarkable understanding of the culture of the seven cities as well as the plight of the Christians in those cities. His letter to Smyrna is no different. Jesus' epithet "who died and came to life" might draw the Smyrnaeans attention to the product (*smyrna*) sold in the marketplace as would certainly the crown of life indicate the pride of Smyrna's crown on Mt. Pagos. Unique to this letter and the one to Philadelphia, Jesus manifests compassion to

23. This raises the interesting possibility that 1 John was written to Smyrna.

24. Tertullian, *Prescription Against Heretics* 32 (*Ante-Nicene Fathers* [*ANF*] 3:258).

25. Irenaeus, *Against Heresies* 3.3.4.

26. Ehrman, "Martyrdom of St. Polycarp," 9.3.

the church in preparation for a period of persecution. William Ramsay notes the difference of the tone of Jesus' letter to Smyrna as compared to the one before to Ephesos. He writes, "The writer is in thorough sympathy with the Church which he is addressing; he does not feel towards it merely that rather cold admiration which he expresses for the noble history of the Ephesian Church, a history which, alas! belonged only to the past: he is filled with warm affection [for Smyrna]."[27]

Notably absent, however, is a reference to emperor worship. Even so, the presence of emperors looms large in Smyrna. Recognized as thrice *neokoros*, the city was proud of its affiliation with Rome for they were the city that stood in the gap when the empire battled against the Macedonians in the second century BC. Subsequently, the city became the first to erect a temple dedicated to Rome and underscored Smyrna's status as "First in Asia" even though a self-proclaimed status in competition with Ephesos and Pergamon. One notable example of the utter dedication to emperors lies in plain sight at the *agora*. A marble base about a meter and a half tall, proclaims Emperor Hadrian as not only Caesar Augustus but among the other Olympian gods as well as savior (Figure 4.11). Certainly a provocative declaration that challenged the Smyrnaean church of the second century.

CHRISTIANITY IN THE MARKETPLACE

Whatever its status, whether self-proclaimed or not, Smyrna held many notable qualities, not the least of which was its monumental *agora* introduced at the beginning of the chapter (Figure 4.4). Among its features are the rather conspicuous graffiti located along the walls and piers of gallery 2 in the basement of the *basilica agora* (Figure 4.12). Notable among the graffiti is a unique Greek word square on the north side of the plaster wall of Bay 12 (Figure 4.13). A second example of the square is less well preserved but utilizes the same words (Figure 4.14). Word squares are not uncommon, but were often four palindromic words.[28] In our case, five by five letters forming five words horizontally and the same five vertically are not palindromic as the famed *rotas-sator* word square of Pompeii. The fact that there are two such examples in the Smyrna *agora* seems

27. Ramsay, *Seven Churches of Asia*, 268.

28. A palindromic word is a word that reads the same forward and backward, such as "level" or "radar."

curious if not significant. Roger Bagnall dates the graffiti to AD 125.[29] He comments, "Our square is the earliest such letter square known in Greek, as far as I can tell, by a matter of more than two centuries, and indeed the only five-letter Greek square known from antiquity."[30]

Written with charcoal in a *tabula ansata*,[31] only the top two words in Bay 12 of gallery 2 are distinguishable as are four letters of the last word at the bottom of the square. Reconstructing the word square in Bay 12 by using the second one found in Bay 9 provides the following:

Μ	Η	Λ	Ο	Ν
Η	Δ	Ο	Ν	Η
Λ	Ο	Γ	Ο	C
Ο	Ν	Ο	Μ	Α
Ν	Η	C	Α	C

1. ΜΗΛΟΝ (*mēlon*)—apple tree, apple, fruit
2. ΗΔΟΝΗ (*hēdonē*)—taste, delight, pleasure
3. ΛΟΓΟC (*logos*)—word, reason
4. ΟΝΟΜΑ (*onoma*)—name
5. ΝΗCΑC (*nēsas*)—floating, swimming, weaving, spinning

Figure 4.15: Recreated *Logos* word square.

Four of the five words are nouns while the last word Bagnall takes as the aorist participle of *neō*.[32] Bagnall does not see a Christian vocabulary here, yet leaves open a "counterargument, to be sure, point[s] to the cross

29. Bagnall, *Everyday Writing*, 22.
30. Bagnall, *Everyday Writing*, 18.
31. A *tabula ansata*, meaning "tablet with handles" in Latin, is a tablet, plaque, or drawing, usually rectangular, with two handles or wings on either side.
32. Bagnall et al., *Graffiti from the Basilica*, 270.

formed by ΛΟΓΟC in the center."[33] As a unique characteristic of the word square, the location of *logos* at the center forming a cross certainly requires a counterargument. The shape, along with the christological relationship of the other words, appears to be a clear indication for the connection to Jesus Christ as the *logos* of God (John 1:1; Acts 19:10). *Logos* is not unfamiliar to the Christian community in Smyrna. Besides being acquainted with John, the author of the fourth gospel, Ignatius of Antioch writes a letter to the church around AD 110. After having already mentioned God, Ignatius now completes the Trinitarian greeting: "Many greetings of happiness through the spotless Spirit and Word [*logos*] of God."[34] In the closing of the letter he makes clear that two deacons visiting Smyrna are conducting the work of Christ. He writes, "You have done well in receiving Philo and Rheus Agathopus as deacons of Christ our God. They have followed me in the Word [*logos*] of God and give thanks to the Lord on your behalf because you have in every way refreshed them."[35] In both instances, *logos* must be taken as a reference to the Word which became flesh, namely Jesus Christ (John 1:14).

The significance of the other four words (*mēlon*, *hēdonē*, *onoma*, *nēsas*) is open to interpretation. Bagnall sees no Christian relationship to these words.[36] Whatever their meaning, contrary to Bagnall, I suggest that their relationship to the center word *logos* must be maintained. If in fact the *logos* indicates a Christian provenance of the graffiti, a possibility Bagnall leaves open, then we have other resources to utilize for understanding its relationship with the other words. These tools, namely literary, include the Septuagint (LXX) as well as the writings of Ignatius of Antioch and Polycarp of Smyrna. So, with this help, along with the presupposition that second-century Christianity was just as vibrant and committed to Christ as first-century Christianity, I offer the following plausible interpretation.

ΜΗΛΟΝ: The Fruit of Life

ΜΗΛΟΝ (*mēlon*), appearing at the top of the word square, means apple tree, apple, or fruit. It evokes strong biblical associations. In Christian

33. Bagnall et al., *Graffiti from the Basilica*, 141; cf. Bagnall, *Everyday Writing*, 18.

34. Ignatius of Antioch, *To the Smyrnaeans* 1 (author's translation).

35. Ignatius of Antioch, *To the Smyrnaeans* 10 (author's translation).

36. Bagnall, *Everyday Writing*, 44.

thought, fruit is a common metaphor for both life and spiritual nourishment. One of the most intriguing interpretations of *mēlon* comes from the third-century Christian philosopher Origen, who, in his allegorical reading of the Song of Solomon, identified the apple tree (*mēlon* in LXX) with Christ (Song 2:3). Just as the apple tree provides shade and sustenance, so, too, does Christ give life and refreshment to his followers.[37] As a rhetorical device, allegory factored significantly in interpretation of sacred as well as philosophical works all across the Greco-Roman world. Indeed, we might even suggest that Jesus' letters to the churches used allegory as a function of communicating spiritual truth. Perhaps more convincing, however, is the fact that Homer was frequently interpreted allegorically as a defense against opposing philosophers for his epic poems.[38]

The word might also remind us of the tree of life in the garden of Eden, the fruit of which grants eternal life (Gen 2:24; Rev 2:7; 22:2). In contrast to the forbidden fruit from the tree of the knowledge of good and evil, Christ, as the tree of life, offers salvation and redemption. This reversal of the fall would be a powerful image for early Christians, who understood Christ's death and resurrection as the means of restoring what had been lost in Eden. Yet, as a part of the Christian testimony about Christ, *mēlon* could evoke the memory of the first couple's fall into sin and the *protoevangelium* in Gen 3 even though the word in the LXX is *karpos*. Alternatively, *mēlon* could symbolize the fruit of the Spirit (Gal 5:22–23), highlighting the virtues that the Holy Spirit produces in believers, although, again, the Greek word is *karpos*.

While this word seems simple, the layers of meaning that could be attached to it are quite profound and arguably Christian. If so, given the *mēlon* connection in Song 2:3, Origen's identification with Christ is a favorable interpretation.

HΔONH: Spiritual Delight or Worldly Pleasure

The second word, HΔONH (*hēdonē*), means pleasure or delight. This word could immediately remind us of Ps 37:4 (36:4 in the LXX)—"Delight yourself in the Lord"—a phrase that invites believers to experience the joy and goodness of God. In Christian thought, spiritual pleasure or delight often contrasts with the fleeting pleasures of the world. Here, *hēdonē*

37. Origen, *Song of Songs* 3.5:179–82.

38. Small, "On Allegory in Homer."

may represent the deep, abiding joy that comes from knowing Christ and living in the Spirit. This kind of pleasure is not superficial or temporary, but rooted in the satisfaction of the soul, the kind of delight that can only come from a relationship with God. The inclusion of *hēdonē* in the word square could be emphasizing the fullness of life that Christians find in their relationship with God.

Yet, *hēdonē* also holds the meaning of ill-gotten pleasure or self-gratification as in Luke 8:14. The parable of the sower warns that the word sown among the thorns are choked due to such worldly pleasure (*hēdonē*). Indeed, the five instances of the word in the NT all relate to hedonistic desires (Luke 8:14; Titus 3:3; Jas 4:1, 3; 2 Pet 2:13). As the second word in the square, it follows *mēlon* and could evoke allusion to the fall of Adam and Eve, who substituted delight in the Lord for the pleasure of the fruit of the forbidden tree. Either way, *hēdonē* and *mēlon* provide powerful christological references for discovering our complete satisfaction solely in Jesus.

ΛΟΓΟC (*Logos*)at the Center: Christ as the Word

As already noted, at the center of the word square, and ostensibly the central theme, is ΛΟΓΟC (*logos*). Theologically, this word is deeply significant, particularly in Christian thought of the first and second centuries. In the opening of the Gospel of John, *logos* refers to Christ—"In the beginning was the Word, and the Word was with God, and the Word was God" (John 1:1). John goes on to say that the *logos* became flesh and dwelt among us, clearly identifying Christ as the divine Word who created and sustains all things.

Since *logos* occupies the central position, it suggests the centrality of Christ in the faith and life of those who created this charcoal testimony. As Bagnall pointed out, the *logos* appears in the form of a cross in the square, and that seems to align well with the way early Christians discussed Christ's crucifixion in their writings and symbols. Indeed, throughout Asia Minor, the *staurogram*, the Greek tau-rho pointing to the cross, factors prominently at sites of Roman and Greek worship (Figures 4.16; 4.17).[39] The ΛΟΓΟC at the center of the word square holds the other words together, much as Christ holds all things together (Col 1:17).

39. Hurtado, *Earliest Christian Artifacts*, 135–54.

Indeed, as Smyrna's bishop Polycarp wrote to the Philippians, "To him all things 'in heaven and on earth are subject.'"[40]

Of course, it's important to remain open to other possibilities. Could *logos* here simply represent the more general Greek idea of reason or speech? In the ancient world, *logos* also had a philosophical dimension, referring to the organizing principle of the cosmos. It's possible, though perhaps less likely in this context, that *logos* was meant more generally as the principle of reason. But knowing what we do about early Christian communities, I find it hard not to see Christ at the center of this square. This is especially true when we consider the prominence of *logos* in the writings of the apostolic fathers and apologists. For instance, while in Smyrna on his way to martyrdom in Rome in AD 110, Ignatius of Antioch wrote a letter to the Christians in Magnesia, about one hundred kilometers to the south. In it, he clearly equates *logos* with Christ: "There is one God, who has revealed himself by Jesus Christ his Son, who is his eternal Word."[41]

ONOMA (*Onoma*): The Name of God or Christ?

Below *logos* we find another significant word in the square, ONOMA (*onoma*), meaning "name." In Scripture, the name of God carries profound theological weight. In Exod 3:14, God reveals his divine name to Moses—YHWH, meaning "I AM WHO I AM." This name is not just a label, but a revelation of God's eternal, self-sufficient nature. The divine name was held in the highest reverence in Jewish tradition, and early Christians understood Jesus as sharing in that divine identity. John's Gospel, for example, highlights twenty-one instances where Jesus uses the LXX version of Exod 3:14—εγω ειμι (*egō eimi*)—six of which are explicit declarations that Jesus is YHWH (John 4:26; 6:20; 8:24–28; 8:58; 13:19; 18:5).

In the NT, *onoma* is also linked to Jesus. Philippians 2:9–11 declares that after his death and resurrection, God exalted Jesus and gave him the name that is above every name, so that at the name (*onoma*) of Jesus, every knee should bow. So, *onoma* could refer to either God the Father or to the exalted Jesus Christ, who shares in the divine identity and authority. So, it should not surprise us that Polycarp, writing to the Philippians, appeals to the name of Christ: "Let us be passionate in the pursuit of

40. Polycarp, *Letter of Polycarp* 2 (author's translation).

41. Ignatius of Antioch, *To the Magnesians* 8 (author's translation).

that which is good, keeping ourselves from causes of offense, from false brethren, and from those who in hypocrisy bear the name (*onoma*) of the Lord and lead foolish people into error."[42] Since the word is situated under *logos*, this name is above every *onoma*.

In a public square in Smyrna, where loyalty to Rome and the emperor was paramount, the use of *onoma* could have been a hidden way of declaring that there is only one true name worthy of worship—the name of the *logos* of God (Rev 19:13). For Christians living under Roman rule, this would have been a significant and subversive statement of allegiance. But again, we should keep in mind that this is only one possible interpretation. Could *onoma* have a more mundane meaning in this square? It's hard to say, but the christological possibilities are worth considering.

NHCAC (*Nēsas*): The Holy Spirit?

Perhaps the most intriguing word in the square is NHCAC (*nēsas*), the only verb (an aorist active nominative masculine participle of *nēthō*),[43] which can mean floating, spinning, or swimming. In the NT, the word appears twice (Matt 6:28; Luke 12:27) and means to weave or spin. At first glance, this seems like an odd word to include in such a context, but it opens up some fascinating symbolic possibilities.

In the Gospels, we read about the Holy Spirit descending upon Jesus at his baptism, floating down like a dove (*katabainō*, Matt 3:16). The imagery of floating can also remind us of Gen 1:2, where the Spirit of God is hovering over the waters at creation (*epipherō*) bringing life and order out of chaos. If we interpret *nēsas* as representing the Holy Spirit, then the square might be reflecting a Trinitarian structure: *logos* (the Son) at the center, *onoma* (the Father) nearby, and *nēsas* (the Holy Spirit) completing the triad upon which the entire Christian faith rests. The idea that the Holy Spirit hovers, floats, or descends upon Christ and the church fits beautifully with early Christian theology, which saw the Spirit as the empowering presence of God in both Christ's ministry and the life of believers. Supporting this idea, we know that the Christians in Smyrna held to the doctrine of the Trinity. After departing Smyrna for Rome, Ignatius writes back to the church: "Ignatius, who is also called Theophorous, to

42. Polycarp, *Letter of Polycarp* 6.3 (author's translation).

43. Cf. Bagnall et al., *Graffiti from the Basilica*, 161 who suggests the word is *neō*, the verb meaning to swim.

the church of God the Father, and of the beloved Jesus Christ . . . through the spotless Spirit and Word of God."[44] The word square might very well be a Trinitarian declaration. However, the Greek verbs in Gen 1:2 and Matt 3:16 do not support the equivocation.

Nevertheless, the christological focus is equally compelling. Since the verb is used in Jesus' Sermon on the Mount, it could be a reference to God's provisions for the disciples (Matt 6:28; Luke 12:27). This has interesting possibilities since the word square is located in a marketplace full of provisions for the community's sustenance. Of course, *nēsas* might also have other, less spiritual meanings. Could it refer to the idea of floating or swimming as a metaphor for navigating life's challenges? Or perhaps it's an allusion to something cultural, philosophical, or even nautical that we haven't yet uncovered. Whatever the case, NHCAC opens up some interesting possibilities when read through a christological lens.

A Missiological Masterpiece in Plain Sight

As we consider this word square, the striking archaeological testimony as well as the rich Trinitarian and christological possibilities offer a unique missiological lens through which to consider the early church in Smyrna. Could this be an early example of a way in which Christians engaged people in the marketplace, an early gospel presentation if you will? Could it be a subtle proclamation of Christian faith—a coded declaration of the Trinity? Or a second-century Christology expressed in *graffito*? Even a theological lesson for disciples who might be in the market to purchase food? Given that the early *ekklēsia* was founded upon Jesus Christ, whatever the word square might mean, we can be encouraged by the faithful saints in Smyrna and their proclamation of Jesus Christ as the eternal Word in the marketplace of this important city.

Yet, when it comes to interpreting the material culture, archaeology is not a precise science. The word square could easily refer to the succulent produce sold in these particular bays of the *cryptoproticos*. Additionally, it might refer to the means by which the produce arrived by ship as there are numerous pictures of nautical vessels in the various bays. Still, the most curious word is *logos* in a cross shape; a compelling reason that could easily identify the keepers of these particular shops as Christians. Whatever the case, assuming that *logos* is a Christian reference—and I

44. Ignatius of Antioch, *To the Smyrnaeans*, intro. (author's translation).

believe it is a reasonable assumption—it would be the earliest archaeological reference to Jesus Christ as the Word whose name is above every name.

If it were only these two word-square graffiti written on the walls in Smyrna, we might disregard any attempt to connect them with the early Christ followers. However, there are others that provide clarity to the Christian witness in the marketplace. For example, Bagnall suggests that *zōē* on Pier 63 in the gallery 2 might be a reference to Eve as the LXX translates her name (Gen 3:20).[45] Perhaps most compelling is the isopsephism on Pier 100. According to Bagnall, the incised *graffito* in the plaster of the pier is among the clearest examples of early Christian symbolic expression in Smyrna. This striking illustration represents a numerological practice deeply rooted in the Greco-Roman world. The inscription simply reads:

ισοψηφα
κυριος ω
πιστις ω

Numerically speaking κυριος and πιστις are of equal value (ισοψηφα): lord (eight hundred); faith (eight hundred). The number eight hundred is indicated by the ω at the end of each word in Greek numerology. According to Bagnall, at its core, this equation reflects a distinctly Christian impulse to associate linguistic expression with theological significance. He notes that while isopsephism was a well-known phenomenon across the Eastern Mediterranean, with parallels such as the infamous equivalency between Nero's name (*Nerōn*) and the phrase "he killed his own mother," this particular pairing of *kyrios* and *pistis*—both numerically and conceptually aligned—has no known precedent in the ancient record. Yet once observed, the formulation seems theologically obvious as it reveals a layer of Christian reflection that moves beyond mere wordplay into the realm of confessional identity. Christians in Smyrna, no doubt familiar with the writing of Paul, would be well versed in the Pauline concept of one Lord and one faith (Eph 4:5). Additionally, the omega (ω) plays an important role in Revelation as it is identified with Christ (Rev 22:13) and the Smyrnaeans would be well aware of its significance. The number eight hundred represented by the letter ω could easily imply finality, completion, or fulfillment.

45. Bagnall, *Everyday Writing*, 77.

What makes this *graffito* especially compelling is its permanence and intentionality—it is not scrawled in charcoal or ink, but incised into the architecture itself. In doing so, it asserts a theological claim in public space: that "lord" and "faith" are not only linguistically isomorphic but ontologically linked in early Christian thought. Bagnall suggests that such usage was not limited to scholarly elites but was part of a broader Christian cultural engagement.[46] This Christianization of Greek numerology testifies to the embeddedness of theological ideas in the daily lives of believers, and further underscores the early church's imaginative engagement with inherited cultural forms to express their convictions in meaningful ways.

FROM GRAFFITI TO APPLICATION

Naturally, the *agora* functioned as one of the most popular gathering places in the ancient world. Paul's presence in the *agora* in Acts 17:17 represents a strategic moment of public engagement, where he reasons daily with Athenians in the social and intellectual heart of the city. While this is the only explicit reference to the *agora* in Acts, the pattern of Paul's ministry consistently reflects a deliberate use of public spaces—whether trade guilds, marketplaces, or lecture halls such as the hall of Tyrannos (Acts 19:9). These venues functioned as civic and cultural centers, offering access to diverse people and opinions. In Philippi (Acts 16:19–20) and Lystra (Acts 14:8–18), Paul's encounters unfold in similar public settings, underscoring his adaptive and missional posture. Even in Corinth he no doubt sold leatherworks in the marketplace (Acts 18:4), and he stood before Gallio in a public space (Acts 18:12) further illustrating the importance for Christians to be in those spaces.

Smyrna offers a brilliant archaeological example of how this practice continued. Early Christians deliberately placed themselves in the proximity of the people they engaged. Rather than waiting for the people to come to them, they took the initiative to share the gospel where people worked and shopped. Such an open and public display of faith testifies to the fearlessness of Christians who faced opposition at nearly every segment of society. In spite of this, the clear application today underscores the sense that Christians are Christian where they live, work, and play. What is striking, nevertheless, is the fact that marketplace engagement is

46. Bagnall, et al., *Graffiti from the Basilica*, 76.

never taught in the Epistles. It might be assumed, even inferred, but there is no explicit reference to this sort of ministry. Even so, it was observed and therefore modeled while ultimately replicated around the empire.

Finally, if I am correct in suggesting that the word-square holds christological significance, the *graffito* displays a manner in which Christians communicated in meaningful language. Contrary to Bagnall, the vocabulary appears uniquely Christian when interpreted through the lens of *logos*, the focal point of the square. Even the use of allegory connects with the normative means of interpretation of philosophy and religion in the early centuries of Christianity. After all, the Smyrnaean Christians held fast to the promise of "the first and the last, who died and came to life. . . . Be faithful unto death, and I will give you the crown of life" (Rev 2:8–10). I can imagine this as a clear encouragement emboldening the body of Christ as they gazed upon Mt. Pagos, the crown of Smyrna, on their way to the *agora*.

In the last chapter, we departed from Ephesos with a clear sense of the importance for communicating the gospel with precision. We arrived in Smyrna and have seen the creativity in communicating the gospel in the marketplace. Now, we journey onward to Pergamon where we will meet what I believe to be the strongest opposition to the claims of Christ. While we certainly see the polemical parallels in Ephesos and might imagine them in Smyrna, they are utterly acute in the primary city of the Roman Empire. Pergamon will be without equal in Asia Minor well into the Byzantine period. Let's see what we might dig up there.

Chapter 5

The Puzzling Disappearance of Christianity: Pergamon

Recently I traveled to North Africa to begin another archaeological research project. Accompanying me were two colleagues. Our goal was to explore whether the patterns we had been observing in the archaeological record of Christianity in Asia Minor also applied to the North African context. This region, after all, boasts a long and illustrious Christian heritage. From Tertullian to Cyprian to Augustine, North Africa helped shape Christian theology in ways still felt today.

On our first visit to ancient Thugga, we made an unexpected discovery: a Christogram etched in marble near the temple of Mercury in the Wind Rose square, a small but telling symbol that assured us of the Christian presence in this space. Our excitement over the find compelled us to ask a passing tour group about it hoping to spark a conversation regarding its significance. I pointed and asked their guide, "Do you know what this is?"

The response was abrupt and dismissive: "It's just a sundial." And they walked on.

That moment lingered with us. Here, in a land once so foundational to Christian theology—doctrines of the Trinity, church unity, predestination were solidified here—the memory of Christianity had all but vanished. Its absence wasn't just spiritual; it was physical, historical, intellectual, and cultural. And in that unsettling silence, we were reminded of Pergamon. Like North Africa, Pergamon once stood as a beacon of Christian witness, a city that Revelation remembers for the martyrdom of Antipas. However, not long after Jesus sent the letter to the Christians there, Christianity was silenced too. The stones remain, but the story has faded. What happened? How did such a formidable Christian presence disappear? And more to the point, what can that disappearance teach us about our own cultural moment?

Pergamon, the ancient city, is located in modern-day Bergama, Turkey. We've examined different parts of the site on various occasions, particularly the acropolis. This is where we find the Temple of Zeus/Trajan, the Altar of Zeus, an incredible theater dedicated to Dionysos—the steepest in Asia Minor (Figure 5.1)—and other significant structures and inscriptions. What makes the site particularly puzzling is the complete lack of evidence for Christianity. In nearly every other site we've explored, we've found some indicator of Christian presence—whether graffiti, repurposed temple structures, or other material evidence. In Ephesos, for example, there is a column capital at the site of the Temple of Artemis bearing a Christian cross (Figure 5.2). This suggests that Christians repurposed architectural elements from the pagan temple and incorporated them into the nearby Church of John (Figure 5.3). In Didyma, the Temple of Apollo is covered in Christian graffiti, including the Christogram and tau-rho monogram, both common symbols representing Christ in the early church.[1] Yet in Pergamon, there appears to be nothing; not a single marker identifying the presence of Christianity at least until the Byzantine period when Christianity was legalized. This absence is striking. It might suggest that Christianity never took deep root here, which raises the question: Why? Why does Pergamon stand in contrast to other cities in Asia Minor where Christianity seemed to thrive? This is the puzzle I want to explore.

In this chapter, we'll examine what the book of Revelation says about Pergamon and consider what it might reveal about the city's Christian history. What we do know is that, unlike Ephesos and Smyrna, Pergamon never developed into a major Christian center. By the third and fourth centuries, Christianity had largely vanished from the city. A number of other cities in the region flourished as Christian strongholds. Sardis, Laodicea, Hierapolis, and Colossae all had Christian communities, though Colossae may have been destroyed by an earthquake before the writing of Revelation and had yet to recover. Still, Christianity expanded across Asia Minor even into the villages, yet somehow Pergamon remained an exception. Why? I think the archaeological record helps answer this question.

1. Hays, *Ichthus Christogram.*

So, this is the puzzle we need to solve, and it will provide a lesson for church planting today. First, let's explore some important background.

BACKGROUND

The Jewish presence in Pergamon is attested in Josephus.[2] In spite of the number of allusions to familiar Jewish traditions in Jesus' letter, however, Colin Hemer notes, "The evidence suggests that there was actually less Jewish presence in Pergamon than in most of the other cities [of Asia Minor]."[3] The political, intellectual, and religious climate in Pergamon was profoundly challenging for Christians if not also for Judaism. The city was a stronghold of imperial power, pagan worship, and philosophical thought, all of which stood in direct competition with Christianity. In relationship to emperor worship, borrowing the term from Adolf Deissmann, Hemer describes this as a polemical parallelism. He writes, "We note the strong hints of the growth of 'polemical parallelism' between Christ and Caesar. The claims of Caesar are viewed by John as a Satanic parody of those of Christ. And some of the imagery of the later chapters [of Revelation] may rightly be seen to refer to Rome as a persecuting power and so to reinforce our picture."[4] Yet, such polemical parallels can also be extended to the juxtaposing of Jesus to both pagan worship and philosophical thought as we might expect (Table 5.1). So, let's consider these polemical parallels, beginning with the cult of *sebatos*, what we typically call emperor worship.

Pergamene Identity	**Jesus Christ**
Allegiance to the emperor—the people of Pergamon were expected to worship the emperor as a god, demonstrating political and religious loyalty to Rome	Allegiance to God's kingdom—Jesus proclaimed the kingdom of God (Mark 1:15), teaching that ultimate allegiance belongs to God alone, not earthly rulers (Matt 22:21)
Worship of savior Gods (Zeus and Asklepios)—Zeus was worshiped as the chief deity, while Asklepios was honored as the god of healing; both were called Soter (Savior)	Jesus as the true Savior—Jesus is the one true Savior (Luke 2:11), who brings both salvation from sin and healing (Matt 9:35)

2. Josephus, *Antiquities* 14.20.5.
3. Hemer, *Seven Churches of Asia*, 89.
4. Hemer, *Seven Churches of Asia*, 87.

Pergamene Identity	Jesus Christ
Zeus as a friend (*philios*)—Zeus was venerated as Zeus Philios, a god of friendship, protection, and hospitality	Jesus as the true friend—Jesus calls his disciples friends (John 15:15) and offers divine protection, love, and hospitality (Matt 11:28)
Asklepios as healer—pilgrims flocked to Pergamon to seek healing at the Temple of Asklepios, known as the "god of medicine"	Jesus as the great physician—Jesus heals the sick, raises the dead, and brings spiritual healing (Matt 9:12, Luke 4:18–19)
Syncretism of politics, worship, and philosophy—the Aristotelian peripatetic tradition of Pergamon merged intellectual rigor, civic duty, and religious worship, blending political allegiance with devotion to the gods	Jesus as the Logos (Divine Wisdom)—Jesus embodies true wisdom (John 1:1, 1 Cor 1:24), offering a way of life that transcends human philosophy, calling his followers to worship God in spirit and truth (John 4:23–24)

Table 5.1: Polemical parallels in Pergamon

Cult of *Sebastos*

Pergamon boasts a long history of kings being identified as gods and saviors. Beginning with Eumenes I (263–241 BC) after defeating the Seleucid king Antiochus I at Sardis, Pergamenians bestowed upon him divine honors although he never accepted the title of king.[5] Attalos I (241–197 BC) followed with accepting the titles "king" and "savior" after defeating the Gauls. Later, Eumenes II (197–159 BC) accepted both "savior" and "divine benefactor."[6] Of no consequence, these pre-Roman kings bore their monikers alongside of both Zeus and Asklepios, who were considered savior gods. Eventually, as Hemer notes, "To the earlier strata of Anatolian and Olympian religion and of ruler-cult was added the worship of the Roman emperor."[7] Such worship of a divine ruler deeply marked the identity of the Pergamenians and ultimately contributed to the Roman cult of *sebastos*.

Indeed, the numismatic record beginning with Tiberius, the adopted son of Augustus, testifies to the deification of living emperors.

5. Hemer, *Seven Churches of Asia*, 80.

6. See inscriptions 302 (ΥΠΕΡ ΒΑΣΙΛΕΩΣ ΕΥΜΕΝΟΥ ΦΙΛΑΔΕΛΦΟΥ ΘΕΟΥ ΕΥΕΡΓΕΤΟΥ ΔΗΜΗΤΡΙΟΣ ΠΟΣΕΙΔΩΝΙΟΥ) and 305 (ΒΑΣΙΛΕΙ ΕΥΜΕΝΕΙ ΤΩΙ ΣΩΤΗΡΙ) in Dittenberger, *Orientis Graeci inscriptiones selectae*, 1:472.

7. Hemer, *Seven Churches of Asia*, 82.

Tiberius, along with subsequent emperors in the second century—Nerva, Trajan, and Hadrian, especially—were all conferred divine status in Pergamon while still alive. While there are no coins assigning such a status to Augustus when he was alive, later coins do confer on him the status of divine emperor. The obverse legend on RPCI 5423 (Figure 5.4) refers to Augustus as "Caesar Augustus god," indicating his deified status. The reverse legend, "the divine emperor," further emphasizes his deification. The coin's imagery includes a bare head of Augustus facing right on the obverse, and a Capricorn facing right above a globe on the reverse, with grapes or a cornucopia above, symbolizing prosperity and *beneficia*, and incorrectly assumed to be Augustus's astrological sign.[8] The exact mint of this coin remains uncertain with some suggestions pointing to Cilicia, though definitive evidence is lacking.

The epigraphic evidence in the archaeological record of the city clearly indicates the divine status of Roman emperors. After the typical honorific tributes we see ascribed to emperors across Asia Minor (ΑΥΤΟΚΡΑΤΟΡΑ ΚΑΙΣΑΡΑ ΣΕΒΑΣΤΟΝ), an inscription dedicated to Nerva (AD 96–98) and Trajan (AD 98–117) reads "son of the divine Nerva, Trajan the excellent and revered *germanikon* and *dakiko*, the lord of the earth and sea" (Figure 5.5, 6). Of particular note, the epithet ΤΟΝ ΓΗΣ ΚΑΙ ΘΑΛΑΣΣ ΚΥΡΙΟΝ is not only declarative but emphatic as indicated by the definite article and its object surrounding the realm of sovereignty: "Who is, of earth and sea, lord."

All across Asia Minor, Trajan is celebrated by the additional monikers *germanikon* and *dakiko* indicating his defeat of the Germans and Dacians. But here, his adoptive father Nerva is conferred divine status as a god (*theou*) while Trajan is lord (*kyrion*). Later, the "divine" or god Trajan's adoptive son Hadrian, who ruled the Roman Empire from AD 138–161, is likewise declared both god and savior. The inscription highlights his divine heritage stemming from his adoptive grandfather Nerva, through his adoptive father Trajan, and bestowed upon him by a priest and temple guardian of Dionysos (Figure 5.7).[9] No doubt such epithets

8. Barton, "Augustus and Capricorn."

9. Adoption of heirs to the throne were quite common in Imperial Rome and signaled a continuity of sovereignty more than blood ties. In adoption, the heir took on the identity of the emperor and was bestowed all the rights of having been a blood relative. See my discussion of the theological implications for being adopted children in *Ephesiology*, 98–100.

follow in the history of the Pergamene ruler-cult that pre-date imperial Rome.

Adding to these challenges was the reality of Roman persecution for not worshiping the emperor, which intensified in Asia Minor from the late first century into the second century. While persecution was often regional and sporadic, there is strong evidence that it occurred in Pergamon. Pliny the Younger's letter to Trajan, for example, described persecution in Bithynia, which was also home to a Synagogue of Zeus (see chapter 6).[10] Given the broader climate, it is reasonable to believe that similar persecution extended to Pergamon, a judicial center, during the reigns of Trajan and Hadrian. While Trajan appears sympathetic to Christians, the threat of Jesus as Lord and God certainly weighed heavy on the Pergamene identity.[11] Such a polemical parallel could hardly be tolerated in the most important Roman city in Asia Minor.

Zeus and Asklepios

During the reign of Eumenes II (221–160 BC), the great Altar of Zeus (Figure 5.8) became a central feature of the acropolis.[12] Depicting the story of the Gigantomachy—the battle between the Olympian gods and giants—its grandeur and religious significance made it one of the most remarkable structures of the ancient world. The Pergamon Museum in Berlin houses a full reconstruction of the altar, the result of early German excavations conducted in agreement with the Ottoman government. The original remnants of the altar were transported to Berlin, where they were meticulously reconstructed in 1901. If we were to imagine how the altar originally appeared on-site, its scale and prominence would have been unmistakable, particularly with the Temple of Trajan/Zeus looming in the background in the second century AD. The presence of these monumental structures underscores the centrality of religious devotion alongside of emperor devotion in Pergamon.

Pagan traditions were deeply embedded in Pergamon's culture. The rise of Zeus Philios (Zeus the Friend) under Trajan is particularly interesting.[13] The Temple of Zeus Philios and Trajan occupies the most

10. Pliny the Younger, *Letters* 10.96.

11. Evans, *History of Pergamum*, 107.

12. Callaghan, "Great Altar of Zeus," 115.

13. Schowalter, "Zeus Philios."

prominent location on the acropolis (Figure 5.9). Today, its anastylosis, fluted-Corinthian columns can be seen from the modern city of Bergama and the Temple of Asklepios. Yet, the idea of Zeus Philios seems to indicate another polemical parallel Christians navigated. This second-century-AD representation of Zeus is starkly contrasted with the Zeus of Homer. In early Greek mythology, Zeus is depicted as capricious and often morally ambiguous, but by the first and second centuries AD, he had been reimagined in philosophical, if not political, thought as a benevolent and caring deity (cf. Acts 17:28). By this period, Zeus was increasingly perceived as a protector and mediator between the divine and human realms, providing a striking alternative to the Christian God. Marianne Palmer Bonz notes, "Indeed, from the beginning Zeus Philios had been associated with the idea of mediation between the realm of the gods and the world of human beings, and by the Roman period he had come to be looked upon as the guardian of friendship and the promoter of harmony among peoples."[14] Bonz sees that Zeus Philios was closely associated with the idea of mediation between the divine and human realms. By the Roman period, he had come to be seen as a guardian of friendship and harmony, particularly political harmony as Zeus seems to serve the imperial ambitions of Trajan and Hadrian.[15] This conceptual transformation suggests that Zeus had evolved to meet the spiritual needs of his devotees in a way that made him an attractive and enduring figure, if not also a means by which Trajan maintained allegiance from Pergamon. One can imagine the challenge this posed for Christian evangelists. Why would the people of Pergamon embrace the Christian God when Zeus, the patron deity of their city, had already assumed the role of a divine friend and protector?

Alongside Zeus, Asklepios played an equally impressive role in Pergamene religion. In the second century, Galen's influence as a physician to the gladiators in Pergamon helped solidify the Asklepion's status as one of the most important healing centers in the empire.[16] Asklepios was revered as *soter*, placing him in direct competition with Christ; once again, another polemical parallel. Sculptures from Athens and Miletos depict Asklepios with his iconic serpent-entwined staff, reinforcing his role as a divine healer (Figures 5.10, 11). A dedicatory inscription at the temple acknowledges the god as savior, confirming the connection

14. Bonz, "Differing Approaches," 263.

15. Cf. Kampmann, "Homonoia Politics," 374–93.

16. Flemming, "Galen and the Christians," 175.

between religion, healing, and intellectual life in Pergamon (Figure 5.12). The subject of the inscription is Flavia Melitine, who funded the construction of a library at the "temple of the savior Asklepios" (ΤΩΙ ΙΕΡΩΙ ΤΟΥ ΣΩΤΗΡΟΣ ΑΣΚΛΗΠΟΙΥ).

The philosopher Aelius Aristides, writing in the second century AD, provides one of the most compelling testimonies of Pergamon's healing cult. In his work *Sacred Tales*, Aristides recounts his personal experiences with Asklepios, whom he credits with both his physical healing and his success as an orator:

> But it is necessary to try to make clear all of my oratorical career that pertains to the god and, as far as I can, to omit nothing of it. For it would be strange if both I and others would recount whatever cure he gave to my body even at home, but would pass by in silence those things which at the same time raised up my body, strengthened my soul and increased the glory of my oratory.[17]

Aristides describes his unwavering devotion to the god, emphasizing that he owed his well-being, intellectual abilities, and even his voice to Asklepios. His testimony provides a powerful glimpse into the depth of religious allegiance in Pergamon, demonstrating how figures like Asklepios and Zeus occupied spaces in people's lives that left little room for Christianity. Indeed, Asklepios's popularity by the second century compelled Ido Israelowich to note, "Asklepios himself was so popular in Aristides' lifetime in the Roman world that Christianity identified him and his cult as a prime focus of opposition to the newly emerging Christian Church from the second century into late antiquity."[18] Together, Zeus Philios and Asklepios Soter presented a religious identity that may have been more culturally palatable than Christianity, further explaining why Christianity struggled to establish a lasting presence in Pergamon.

Philosophy

Beyond politics and religion, the intellectual climate of Pergamon also played a significant role in shaping the city's identity. Similar to how Aristotle was entrusted with the education of Alexander the Great, Apollodorus of Pergamon accompanied Octavian, who later became Caesar

17. Aristides, *Orations* 51.36, quoted in Israelowich, *Society, Medicine and Religion*, 30.

18. Israelowich, *Society, Medicine and Religion*, 134.

Augustus, in his youth instructing him in Greek studies.[19] Pergamon at the turn of the era rivaled both Alexandria and Athens as the intellectual capital of the empire. Its library, Plutarch records, contained two hundred thousand scrolls at its height, making it a critical repository of Greek thought, philosophy, and scholarship.[20] Gregory Nagy notes, "The development of new technologies in library science involving the media of parchment in place of papyrus, and the codex instead of scroll or roll was, for example, more pronounced in Pergamon than in Alexandria" and it contributed to the prestige of Pergamon as a learning center.[21] In an act of political maneuvering, Mark Antony later transferred many of these scrolls to Alexandria, following Julius Caesar's destruction of part of the Alexandrian collection. Regardless of this shift, Pergamon remained a significant intellectual hub, particularly for Aristotelian and Stoic thought.

While by the second and third centuries the Library of Pergamon (Figure 5.13) was not as dominant as it had once been, out of it came the Pergamene School; an intellectual tradition that emphasized Aristotelian and Stoic philosophy led by Crates in the third century BC. The peripatetic tradition, following Aristotle, engaged in rigorous philosophical inquiry emphasizing empirical observation and dialectical reasoning as foundational to knowledge. In that tradition, Socrates famously held that the streets of Athens were his classroom, and a similar philosophical approach emerged in Pergamon. Eunapius recounts how Chrysanthius experienced the Stoic philosopher, Aedesius, who carried on the peripatetic tradition in the fourth century:

> This is why Chrysanthius used to say to the author of this account that Aedesius' manners were sociable and unassuming, and after their contests in disputation, he would go for a walk in Pergamon accompanied by the more distinguished of his pupils. And their teacher used to instill in his pupils a feeling of harmony and of responsibility toward humanity, when he observed that they were headstrong and arrogant because of their overconfidence in their own opinions (their wings bigger and softer than those of Icarus), he would force them back down, not into the sea, but to earth and to human life. While he thus instructed them, he himself, if he met a woman selling vegetables, was

19. Suetonius, *Lives of the Caesars* 1:4.89.

20. Josephus, *Antiquities* 58.5–59.

21. Nagy, "Library of Pergamon," 213.

> pleased to see her and would interrupt his walk to speak to her and discuss the price she charged, and say that her shop was making a good profit, while at the same time chatting with her about the cultivation of vegetables. He would behave in the same fashion to a weaver, a smith, or a carpenter. Thus, the more prudent of his pupils were trained in this affability, especially Chrysanthius and all who in that school resembled Chrysanthius.[22]

The Stoic influence was particularly important as Stoic thinkers employed allegory and analogy—methods that Jesus himself uses in his letters to the largely Gentiles churches, and especially to the church in Pergamon. Jesus' references to Balaam and Balak might be considered allegory as he extends the meaning of the story to the present situation, whereas his reference to the Nicolaitans would be an analogy as he compares whatever the Nicolaitans were to the sexual immorality occurring in Pergamon. This suggests that Christian intellectuals would have had to engage in similar types of discourse to be taken seriously in the city.

The philosophers of Pergamon played a significant role in shaping the city's intellectual climate, and while this may not seem directly relevant, it is certainly interesting. As mentioned, one of the earliest figures associated with the Pergamene School was Crates, a Stoic philosopher and Aristotelian scholar. Letters were sent to several philosophers inviting them to head the library or philosophical school in Pergamon, and while many declined, Crates was the first to accept the invitation. His work helped establish Pergamon as an important center of Stoic and Aristotelian thought. Later, other notable figures emerged, including the renowned physician Galen, who revolutionized medicine and philosophy. Indeed, Robert Wilken notes the disdain that Galen held for the Christian that was also reflected in Celsus:

> As early as the mid second century the physician and philosopher Galen complained that it was pointless to engage Christians in discussion because they never give arguments for what they believe. They only make appeals to "God commanded" or "God spoke." In *True Doctrine*, written about the same time, Celsus echoed Galen's accusation: "Some Christians," he wrote, "do not even want to give or to receive a reason for what they believe, and use expressions such as 'Do not ask questions, just believe'

22. Eunapius, *Lives of Philosophers* 8.5–8.

> and 'Your faith will save you.' Others quote the apostle Paul. 'The world's wisdom is evil and foolishness a good thing.'"[23]

Of final note, Maximus of Ephesos, another major thinker, would eventually become an advisor to Emperor Julian (AD 361–363)—the nephew of Constantine the Great. Julian, of course, is known for renouncing Christianity and making a determined, though ultimately unsuccessful, attempt to restore the empire to its traditional Greco-Roman religious roots. The observation that Pergamon factored into Julian's efforts speaks to its continued importance as a philosophical and religious stronghold. The rise of Neplatonism in the third and fourth centuries also provided an alternative spiritual worldview, blending philosophy, medicine, and mystical practices. So, what happened to Christianity in Pergamon?

CHRISTIANITY IN PERGAMON

We have only a handful of Christian literary references to Pergamon, and the most significant is Jesus' letter to the church there, which we'll examine shortly. Beyond that, references to Christianity in the city are largely incidental. In the middle part of the second century, during the reign of Hadrian, a group of Greek speaking Christians from Asia Minor made their way to Gaul. Among them travelled the missionary scholar Irenaeus, a disciple of Polycarp. We're not certain if Irenaeus was originally from Smyrna or lived there to study Christianity under Polycarp. Whatever the case, his ability to speak a Celtic language ostensibly led him to Gaul in the second century.[24] If so, Irenaeus might originate from Galatia where Celtic people had migrated as early as the third century BC.

During the reign of Marcus Aurelius (AD 161–180)—a particularly troubling time for Christians in Gaul—Irenaeus traveled to Rome to meet with Pope Eleutherus regarding the emergence of Montanism in Lyon and Vienne (France).[25] While there, persecution broke out in the two cities and members of his community—including one Attalos from Pergamon—were martyred (ca. AD 177).[26] We learn about the martyr-

23. Wilken, *Early Christian Thought*, 162.

24. Irenaeus *Against Heresies*, 1.3; cf. Fox, *Pagans and Christians*, 368.

25. Irenaeus was a presbyter at the time and became bishop of Lyon after the martyrdom of Pothinus (see Tabbernee, *Fake Prophecy*, 34).

26. See Eusebius, *History of the Church* 5.1

dom from a second-century letter to the churches in Asia and Phyrgia preserved in Eusebius.[27] What is particularly intriguing is that Attalos and his family had migrated from Asia Minor, likely in the early second century, raising the question: Why? Could their departure from Pergamon have been due to persecution? Or perhaps for ministry purposes as we see with Irenaeus? Maybe they were Montanists? We know that migration from Asia Minor to Gaul was not uncommon in the second century, so this movement itself is not necessarily unusual.[28] However, it is interesting that a Christian from Pergamon is found among those who were later martyred in Lyon—one of the few clear links between Christianity and the city.

Eusebius also mentions other Christians in the third century, apparently missionaries, who traveled to Pergamon and were arrested. Ultimately martyred, Eusebius remarks that they entered their "glorious fulfillment."[29] The story is preserved in *The Martyrdom of Karpos, Papylos, and Agathonike*, which recounts how Karpos, a bishop from Lydia, and Papylos from Thyatira stood before the proconsul during the reign of Decius (r. 249–251 AD) because they were witnesses of Christ. Karpos boldly denounced pagan gods and refused to offer sacrifices, leading to his horrendous and painful torture. Papylos, a deacon, likewise rejected the demand and suffered the same fate after claiming he had many disciples. Condemned to be burned alive, Papylos died first. As Karpos faced the flames, he smiled and declared he had seen the Lord's glory. He affirmed that Christians endured suffering in hope of divine judgment, then offered a final prayer of thanksgiving. Moved by his vision, Agathonike, who came to faith along with her son as a result of the missionaries' work, also chose martyrdom despite the crowd's pleas to not leave her son behind.[30]

27. Eusebius, *History of the Church* 5.1–2. The fascination with the lives of martyrs held by those in Lydia and Phrygia might suggest the extent of Montanism from Asia Minor to Europe. We will discuss this in the chapter on Philadelphia.

28. Tabbernee, *Fake Prophecy*, 29.

29. Eusebius, *History of the Church* 4.15.

30. Musurillo, *Acts*, 22–37. There are two versions of the martyrdom. The Greek version includes the account of the believers gathering the remains of the martyrs. If true, we have indication of a church in Pergamon into the third century. However, it appears that these believers were the result of the work of Karpos and Papylos who travelled from Thyatira for missionary work in Pergamon. Agathonike and her children become their disciples along with others. Prior to Karpos and Papylos, the question of the church's existence is unanswered. It is curious that these two leaders from a different city would engage in missionary activity where the church already existed.

Another incidental reference is found in Tertullian. In his work *On Fasting*, he makes a passing reference to the wealth of the Attalid dynasty—the ruling family of Pergamon which governed the region when it was the capital of Phrygia prior to its bequest to Rome in the second century BC. He uses Pergamon as a metaphor for material excess suggesting that the city was well-known even among early Christian thinkers. Yet, notably, he does not associate it with Christianity. His knowledge of Pergamon, like that of many others, seems to be purely material, rather than theological or ecclesiastical, which is striking.

Beyond these three references, we have no known bishops from Pergamon attending any of the ecumenical councils after the Christianization of the empire; another indication that the city never became a significant Christian center. Walter Bauer, a NT scholar, argued decades ago that Pergamon simply wasn't important to early Christianity. His reasoning is based, in part, on the fact that Ignatius of Antioch—who wrote letters to several churches in Asia Minor—did not write to Pergamon. If Pergamon had been a major Christian hub, Bauer suggests, Ignatius would have addressed it as he did with cities like Ephesos, Smyrna, and Philadelphia. He writes,

> Is it too much to claim if, on the basis of what Ignatius both says and does not say, and considering the evidence of the Apocalypse, one concludes that in his attempt to stretch the circle of his influence as widely as possible for the sake of his constituency there was nothing Ignatius could hope for from the Christian groups represented at Pergamum, Thyatira, Sardis, and Laodicea, because no points of contact existed for him there—no "bishop" was present whom he could press into service, because the heretics had maintained, or had come to exercise, leadership there?[31]

Well into the Christian era of the Roman Empire, there is an unreliable sixth century text mentioning Theodotus, a bishop of Pergamon in AD 152, who deposed the heresy of the Colarbasians at an undocumented synod.[32] According to Charles Joseph Hefele, a bishop named Dracontius of Pergamon is deposed at a Synod of Gangra (ca. 340), but we have no details of the charge and no mention of his name in extant documents.[33] Consequently, Hefele cannot be trusted as a reliable source.

31. Bauer, *Orthodoxy and Heresy*, 79.
32. Hefele, *History of the Councils*, 89.
33. Hefele, *History of the Councils*, 739.

Even so, with Julian the Apostate's apparent favor of Pergamon as an intellectual center, which ostensibly contributed in part to his inspiration for the revival of worship of Roman gods and goddesses, Christianity was of no consequence in the city. Later, John of Ephesos (ca. AD 507–588), a Miaphysite missionary and historian, traveled to Pergamon to destroy the Altar of Zeus, which had long been a major site of Greco-Roman worship.[34] While he was ostensibly successful in his efforts, there is no mention of a church in Pergamon, no record of Christian inhabitants, and no evidence that Christians resettled there after the altar's destruction. This further reinforces the idea that Christianity either never fully took hold in the city or had already faded into obscurity, if not actually persecuted out of existence, by this time.

JESUS TO PERGAMON

This brings us back to the puzzle of Pergamon. We simply don't know in detail what was happening with Christianity there other than what is recorded in Jesus' letter in the book of Revelation. He says to John,

> And to the angel of the church in Pergamum write: "The words of him who has the sharp two-edged sword. 'I know where you dwell, where Satan's throne is. Yet you hold fast my name, and you did not deny my faith even in the days of Antipas my faithful witness, who was killed among you, where Satan dwells. But I have a few things against you: you have some there who hold the teaching of Balaam, who taught Balak to put a stumbling block before the sons of Israel, so that they might eat food sacrificed to idols and practice sexual immorality. So also you have some who hold the teaching of the Nicolaitans. Therefore repent. If not, I will come to you soon and war against them with the sword of my mouth. He who has an ear, let him hear what the Spirit says to the churches. To the one who conquers I will give some of the hidden manna, and I will give him a white stone, with a new name written on the stone that no one knows except the one who receives it.'" (Rev 2:12–17)

The letter itself is striking. Jesus opens the address saying, "The words of him who has the sharp two-edged sword" (Rev 2:12). This likely refers to imperial authority, a concept deeply relevant to Pergamon's status

34. Kästner, "Great Altar of Pergamon," 145; Evans, *History of Pergamum*, 110; Wilson, *Biblical Turkey*, 278–79.

as a *neokorate* in the Roman Empire. While many assume that Ephesos was the most powerful city in Asia Minor, Pergamon was, in fact, the true political capital, as well as the intellectual, religious, and medical capital of the region.[35] Jesus' reference to a sharp sword may allude to Roman judicial power, as Pergamon was one of the few cities with the *jus gladii*, or "right of the sword," meaning it had the authority to enact capital punishment.[36] We've observed this enforced already with the third-century missionaries who travelled to Pergamon.

Jesus continues by making the bold claim, "I know where you dwell, where Satan's throne is" (Rev 2:13). These early believers, according to Jesus, lived in the very place where Satan had established his throne. Of course, the language of Revelation is allegorical, metaphorical, and analogical, so we need to ask: What did Jesus mean by this? Scholars typically point to one of three referents as the throne of Satan: the cult of *sebastos*, the Altar of Zeus, or the Temple of Asklepios.[37] There is no sure way to determine which referent pointed to the throne. Most likely, due to the conflation of religion, philosophy, and imperial rule, all three served as representative of a city ruled by Satan. Each of these played a role in shaping Pergamon's spiritual, intellectual, and political identity, making it a particularly difficult place for Christianity to thrive.

Nevertheless, despite the opposition, Jesus commends the Christians in Pergamon: "Yet you hold fast my name, and you did not deny my faith even in the days of Antipas, my faithful witness, who was killed among you, where Satan dwells" (Rev 2:13). Antipas is the only named Christian martyr in Revelation, but beyond this verse, we know nothing about him. Later church tradition identifies him as a bishop, but there is no historical or textual evidence to confirm this.[38] It is also unclear whether Antipas was from Pergamon or if he came from another Christian center to spread the gospel there. Ramsay adds, "It is not even certain that Antipas was a member of the congregation: the words are not inconsistent with the possibility that Antipas was brought up for trial from some other city, and killed among the Pergamenians."[39] All we do know

35. Wright and Bird, *New Testament*, 900.

36. Ramsay, *Seven Churches of Asia*, 292.

37. Hemer, *Seven Churches of Asia*, 84–86; cf. Collins, Pergamon," 166–76.

38. Tabbernee, "Asia Minor and Cyprus," 282. A late unreliable tradition makes him the bishop of Pergamon after Gaius, the disciple of John (*Constitutions of the Holy Apostles* 7.46 [*ANF* 7:478]).

39. Ramsay, *Seven Churches of Asia*, 298; Hemer, *Seven Churches of Asia*, 86.

is that he was killed, and his martyrdom is explicitly linked to the city's spiritual and political climate.

Jesus then issues a warning to the church: "But I have a few things against you: you have some there who hold to the teaching of Balaam" (Rev 2:14). The Greek word for "teaching" here is the same term used to describe doctrine (*didachē*), meaning that a defined system of belief was present. Jesus appears to be drawing an allegorical parallel between Balaam—who in the Old Testament led Israel into sin—and certain teachings in Pergamon. This method of allegorical critique is particularly significant given the Stoic influence in Pergamon where allegory was a central feature of philosophical discourse[40] as well as the fact that the Jewish presence in the city was not as large as in others.[41] The Stoic philosopher Crates (ca. third century BC), who became the head of the Pergamene library and school, was known for emphasizing anomalies in language and philosophy in his allegorical interpretation of Homer.[42] If Stoic thought shaped Pergamon's intellectual climate, it's likely that Christians there had to engage with it in some capacity. Certainly, in this cognitive environment, Jesus' use of allegory is deliberate. He then explains that the Pergamene doctrine led to two major issues: eating food sacrificed to idols and practicing sexual immorality. Such behaviors were almost certainly tied to the religious practices surrounding the city's gods and goddesses. Zeus, Asklepios, Dionysos, Demeter, and Athena were all worshiped in Pergamon, and their cults involved sacrificial feasts and ritualized sexuality.[43]

Jesus also condemns the Nicolaitans, a group already mentioned in Ephesos. I tend to agree with Irenaeus, who suggests that the Nicolaitans were exploitative, particularly of women. There are indications in Irenaeus's writings that their practices involved forms of sexual immorality that crossed the boundaries between Christianity and pagan worship.[44] Here again Jesus designates such teachings as *didachē*, which no doubt connects with the intellectual climate of this philosophical center. Adela

40. Nagy, "Library of Pergamon," 214.

41. Hemer, *Seven Churches of Asia*, 89. The midrashic method of interpretation is very similar to allegory. So, even if there were a notable Jewish presence in Pergamon, the interpretation of Balaam holds. That back then is this that is happening now (see Caldwell, *Bible in Culture*).

42. Nagy, "Library of Pergamon," 223–28.

43. Ramsay, *Seven Churches of Asia*, 339. See Strabo, *Geography* 10.3 for references to the orgiastic rituals practiced in Anatolia.

44. Irenaeus, *Against Heresies* 1.15.3; 3.11.1.

Yarbro Collins notes, "Those who followed the teachings of 'Balaam' and the 'Nicolaitans' are the ones who advocated assimilation of the dominate cultural values."[45] To this assimilation, Jesus' message is clear: "Repent, or I will come to you soon and war against them with the sword of my mouth" (Rev 2:16). If they do not repent, judgment will come. Yet, for those who remain faithful, Jesus promises: "To the one who conquers I will give some of the hidden manna, and I will give him a white stone, with a new name written on the stone that no one knows except the one who receives it" (Rev 2:17).

Summary

Reflecting on all of this, I cannot help but wonder if these factors contributed to the decline—if not the disappearance—of Christianity in Pergamon. We see evidence of Christians migrating to other cities, possibly due to persecution or the inability to sustain a community in such an environment. We also see the absence of a strong Christian intellectual presence. Christianity could not compete with the dominance of Stoic, Aristotelian, and later Neoplatonic philosophy, which thrived in Pergamon. Unlike Alexandria, which produced great Christian thinkers like Pantaenus, Clement, and Origen, Pergamon does not appear to have had any significant Christian scholars capable of engaging with the prevailing philosophical traditions. If Galen is representative of the intellectual climate of Pergamon, then Richard Walzer's comment about him is apropos. To Galen, "Jews and Christians learn by authority alone and are satisfied to have their belief prescribed to them by their masters; they do not venture upon a critical examination of their tenets."[46] All of these factors—the imperial cult, the philosophical climate, the dominance of Zeus and Asklepios, and the absence of a Christian intellectual tradition—help explain why Christianity failed to take hold in Pergamon in the way it did elsewhere. If Christianity did exist here, it was likely marginalized and irrelevant, persecuted, and overshadowed by the deeply entrenched religious and cultural forces of the city.

45. Collins, "Pergamon," 184.

46. Walzer, *Galen on Jews*, 49.

FROM ARCHAEOLOGY TO APPLICATION

The Pergamon puzzle serves as a stark reminder that Christianity cannot thrive in a vacuum of cultural detachment. The disappearance of Christianity from this once-prominent city underscores several critical lessons for the church today. While we often assume that the early church grew inexorably, Pergamon challenges that assumption. Its apparent failure to develop into a lasting Christian center is not incidental—it reveals what happens when a church lacks a strong theological and intellectual foundation, fails to develop deep discipleship structures which meaningfully engage culture, and struggles to withstand religious and political pressure.

Challenge	Description
Persecution and political pressure	The city's strong ties to imperial power meant that allegiance to Rome and the emperor cult was expected
Religious competition	Zeus (the Friend) and Asklepios (the Savior) provided competing religious alternatives to Christianity
Intellectual dominance of Greco-Roman philosophy	Unlike in Alexandria, where Christian intellectuals like Origen and Clement emerged, Pergamon produced no major Christian scholars; the city's philosophical traditions may have overshadowed the development of Christian theology
The rise of Neoplatonism	This fusion of philosophy, medicine, and mysticism may have drawn potential converts away from Christianity
Migration of Christians	The lack of episcopal representation and literary references suggest that Christians may have left Pergamon for more hospitable regions
Jesus' warning	Some Christians succumb to the temptations of idolatry and sexual immorality

Table 5.2: The decline of Christianity

The first and perhaps most evident lesson is that Christianity thrives where there is a strong theological and intellectual foundation. Pergamon was a city of ideas, home to one of the great libraries of antiquity and a philosophical tradition that rivaled Athens and Alexandria. Yet, unlike Alexandria, which produced formidable Christian thinkers, Pergamon seems to have lacked a significant intellectual Christian presence. There is no record of a major Christian scholar emerging from the city to engage the dominant philosophical currents of the time. This absence left Christianity intellectually vulnerable. If the faith is not defended and articulated at the highest levels of thought, it becomes susceptible to assimilation or irrelevance, even viewed as anti-intellectual. Indeed, Rebecca Flemming argues that such anti-intellectualism contributed to Galen's philosophical weaponry against Christianity.[47] Today, this remains a pressing issue. Churches that neglect irenic apologetics, biblical literacy, and engagement with contemporary intellectual movements find themselves similarly vulnerable. When the prevailing cultural narratives go unchallenged, the church risks being either absorbed into secularism or dismissed as an anti-intellectual relic.

A second key lesson is that Christianity must build strong communities and discipleship structures. In Pergamon, we have little evidence of an enduring Christian network. Unlike Ephesos, which became a center for Christian teaching and missionary activity, Pergamon appears isolated. Without deep discipleship and interchurch connections, believers are more likely to drift into cultural and religious assimilation. This is precisely what we see in Jesus' letter to the church in Pergamon. Some in the community had begun to embrace syncretistic practices, participating in idolatrous feasts and sexual immorality tied to pagan and emperor worship. In the absence of a robust Christian community, it became far too easy to conform. Today, the church faces similar pressures. Without intentional discipleship, accountability, and strong Christian communities, believers will inevitably absorb the values and ideologies of the surrounding culture.

The third lesson is that Christianity must prepare believers for persecution and marginalization. Pergamon was a city where loyalty to Rome, the emperor, and traditional Greco-Roman religion was deeply embedded in civic identity. To reject these was to invite social, economic, and even legal consequences. The martyrdom of Antipas and others is one indication that Christians faced real opposition. Historically, where the church fails to develop resilience, it withers under social and political pressure. Today, while persecution may take different forms, the reality remains the same: Christians who are not prepared to stand under pressure will compromise or abandon their faith. Churches must cultivate a resilient faith—one that can endure, not only overt hostility but also the subtler pressures of religious nationalism, ideological conformity, and cultural accommodation.

47. Flemming, "Galen and the Christians," 185.

Finally, Christianity must learn to engage culture without compromise. Pergamon offers an example of what happens when the faith is assimilated rather than distinct. The early church was not called to retreat from culture, but neither was it meant to blend in so seamlessly that it became indistinguishable from other religious and philosophical systems. Jesus' critique of Pergamon's Christians was not that they had left the faith entirely, but that they had absorbed the values and practices of the surrounding society. The same danger exists today. If the church fails to offer a compelling and unique alternative to political, philosophical, or religious competitors, it will cease to be a transformative force. The church cannot merely react to culture; it must proactively shape it.

The Pergamon puzzle serves as a sobering story. Christianity must be intellectually defended, communally reinforced, and spiritually resilient. Without these elements, it fades. If we are to learn from Pergamon's failure, we must ensure that the church today is theologically equipped, deeply discipled, prepared for opposition, and culturally engaged without compromise. The case of Pergamon remains a historical enigma. While Christianity flourishes in other cities of Asia Minor, Pergamon appears to have resisted Christian influence. Whether due to political hostility, religious syncretism, or intellectual competition, Christianity ultimately failed to gain a strong foothold in this powerful city. Further archaeological exploration may yet provide additional insights into this compelling mystery. Until then, we can learn an important missiological lesson from its disappearance. This might help us as we think of re-engaging places like North Africa where Christianity was once strong.

CHAPTER 6

Guilds as Places of Peace: Thyatira

THERE IS NOTHING SPECIAL about the city. In fact, the city never rose to a level of prominence like Ephesos, Smyrna, or Pergamon.[1] So, it makes it all the more curious that Jesus would write a letter to a city that was neither the focal point of emperor worship, nor of any other imperial consequence in the first century AD. Yet, what we glean from his letter is disheartening: they follow the path of Pergamon. Here we have another example of an early community of Christ followers contending with false teaching that seduced people to sexual immorality and idol worship (Rev 2:20). This is no real surprise considering what Thyatira offers: insights into one of the most significant economic components of the Roman Empire—the trade guilds. Certainly Jesus alludes to such as he identifies himself with language familiar to metalworking, "The words of the Son of God, who has eyes like a flame of fire, and whose feet are like burnished bronze" (Rev 2:18).

Walking among the ruins, the city's reputation as a focal point of these guilds stands out on the numerous inscriptions found on marble slabs which dot the archaeological site (Figure 6.1). Prominent among those trades were guilds associated with textiles. So, naturally, Lydia, the dealer in purple fabric who we meet in Acts 16, comes to mind. When Paul encounters her while searching for a *proseuchēn* (place of prayer),[2]

1. William Ramsay called it "essentially a handmaid city, built to serve an Empire by obstructing for a little while the path of its enemies and so giving time for the concentration of its military strength" (see *Seven Churches of Asia*, 319). In essence, the city played the role of a pawn and buffer to Pergamon, the first of Asia.

2. Προσευχη is Philo's most common word for a place where Jews gathered.

she is in Philippi. However, her home town was Thyatira (Acts 16:14). Luke describes her as a *sebomenē ton theon* (worshiper of God) whose heart opened to the Lord. It's not difficult to imagine that Lydia, "a woman of independent means,"[3] frequently traveled from Thyatira to Philippi as she owned a house in the city where the early believers gathered (Acts 16:15).

Guilds, popularly known as voluntary associations, vocational associations, or *collegia* (societies), played a significant role in both Hellenistic and Roman society. Their presence not only represented important cultural institutions of craftsmen, but they contributed to mediating relationships, whether economic or social.[4] Their membership, even though comprised of people who came from differing economic advantage, provided a place where members stood on a somewhat level pitch while being afforded opportunities to take leadership positions which would not otherwise be open to them in the *polis*.[5] Women quite frequently associated with or were members of guilds; especially those which were oriented to domestic work.[6] So, Lydia was not unique among guild members. However, Philip Harland contests such a view. He writes, "The most widely attested links between women and guilds are cases where the woman in question was a wealthy benefactor or the recipient of honors rather than an ordinary member";[7] an appropriate description of Lydia.

Similar to cultic associations, many vocational associations performed religious duties to honor a patron deity of the craft, and banquets celebrating such auspicious occasions would sacrifice animals to be eaten in honor of the god or goddess. Members ate these meals at times in the respective temple, dining hall of their meeting place, or in the private dining hall either rented or owned by the *patron/a*. Scholars have traditionally emphasized the debauchery that occurred during these meals. Harland points out, however, that much of the literature depicting such conviviality found its motivation from writing pejoratively about

---

"Generally Philo, writing in the early first century CE, follows Egyptian usage and employs *proseuche* when he wishes to refer to buildings from the Jewish community" (Richardson, "Early Synagogues as Collegia," 94). The New Testament range for the word includes prayer but also "house of prayer" (Matt 21:13).

3. Wright, *Paul*, 178.

4. Kloppenborg, "Collegia and Thiasoi," 17.

5. Such leadership positions bore titles like *diakonos*, *presbyteros*, *archisynagogos*. See Kloppenborg, "Collegia and Thiasoi," 26.

6. Kloppenborg, "Collegia and Thiasoi," 25.

7. Harland, *Associations, Synagogues, and Congregations*, 32.

the social "other."[8] Nevertheless, such depictions often contain a hint of reality as attested by the number of regulations placed on guild members. It is safe to presume that such regulations demonstrated a tendency of members to go to extreme displays of cult honor, including sexual immorality. Nonetheless, Harland warns,

> Though there may be truth in the fact that drunkenness was a part of the religious and social celebrations of some associations on certain occasions, scholars need to refrain from adopting the moralists' critique as a sign that the associations were all about partying and could care less about honoring the gods.[9]

Other honorific inscriptions to deities appear on grave stones, columns, even column bases of guild meeting places such as one excavated, a physicians' guild, at Ephesos in an apsidal building.

> The physicians (*iatroi*) who sacrifice to ancestor Asklepios and to the Augusti (*Sebastoi*) honored T. Statilius Kriton, chief–physician (*archiatros*), procurator of emperor Nerva Trajan Caesar Augustus, victorious in Germany and Dacia, and priest of the Lords (*Anaktores*), of King Alexander, and of Gaius and Lucius, (10) the grandsons of Augustus. When Tiberius Claudius Demostratos Caelianus was priest and L. Atilius Varus was leader (*archon*) of the physicians, C. Arius Hermeros and his sons, Arius Celsianus and Arius Celsus, set up the honor from their own resources as he (Hermeros) had promised the physicians.[10]

Such honorific practices ensured the favor of the god or goddess responsible for assisting them in their work.

Singing hymns or shouts of acclamation to the gods and goddesses also comprised a part of the way a guild might honor a patron deity.[11] Such honorific duties demonstrated the membership's piety and fidelity to the god. These songs or shouts were as much inscribed for posterity as they were vocal. Indeed, we see such vocal acclamation when the silversmiths' guild, coppersmiths' guild, and other guild members gathered in the theater in Ephesos (Figure 6.2). Harland points out,

8. Consider, for example, the false claims made about the early church: cannibalism related to the eucharistic meal of eating flesh and drinking blood; and incest related to the holy kiss. Such "fake news" often grabbed the attention of an audience determined to be against something that is different from themselves.

9. Harland, "Banqueting Values," 78.

10. Harland, trans. "Honors by Physicians."

11. See Bitner, "Acclaiming Artemis in Ephesus."

> The silversmiths of Ephesos who, according to the author of Acts (19:23–41), gathered together a crowd of craftsmen and others in defense of the reputation of Artemis, patron deity of their hometown, would not be exceptional in this regard: "Great is Artemis of the Ephesians!" they shouted.[12]

While we do not know much about Thyatira, Jesus' letter to the church certainly alludes to the fact that Christians appeared to be participating in these types of guild activities (Rev 2:18–29). To not participate threatened both their social standing and economic well-being. Consequently, the church fell prey to the deceptive teaching of Jezebel.[13] Grant Osborne suggests that Jezebel taught,

> There was nothing wrong with a Christian taking part in the guild feast and celebrations, for it was merely civil. Since idols were nothing, Christians would not destroy their faith by participating. It is also possible that she used some form of Pauline teaching on Christian liberty similar to 1 Cor. 8:4–8, "We know that an idol is nothing at all in the world and that there is no God but one. . . . But food does not bring us near to God; we are not worse if we do not eat, and not better if we do." In other words, the Christian is free to eat meat offered to idols.[14]

The Son of God, as opposed to the Son of Zeus, Apollo the patron god of Thyatira, would not tolerate such syncretism in the church of Thyatira. Yet another example of polemical parallelism.

While much about guilds in Thyatira eludes us, the early Christian mission in Corinth and Ephesos in Acts 18–19 met resistance, not only from Jews, but also from the members of these occupational associations. Yet, such opposition curiously connects with people and places where Paul and his missionary band experienced great fruit. As Harland notes, "In fact, cities like Ephesos were dotted with such groups, groups which may open a new window into the world of early Christians and diaspora

12. Harland, *Associations, Synagogues, and Congregations*, 51.

13. "Jezebel" is a euphemism for someone in Thyatira deceiving Jesus' "slaves." Certainly an allusion to the Phoenician wife of Ahab in 1 Kgs 16:31–34, the woman in Thyatira led the Christians to eat food sacrificed to idols by declaring that she was a messenger of God. Speculations about the identity of this woman have led some to suggest that she was the wife of the leader of the church, Lydia who Paul met in Philippi, the Sibyl Sambathe, or simply an allegorical representation of the cultic activities of the Nicolaitans (see Osborne, *Revelation*, 234–38).

14. Osborne, *Revelation*, 237.

Judeans."[15] In this sense, guild members and the spaces they occupied provide a new framework for how we understand the "person of peace." First, we set the context by introducing an area of study that is largely ignored by missiologists mostly due to the weight of scholarly tradition toward a widely held assumption about the word *synagōgē* in the NT and especially in the Acts of the Apostles. Ultimately, we will address the missiological implications as we attempt to answer the questions of why Jesus had many followers in Corinth and why did the word of the Lord spread so effectively in Roman Asia.

TRADITION AND EVIDENCE

The absence of archaeological evidence for Jewish places of worship in Asia Minor draws into question the long traditional view that Paul visited the *synagōgē* of the Jews as a first engagement of a city during his missionary journeys.[16] The presumption that Paul prioritized the Jews first then the Gentiles[17] is equally challenged by his ministry in the Lycus Valley, which seemed to place the Greek first then the Jew (Col 3:11). This "Jew first" mission paradigm has a long and illustrious history.[18] While there is no denying that Paul's mission to the Jews provided a natural inroad to his missionary strategy for reaching metropolises, it also misunderstands the meaning of *synagōgē* much in the same way *ekklēsia* is misunderstood today, a point we will take up momentarily.

Nevertheless, scholars agree that the presence of Judaism in the Greco-Roman world appears in the literary, epigraphic, and material records. Based on these records, Steven Fine asserts that there were 150 Jewish synagogues attested in diaspora Judaism.[19] Out of those, Mark Wilson claims that there are sixty cities known to have Jewish synagogues attested to by the extant evidence in Asia Minor and Greece. In regards to the archaeological record in Asia Minor, however, he admits to a lack of archaeological evidence pointing to buildings: "In Asia Minor synagogues have been identified at three sites—Sardis, Priene, and Andriake. Limyra is the latest city where excavators have discovered a possible synagogue.

15. Harland, *Associations, Synagogues, and Congregations*, 2.
16. Schnabel, *Early Christian Mission*, 937–38.
17. Wright, *Paul*, 334.
18. Allen, *Missionary Methods*, 30; Bosch, *Transforming Mission*, 172–74.
19. Fine, "Synagogues," 117.

Tentative identifications have also been made at Miletus, Pergamum, and Mopsuestia."[20]

Both Fine and Wilson concede that the architectural evidence for Jewish synagogues is sparse.[21] Lee Levine acknowledges that the evidence is "woefully fragmentary."[22] Nevertheless, all insist that the literary testimony provides sufficient claims for Jewish synagogues even though there is very little material evidence. While certainly earthquakes and Christian usurpation of the Jewish synagogue might provide some reasonable explanation for the archaeological deficit,[23] the uncomfortable lack of evidence suggests either an absence of Jews in Asia Minor, which is certainly preposterous,[24] or the word *synagōgē* does not necessarily equate to a building nor to a place of Jewish worship. Indeed, as Anders Runesson muses, "It is not uncommon that scholars go on to reconstruct the history of the 'synagogue' as if the problems involved in this enterprise were of minor significance."[25] So, perhaps the word itself holds clues to the lack of evidence.

Defining Synagogue

Defining *synagōgē* is not an easy task. For instance, the lexical range of the English translation of *synagōgē* encompasses more than the typical student of the Bible knows. In an extended footnote, Runesson, Binder, and Olson highlight the challenge we face when confronted with the word in the context of ancient Judaism:

> What in English is translated synagogue went under several different names in antiquity (in Greek, Latin and Hebrew): *synagoge, proseuche, ekklesia, oikos, topos, hagios topos, hieros peribolos, hieron, synagogion, sabbateion, semneion, didaskaleion, amphitheatron, eucheion, proseukterion, thiasos, templum, proseucha, bet mo'ed, bet ha-Torah, bet ha-kneset.*[26]

20. Wilson, "Ancient Synagogues," 122.
21. Fine, "Synagogues"; Wilson, "Ancient Synagogues."
22. Levine, *Ancient Synagogue*, 250.
23. Wilson, "Ancient Synagogues," 122–23.
24. See Ramsay, *Seven Churches of Asia*, 151.
25. Runesson, *Origins of the Synagogue*, 22.
26. Runesson et al., *Ancient Synagogue*, 10n21.

As reflected in the number of synonyms for "synagogue," Stephen Wilson acknowledges that "in the ancient world the boundaries and the terminology were fluid."[27] Adding to the complexity of the word, Ralph Korner asserts in his study of *synagōgē* and voluntary associations, "It has become clear that *synagōgē* is an ethnically neutral term that is used for group modalities of non-Judean and Judean associations, and of non-Judean and Judean communities of Christos followers."[28] Yet, there are many words used for such associations. According to Kloppenborg, both the Latin and Greek forms of *synagōgē* are used for cultic associations (religious guilds) along with several additional synonyms. He notes the following:

> The Greek terms used for cultic associations (and their members) are numerous, the most common being *koinon*, *thiasos* (*thiasotai*), *orgeones*, *eranos* (*eranistai*), and *synodos*; less common, but still well attested, are *doumos*, *familia*, *mystai*, *hoi peri NN*, *xystos*, *philoi*, *plethos*, *speira*, *stemma*, *synagoge*, *synedrion*, *synklitai*, *systema*, and *therapeutai*. Other names are formed from the name of the deities reverenced (e.g., Sarapiastai, Dionyiastai). In Latin the most common terms are *collegium*, *coetus*, *corpus*, *cultores*, *curia*, *familia*, *synagoga*, and *sodalis*.[29]

In their extensive study of Greek inscriptions, Ascough, Harland, and Kloppenborg also recognize additional uses for *synagōgē* evidenced in the epigraphic record.[30] For instance, an eighty-three centimeter by thirty-nine centimeter second-century-BC slab discovered at Triglia in Bithynia of Asia Minor depicts an honorific sacrifice to the mother of the gods, Cybele, and to Apollo. The priestess Stratonike raises her hands in adoration as she approaches the altar accompanied by a girl playing a double flute and a boy leading a sheep. The middle panel shows the group enjoying a meal and drinks, and the lower panel displays musicians and a dancer. The inscription provides a clear reference to the use of *synagōgē* as a place for worship of Zeus:

> The male (*thiasitai*) and female (*thiasitides*) members of the society crowned Stratonike daughter of Menekrates, who was priestess of Mother Cybele and Apollo in the 178th year, with

27. Wilson, "Voluntary Associations," 4; cf. Kloppenborg, "Collegia and Thiasoi," 18.

28. Korner, "Συναγωγη and Semi-Public Associations," 241

29. Kloppenborg, "Collegia and Thiasoi," 357n23.

30. Ascough et al., *Associations*.

> a crown with a band engraved on a plaque that was announced and another crown with a band that was announced in the synagogue (*synagōgē*) of Zeus, since she acted in a benevolent manner.[31]

Not only do we possess inscriptions in reference to the worship of Greek deities at a *synagōgē*, we also possess inscriptions where *synagōgē* is a trade guild. On a first-to-second century-AD altar excavated at Perinthos-Herakleia in Thrace, an inscription reads,

> To good fortune. . . . Drakon who is also called (?) . . . Chrestos, son of Chrestos, set this up for the synagogue (*synagōgē*) of small-wares dealers (ropopolai; or: orkopopolai = oar-dealers) who are gathered around Sokrates, son of Meniskos.[32]

Similarly, a first-century-AD marble altar also discovered at Perinthos-Herakleia in Thrace reads,

> Name . . . the administrator (*dioiketes*) and Marcus Pompeius Comicus, son of Comicus, restored the altar to the synagogue (*synagōgē*) of barbers—namely those gathered around the head of the synagogue (*archisynagōgos*) Gaius Julius Valens—and provided the location.[33]

More common than references to *synagōgē* as a religious guild for worship of Greek deities and as a trade guild are references to *synagōgos* or occasionally *archisynagōgos* (head of a synagogue). For instance, a second-century marble slab found in Bosporos contains a relief of Zeus holding a scepter. The inscription reads,

> To good fortune. During the reign of king Tiberius Julius Rheskouporis (I), friend of Caesar and friend of the Romans, pious one, this was dedicated to the deities . . . Zeus (?) . . . and Hera, Saviors, according to a vow (euche). Menios son of Bradakos was synagogue-leader (synagogos), Antimachos son of Chariton was the goodness-loving official (philagathos), and Pasion II was supervisor (epimeletes).[34]

31. Harland, "Honors by a Society."
32. Harland, "Altar for a Synagogue."
33. Ascough, "Dedication of an Altar."
34. Harland, "Dedication to Zeus."

Yet there is a third general possibility for the word: a gathering of students of a philosopher or a philosophical school.[35] In chapter 9 of his *Lives of Eminent Philosophers*, Diogenes Laertius discusses the life and teachings of the fourth-century-BC-Greek philosopher Pyrrho. In section 11.102 we meet the word *tēs synagōgēs* used as the gathering or school of his followers. He writes, "It is possible to understand the overall manner of their assembly (*synagōgē*) from the remaining compositions. For Pyrrho himself left nothing behind, but his associates Timon, Aenesidemus, Numenius, and Nausiphanes, among others, did."[36] The passage highlights Pyrrho's skepticism as well as his philosophical school which left no written records by Pyrrho himself. Instead, the understanding of Pyrrho's teachings comes from the works of his followers, such as Timon, Aenesidemus, Numenius, and Nausiphanes. The text emphasizes how the doctrines and practices of Pyrrho's school (i.e., *synagōgē*) were preserved and conveyed through these disciples rather than through any direct writings by Pyrrho.

So, we have *synagōgē* as: 1) a Jewish and/or Christian gathering (cf. Jas 2:2; Heb 10:24); 2) a Pagan gathering as a religious guild; 3) a trade guild; and 4) a philosophical school or tradition. Using Korner's categories of Judean and non-Judean associations, we arrive at a definition for a Judean synagogue with the help of Runesson, Binder, and Olson. Simply stated, a Judean synagogue is a formal assembly which exercises authority in matters of liturgical and non-liturgical practices of Judaism, including the reading of the Torah and prayer, judicial courts, and school that are conducted in a space designed for these functions.[37] That space could be a dedicated physical structure or the hall in a private house. In terms of a non-Judean association, *synagōgē* functions in a similar manner. That is, the four aspects of the Judean synagogue are also present. Thus, a non-Judean synagogue possesses formal structure as a cult, guild, or school and exercises authority corresponding to each whether liturgical or non-liturgical. The gathering of the non-Judean synagogue might occur in a home or a dedicated building.

Consequently, if epigraphical references to *synagōgē*, *synagōgos*, or *archisynagōgos* (ruler of the synagogue) in Greek inscriptions do not

35. Mason, "Philosophiai."

36. Diogenes Laertius, *Lives of Eminent Philosophers* 9.11.102:513 (author's translation). Cf. R. D. Hicks's translation where *tēs synagōgēs* is used functionally rather than nominally.

37. Runesson et al., *Ancient Synagogue*, 34–35.

refer to the Jewish gathering for cultic purposes or a Jewish building used for the observance of religious traditions, can we assume that references in the NT always refer to the same? This question is important in light of the fact that the NT uses the word more than any other piece of ancient literature.[38] Considering the lexical range of *synagōgē* and its cognates, we are presented with quite an interesting variety of possibilities when encountering the word in the biblical record, especially in the Acts of the Apostles.

Synagōgē in the Acts of the Apostles

The English word "synagogue" is used twenty-two times in Acts in the English Standard Version (ESV) while the Greek word *synagōgē* is used nineteen times. In addition to *synagōgē*, one other compound cognate is used three times for the ruler of the synagogue (*archisynagōgos*). When the Acts context for *synagōgē* refers explicitly to the "synagogue of the Jews" (*synagōgē tōn Ioudaiōn*, Acts 13:5; 14:1; 17:1, 10), it is clearly referring to the gathering of the people who are practicing the Judean traditions as defined above. Similarly, when the word is used in conjunction with a gathering on the Sabbath (Acts 13:14; 15:21; 18:4), it seems to be another explicit reference to the Jews.[39] However, the Corinthian context of trade guilds in Acts 18:4 leaves the issue open as we will discuss below.

The first occurrence of *synagōgē* in Acts is a curious reference to a "synagogue of freedmen" along with various synagogues of different ethnic groups who disputed with Stephen (Acts 6:9). Clearly these people were Jewish as Stephen addresses them as "brothers and fathers" (Acts 7:2). In this context, it would be difficult to connect *synagōgē* with a building as it appears it is in reference to gatherings of affinity and ethnic groups who happened to be religiously Jewish.

The Talmud's suggestion that there were 394 Judean synagogues in Jerusalem before the destruction of the temple in AD 70 certainly fits the Acts 6 scenario.[40] However, the physical evidence for distinct buildings is

38. According to a word frequency study of *synagōgē* at Perseus Digital Library, the NT uses the word eighty-five times compared to Diognees Laertius at twenty-seven times, Athenaeus sixteen times, Strabo fourteen times, and Josephus, surprisingly, ten times. See Perseus Digital Library, "Word Frequency Information."

39. Additionally, in other contexts it appears clear that the reference is likewise an explicit Jewish place of worship (Acts 6:9; 9:2, 20; 13:43; 24:12; 26:11).

40. b. Ketubbot 105a.

sparse in comparison. This does not infer that the Talmud exaggerates the numbers. It simply indicates that the numbers do not relate to architecture as much as they relate to groups who gathered together like we see in Acts 6:9. At the same time, 394 might refer to architectural spaces as the Talmud's numbers included courts and schools. Yet, the word *synagōgē* itself does not explicitly refer to such a space. Indeed, *synagōgē* could be a gathering that takes place in a private house since it does not necessarily refer to a dedicated physical structure. Due to the sparse archaeological records, the same might be assumed for other cities.

After the martyrdom of Stephen when Saul continued his threats against the followers of Christ (Acts 8:1), he asked the high priest in Jerusalem for letters addressed to the "synagogues" of Damascus where apparently men and women of "the Way" (*tēn odon*) still gathered alongside the Jews (Acts 9:2). Ultimately, after his encounter with Christ and subsequent restoration of sight, Saul proclaims Jesus among the same "synagogues" (Acts 9:20). While it seems unlikely that *synagōgē* meant anything more than a gathering of Jews and Christian converts rather than a building, it appears that the written record undoubtedly testifies to multiple gatherings, presumably in private homes (*domus-synagōgē*) or perhaps dining halls of Jews of the same trade guild. Just as in Acts 6, the emphasis of the word *synagōgē* in Acts 9 is clearly on the gathering of groups of people who share a common affinity that includes religious customs as well as groups who share a common ethnic, social, or perhaps vocational identity. Again, the lexical range of the word must be taken into consideration.

During Paul's missionary journeys, Luke records two places where he refers to a "synagogue of the Jews" (Acts 13:5; 17:1). Additionally, while in Pisidian Antioch, Paul and his companions sat down in a *synagōgē* which appears to be of the Jews until invited to stand and address the congregants who were "Men of Israel" (Acts 13:14). Where the word feels more ambiguous is in contexts that indicate no reference to the Sabbath or to delineating the *synagōgē* as an explicit place of Hebrew gathering (Acts 17:17; 18:4, 7, 26; 19:8). Jews might have still gathered in these places but they often gathered with Greeks (Acts 18:4) and devout persons (*sebomai*, Acts 17:17). In the Corinthian context, Paul's ministry in a *synagōgē*, together with two references to *archisynagōgoi* in the city (the Roman Crispos, Acts 18:8; the Greek Sosthenes, Acts 18:17) could just as easily be understood as leaders of guilds. To this we briefly turn.

The "Synagogues" in Corinth: Crispos and Sosthenes

On the second missionary journey, Luke makes a transition away from a ministry whose first engagement was with the Jews (Acts 13–14) to one whose engagement connected Paul with people vocationally, religiously, politically, and philosophically (Acts 16–19). Such a connection reflected the integral nature of the Greco-Roman world where one's identity encompassed multiple sodalities. We see a transition from a focus on Jews to all cultural actors alluded to in the letter Paul addresses to the Corinthian believers. Written while in Ephesos, Paul declares, "For Jews demand signs and Greeks seek wisdom" (1 Cor 1:22), indicating the breadth of his cultural engagement. Certainly this is what we observe in the ministry in Ephesos. Among the Jews there: John the Baptist's disciples received the sign of the Holy Spirit (Acts 19:6); Seven sons of Sceva, the Jewish high priest, encountered an evil spirit (Acts 19:14–15). Among the Greeks, Paul taught in the lecture hall of Tyrannos (Acts 19:10); Paul persuaded many to turn from the worship of Artemis (Acts 19:26); Paul reasoned from house to house (Acts 20:20).

After stints in Philippi, Thessalonica, Berea, then Athens, Paul visits Corinth in AD 51 where he resides for nearly two years.[41] After connecting with Aquila and Priscilla who practiced the same trade (*omotechnos*),[42] Paul reasoned with Jews and Greeks at a *synagōgē* located next to the house of Titius Justus, a *sebomenou ton theon*, each Sabbath (Acts 18:4, 7).[43] We learn that this particular *synagōgē* was ruled by Crispos (1 Cor 1:14). As previously mentioned, the Greek *archisynagōgos* (synagogue ruler) is used for both the leader of a cult association, whether Jewish or otherwise, as well as for the master of a guild. The proper name, Crispos, sheds some light on the Corinthian context of this *synagōgē*. Its Latin origin was often used as a nickname for someone with curly hair. It seems reasonable to suggest that Crispos was not religiously Jewish but likely a God-fearing Roman who was the master of a guild, perhaps

41. According to Gideon Foerster, "The history of the Jewish community there [Corinth] is obscure, and archaeological discoveries provide little illumination" See Foerster, "Remains of a Synagogue at Corinth," 185.

42. In a sixth century AD Egyptian papyrus, Kloppenborg translates ομοτεχνος as "guild." See Kloppenborg, "Aphrodito Village."

43. "While Judaism was attractive to many Gentiles in antiquity (Josephus, *A.J.* 14:110), it is not easy to describe the relations between these sympathatic [*sic*] Gentiles and the Jews: there is still a lively debate about the God-fearers both in Luke and in other ancient sources." See Runesson et al., *Ancient Synagogue*, 121.

a guild of leather workers or barbers (see above).[44] Similarly, the ruler of a different *synagōgē*, Sosthenes, a Greek proper name, must hold no Jewish sympathies as the Jews beat him in front of Gallio, the proconsul of Achaia (Acts 18:17). It seems unimaginable that Jews would beat their own religious leader.[45] Conversely, if Sosthenes is associated with Paul, which he ultimately is (1 Cor 1:1), it seems more plausible to suggest that he was the master of a guild whose members included Jews and Greeks. If a guild master, the proconsul Gallio's apathy toward Sosthenes's beating is understandable as he no doubt held a lower social status (Figure 6.3),[46] as well as the fact that the Roman emperor Claudius held no consideration for vocational associations of any sort since they could be a political threat.[47]

Considering the range of the word, a door opens for understanding the Corinthian context and use of *synagōgē* as situated among trade guilds, which would be familiar to Paul as well as Aquila and Priscilla who were members of a leatherworkers' guild (Acts 18:3). Indeed, on the road to Lechaion, a lintel block was discovered in 1898 (Figure 6.4). Dating to the third century AD, the block clearly indicates the existence of a [συνα]γωγη Εβρ[αιων]. Its presence on a road lined with guild shops seems to suggest that it marked a Jewish trade guild which might have included the observance of traditions on the Sabbath.[48] No doubt, Paul dialogued with the Jewish and Greek members of these *synagōgai* which were led by guild masters Crispos and Sosthenes.[49] Likewise, there is no doubt that Paul went to the *synagōgē* on the Sabbath, whether a physical

44. The traditional view exemplified by William Larkin maintains that Crispos was the ruler of a Jewish synagogue where he supervised liturgical services (Larkin, *Acts*, 264). As I'll argue later, there were Roman and Greek converts to Judaism, so having Roman and Greek names would not be unusual. However, as is common among converts, the usual pattern is for the new adherent to take on the name suited for their religious identity.

45. Similar to Crispos, Sosthenes is often portrayed as a Christian sympathizer beaten or disciplined by his own religious community (Keener, *IVP Bible Background Commentary*, 381).

46. See Harland, *Associations, Synagogues, and Congregations*, 31. By lower social status, I mean in relationship to the Roman political elites. Among the tradespeople, Sosthenes certainly held some status as *archisynagōgos*.

47. Cotter, "Collegia and Roman Law," 80.

48. The block's crude engraving, along with its mixed use of lower and uppercase Greek letters, suggests that this mostly likely was not a marker for a Jewish place of worship. A Jewish dedicated place of worship has not been discovered in Corinth.

49. Both of whom eventually change their allegiances to Christ (1 Cor 1:1, 14).

building (perhaps a trade shop), a hall in a private residence, or some other location, as, on the one hand, that was the only day he had free while working in his guild with Aquila and Priscilla, or, on the other hand, he conducted his dialogue while working on the Sabbath (1 Cor 9:19–23).[50] However, another understanding might be as plausible. Due to the syncretistic tendencies already present in Corinth among Jews,[51] a gathering at a dining hall is within the realm of possibilities as Jewish and Greek guilds practiced such a custom with some regularity, ostensibly alongside of each other (1 Cor 8:7–13). In view of Paul's first extant epistle to the troubled believers in Corinth, the guild understanding seems all the more plausible as Paul reasoned with both Jews and Greeks (not *sebomenou ton theon* or *phoboumenos ton theon*) at a particular location in Corinth.

The Synagogues in Ephesos: Demetrius and Alexander

After the unfolding of events in Corinth, Paul departs the city around AD 52 leaving an assembly of Christ followers. Along with him travel Priscilla and Aquila, his fellow trade workers. Arriving in Ephesos, Paul curiously leaves "them there" and enters a *synagōgē* to dialogue with the Jews (Acts 18:19).[52] Later, after Paul's departure from Ephesos, Apollos of Alexandria arrives.[53] He knew about Jesus and taught eloquently about

50. I propose that Paul would not submit to Jewish law if it meant that he could win those who were not under Jewish law.

51. Philo of Alexandria conceded that Jews were permitted to take part in the banquets of Greeks (*On Drunkenness*). "Philo, for example, warns his fellow Jews about the dangers of joining in pagan symposia, clubs, and schools, and notes that some became apostates in this way. Clearly some Jews were socially adventurous and, despite his warnings, Philo surprisingly suggests that he (and others who were morally mature) could participate in certain pagan gatherings providing they did not drink or eat to excess" (Wilson, "Voluntary Associations," 10; cf. Seland, "Philo and the Clubs"; Hadas-Lebel, *Philo of Alexandria*). The Old Testament clearly documents the Jewish tendency toward syncretism and idolatry (Isa 1:4; 57:3–8; Hos 2:2–13). Indeed, as we've already indicated in chapters 2 and 5, Philo readily admits to sacrificing in honor of the emperor Gaius Caligula on three occasions (*Embassy to Gaius*, 356).

52. Presumably, Paul leaves Priscilla and Aquila. We do not know where Silas and Timothy are. Perhaps they remained in Corinth and came to Ephesos later.

53. The fact that Apollos knew about Jesus but did not know about the Holy Spirit seems to indicate that he would not have been present in Jerusalem in Acts 2. Being from Alexandria, home of Philo who articulates a Jewish understanding of *logos*, it is interesting that Apollos arrives in the city where the *logos* philosophy originates with the philosopher Heraclitus in the sixth century BC.

him in the *synagōgē* where Priscilla and Aquila continued gathering or perhaps working. Subsequently, they instructed him more accurately about *tēn odon* ("the Way") of God (Acts 18:26; 19:9, 23).[54] In light of the *synagōgē* experience in Corinth, the introduction of the work in Ephesos raises at least four questions. First, Paul certainly goes to the Jews, but where were the Jews gathering? Second, Luke does not indicate the day that Paul enters the synagogue as he frequently does in other cities (Acts 13:14; 17:2; 18:4), so was it the Sabbath or did he reason with the Jews daily during a three-month period (Acts 19:8)? Third, Priscilla and Aquila continued to gather with those of this particular *synagōgē*. Does this indicate a specific Jewish guild rather than a cult association where they would have engaged in dialogue more frequently? Fourth, in the context of the work in Ephesos, we meet the Jewish coppersmith (*chalkeus* in 2 Tim 4:14) Alexander who appears to be esteemed by the Jewish community (19:33–34). Could the *synagōgē* be a Jewish coppersmith guild? We'll address the latter question when we consider Paul's second encounter with a *synagōgē* in Ephesos. The former three questions can be summarized together.

There is no doubt that Paul reasons with Jews in a *synagōgē*. According to the archaeological and literary records, Jews have been in Asia Minor since at least the Seleucid king Antiochus III (223–187 BC) and most likely before as the Ephesian constitution infers their presence during Antiochus II.[55] When, precisely, they came to Ephesos, however, is difficult to ascertain.[56] Their much-debated dispersion across the Roman Empire led to the establishment of Jewish communities in many cities, as well as their influence on (if not influence by) local cultures while maintaining their own religious and cultural identity. In the first century AD, Josephus, quoting Strabo, notes, "Now these Jews are already gotten into all cities; and it is hard to find a place in the habitable earth that hath not admitted this tribe of men, and is not possessed by them."[57] Their well-attested missionary activity resulted in many Greeks and other ethnic populations either converting to Judaism or becoming so-called *theosebes* (see chapter 2) as their form of monotheism attracted those disenchanted with polytheism (Esth 8:17). Quoting a 1965 doctoral study,

54. While Christ followers were first called Christians in Antioch (Acts 11:26), Luke uses the moniker "the Way" more frequently (Acts 9:2; 19:9, 23; 22:4; 24:14, 22).

55. See Ramsay, *Seven Churches of Asia*, 151–52.

56. Sand, *Invention*, 145.

57. Josephus, *Antiquities* 14.7.2.

Shlomo Sand agrees: "Given its great scale, the expansion of Judaism in the ancient world cannot be accounted for by natural increase, by migration from the homeland, or any other explanation that does not include outsiders joining it."[58] Convinced of this, Sand notes, "A careful reading of ancient Roman literature and Jewish writings soon revealed to me an open secret: from the time of the Hasmonaeans, in the second century BCE, Judaism was clearly a proselytizing monotheism that experienced rapid expansion within the Hellenistic world."[59]

Nevertheless, by the first century BC, when John Hyrcanus II became *ethnarch* of the Jews under Julius Caesar, the Roman republic provided many concessions for those following the Jewish tradition. In this period, Josephus informs us that the Jews in Ephesos, citizens of Rome (perhaps Roman converts), were granted the right to conduct their own religious ceremonies and were exempt from military service.[60] Such an honor no doubt was granted due in part to the Jewish Roman loyalty during Julius Caesar's military exploits in Egypt.[61] All that to say, Jews in Ephesos, including Roman and Greek converts, are well established by at least the first century BC if not before. By the time Paul arrives in Ephesos, those following the Jewish religion would be near two thousand adherents.[62]

In spite of the literary record of the presence of Judaism in Ephesos, the archaeological record is rather sparse: no synagogue has been excavated.[63] Such a curious limit of artifacts might indicate that many if not a majority of the Judeans actually converted to Christianity. In such a case, a Jewish meeting place might have been usurped by the Christians. Given that only twenty percent of Ephesos has been excavated to date, many hold out hope that a Jewish building will be unearthed. Even so, the lack of current material evidence opens another door like the one in Corinth. It seems reasonable to suggest that Paul did indeed enter a Jewish trade guild that Luke called a *synagōgē* where many felt persuaded by his reasoning. Priscilla and Aquila continued that work in the *synagōgē*

58. Rapaport in Sand, *Invention*, 153.

59. Sand, *Invention*, 253.

60. Josephus, *Antiquities* 14.10.13.

61. Josephus, *Antiquities* 14.8.

62. Cooper, *Ephesiology*, 142.

63. A least two grave markers indicating that Judeans were the caretakers, five menorahs, and a few minor artifacts attest to the Jewish presence in Ephesos (Wilson, *Biblical Turkey*, 213; cf. Trebilco, "Jewish Community in Ephesos"; Figure 6.7).

after Paul's departure.[64] It is noteworthy that we have very little textual evidence that the *synagōgē* in Ephesos (or in Athens and Corinth) had any distinctly religious affiliation. Luke does not mention prayer, reading from the Torah, meeting on the Sabbath (except Corinth), nor does he indicate that Paul as a Pharisee had a place to sit. Indeed, Paul's status as a Pharisee does not even factor into his ministry in Athens, Corinth, or Ephesos. So, I suggest that the context of Acts 18:18—19:41 relates more to trade guild opposition than it does to Jewish opposition.

Turning to the circumstance leading to Paul's departure from a *synagōgē* in Ephesos only reinforces the suggestion above. In Acts 19, Paul returns from his visit to Antioch in Syria, making his way through the Lycus Valley to Ephesos tucked away between the mountains. After encountering some of John's disciples, Luke tells us that he goes to a *synagōgē* where he reasons with its members for three months. Paul's reasoning focused on the kingdom of God as he attempted to persuade the *synagōgē* members (Acts 19:8).[65] Knowing Paul's propensity for connecting the message to the culture, such a focus on the *basileia* ("kingdom," "rule") of God fits in a cultural environment where the political climate was accustomed to the language of a *basileia*.[66] Additionally, the Jews would hardly need to be persuaded about God's rule. However, the Ephesians, who took great pride in their city, would no doubt be intrigued if not ultimately offended by Paul's assertion that God's rule was superior to anything the Ephesians might consider as a kingdom.

Ultimately, as Luke writes, some people became stubborn but which people and from what synagogue? One might assume Jews based on Paul's prior experience with them in places like Thessalonica and Corinth. However, given the evidence for a *synagōgē* being a trade guild, it appears more likely that both Jews and Greeks were members of this guild and they both spoke evil of "the Way" (*tēn odon*, Acts 19:9). If Paul dialogued with people at a silversmiths' or coppersmiths' *synagōgē*, or perhaps it was

64. Sardis might provide evidence for this argument where archaeologists have excavated what has been called the largest synagogue in the Judean diaspora. The synagogue is adjacent to the gymnasium and shares a wall with an agora where pagans, Judeans, and Christians sold their wares (see chapter 7).

65. There is no indication that these members were restricted to Jews.

66. See Eph 5:5, where Paul uses the same language for the predominantly Gentile audience. Of note, Ephesos was no stranger to the rule of various despots: Croesus of Lydia, Cyrus of Persia, Lysimachus of Macedonia, Antiochus the Great of Seleucid, Mithridates of Pontus, Attalos III of Pergamon, Quirinius of Rome (see Ramsay, *Seven Churches of Asia*, 225–27; Yamauchi, *New Testament Cities*, 82).

simply a metalworkers' guild, this would explain Demetrius's opposition to "the Way" (Acts 19:23) and the great harm Paul experienced by the hand of Alexander (2 Tim 4:14; Acts 19:33). While some did join Paul, we have to note the modification of his message from the rule of God to the word (*logos*) of the Lord (Acts 19:10) in Paul's ongoing attempt to connect with culture.[67]

Eventually, the opposition to "the Way" precipitates a near riot. Those who became stubborn must be the focus of the opposition if we are to remain faithful to the context. Led by Demetrius, a silversmith who no doubt shared a profound sense of pride in his craft of casting statuettes of Artemis sold in the Tetragonus Agora (Figure 6.5) in order to be offered to the goddess at her temple, the crowd grew to a frenzied chant: "Great is Artemis of the Ephesians!" (Acts 19:28). In spite of the fact that some did not know why they had gathered, this would not have prevented the crowd from joining in a chorus of acclamation to Artemis. Bitner notes,

> In the acclaim for Artemis there was not only commercial and cultic rage; there was also a growing political-theological expression of identity. For the gathered populace, this "Great is Artemis of the Ephesians!" and the linked acclamations for the local benefactors and for the house of the Caesars, which surely accompanied it according to script, expressed what it means to be gloriously Ephesian.[68]

Yet, curiously, the opposition also includes the Jews who were present, if not also participating in the chant "Great is Artemis of the Ephesians!" As we have seen (above n. 51), Philo acknowledges that Jews participated in Greek banquets. Indeed, he participated as well, albeit he reasoned that one could participate when they were in the right state of mind.[69] Additionally, as I've argued in chapter 2, Jews accommodated to the culture. We are relatively confident that they participated in sacrificial meals (1 Cor 8:7–13; 11:17–22). So, Luke is clear that the Jews gathered with others in the theater and put Alexander the coppersmith forward as their spokesperson. One might suggest that these Jews were sympathetic to Paul and his disciples, which is certainly plausible. It seems apparent that Paul has some relationship with Alexander, albeit contentious. Yet, the context seems to fit a scenario where both Jewish and Greek trade

67. Cooper, *Ephesiology*, 47–53.

68. Bitner, "Acclaiming Artemis in Ephesus," 154.

69. Philo, *Allegorical Interpretations*, 3.156.

guild members were vehemently in opposition to Paul as the activities of "the Way" threatened, not only the economic livelihood of Ephesos but also its identity as the cultic center for the worship of Artemis (Figure 6.6). So, for two hours, Luke tells us, the Ephesians chanted the foundational element to who they were: "Great is Artemis of the Ephesians!" (Acts 19:34).[70] Economics and religion were intimately tied, and the fact that all the residents of Asia heard the *logos* of the Lord categorically threatened Ephesian identity (Acts 19:10, 20).

FROM EPIGRAPHIC TO APPLICATION

The epigraphic and literary evidence clearly demonstrates the breadth of the lexical range of the Greek word *synagōgē*. In both Corinth and Ephesos, Paul engaged members—Jewish and Greek—of trade guilds. From this study, we can conclude at least four implications for contemporary missionary work summarized by the overarching notion that missions occurs in the context of relationships. Paul clearly developed relationships in the cities of the Roman world, and they were significant relationships with trade leaders, religious leaders, philosophical leaders, and political leaders. Not only were they significant relationships, but they were relationships that he was intellectually and culturally prepared to engage. So, the first missiological implication is that missionaries must prepare to engage people from a position of knowledge. Noticeably absent from Paul's method of engaging culture are pithy, simplistic gospel presentations. Instead, Luke's testimony about Paul's ministry infers that Paul held a profound understanding of both Greek and Jewish identity (including culture, philosophy, customs, language, and more). That knowledge afforded him the opportunity to connect with people on deeply meaningful levels.

Second, the implications for Paul's engagement of people in trade guilds provides a model of a potential place of first contact in new areas. As John Kloppenborg notes,

> If the description in Acts are regarded as Lukan idealizations, it is quite conceivable that Paul regularly began his activities in the context of local tentmaker's guild. Indeed Acts 18:3 uses the

70. Bradley Bitner points out that "Great is Artemis of the Ephesians!" would have been the beginning of a chain of acclamations that included acclamation for the emperor as well as the political elite of Ephesos. See Bitner, "Acclaiming Artemis in Ephesus."

term *homotechnon* which is attested along with *synergasia* and *syntechnia* in conjunction with professional guilds.[71]

Paul engaged in his craft of leatherworks which placed him in the proximity of people who needed to hear about Jesus Christ. Exactly how much time he spent practicing his trade remains unanswerable. However, we can say that the practice of his trade provided him a level of credibility with those he engaged even when his attention ultimately turned to full-time ministry. In our modern missions, this should empower those in co-vocational service with courage to engage the people they are with on a daily basis just as Paul engaged those in his *synagōgē* on a daily basis.

By extension of the second implication, the third recognizes that the workplace environment provides a natural place of peace. Modern missions rightly gives attention to the idea of a person of peace. Simply stated, a person of peace (Luke 10:6) is a gateway person who maintains relationships in a personal network of people and opens doors of opportunities for missionaries to establish a presence in a city or region. Some might refer to this person as a key figure connecting the missionary with people of a culture. While others have noted the shaky exegetical and missiological foundation of the idea,[72] we certainly witness such people in the book of Acts (Sergius Paulus in Cyprus; Lydia in Philippi; philosophers in Athens; Crispos and Sosthenes in Corinth; Asiarchs in Ephesos). Nevertheless, just as important as a gateway person is a gateway place. In Athens, the Areopagus was a gateway place. In Corinth and Ephesos, those gateway places were guilds. In other places like Thessalonica and Berea, it was the Jewish place of gathering. Identifying such places means that the missionary should have knowledge and experience in these places. Perhaps this is the reason why Paul writes to the Corinthians, "Only let each person lead the life that the Lord has assigned to him, and to which God has called him. This is my rule in all the churches" (1 Cor 7:17). So, if you are an engineer, remain an engineer. If you are a teacher, remain a teacher. If a videographer, remain the same. If a nurse, remain a nurse. If a social worker, do the same. We are all in places of peace where God works.

Finally, what we learn in Corinth and Ephesos, we also see in other cities. Paul uses indigenous spaces to engage and gather people. He did not create the space. Rather, he observed God at work in those spaces

71. Kloppenborg, "Collegia and Thiasoi," 24.

72. Matthews, "Person of Peace Methodology."

and joined with him in what he was doing. No other location pictured this reality like Corinth. Jesus spoke to Paul, "Do not be afraid, but go on speaking and do not be silent, for I am with you, and no one will attack you to harm you, for I have many in this city who are my people" (Acts 18:9–10). Yet, just like in Corinth, Jesus continues to engage the world, preparing the hearts of people where they are. In Ephesos, he used not only the trade guilds but also the hall of Tyrannos—a philosophical guild perhaps. So, the awesome privilege of the missionary is to join with him in his work and connect with people *in situ*. This is the epitome of the *motus Dei* (movement of God): God making the missional move to people and calling us to do the same.

About 160 kilometers to the north of Ephesos, we arrive back in the inland city of Thyatira. Ramsay describes it: "Thyatira, with its low and small acropolis in its beautiful valley, stretching north and south like a long funnel between two gently swelling ridges of hill, conveys the impression of mildness, and subjection to outward influence, and inability to surmount and dominate external circumstances."[73] Perhaps that was the appeal for Jesus in addressing the Christians there. Yet, like the larger cities designated *neokoroi* with elaborate temples and vast imperial resources, Thyatira was not impervious to the same vices: sexual immorality and eating food sacrificed to idols. Only here, the focal point of such practices, were the trade guilds. Everyday people gathering for work and seeking to earn a living by their hands were just as important in his eyes and just as vulnerable to cultural influences. Still, there were those in Thyatira who had not learned the deep things of Satan as had four of the other churches Jesus admonished. Indeed, Jesus, in the longest of the seven letters, promises, "The one who conquers and who keeps my works until the end, to him I will give authority over the nations, and he will rule them with a rod of iron, as when earthen pots are broken in pieces, even as I myself have received authority from my Father" (Rev 2:25–27).

The Thyatirans related to hard work and they knew how a bronze rod could easily break their wares. And Jesus related to them. His self-description as the one whose eyes like fiery flames and feet like burnished bronze no doubt testifies to the fact that he knows the Thyatirans intimately. In fact, there is something about him that is already present in

73. Ramsay, *Seven Churches of Asia*, 44.

their identity. For the missionary, this brings great hope that we, too, might discover in the places where we work something of Jesus already present so that we can make him explicitly known to a people to whom he reveals himself implicitly. In order to do so, it demands that the missionary remains curious, ever wondering at the incredible extent to which Jesus will go to make himself known. He indeed makes the missional move to people. Do we have the eyes to see it?

Chapter 7

A Place of Worship: Sardis

I had the wonderful privilege to accompany Loré as she was conducting research on persecution for her master's program focused on trauma and resilience. Her objective, in part, was to learn what created resilience under hostile circumstances. Through surveys and face-to-face interviews with persecuted Christians in the Middle East and South Asia, she learned that a clear sense of who they were in Christ was a salient factor in the resilient life of a persecuted believer. An issue that she suspected but was confirmed by multiple interviewees was the targeting of Christians because of their connection to the West. She writes,

> In societies where Christians are perceived as socioeconomically privileged or as outsiders, they may face discrimination, exclusion, or violence. This is happening where Western influences and money have shaped the local church to look more foreign and western rather than indicative of local culture and society. We have witnessed this in history in such places as Japan where Japanese Christians were targeted as potential allies of European imperialism. In China, as well, the Chinese government was provoked to "persecute Christians as agents of a foreign power" when the Vatican had prohibited Jesuit attempts to adapt the liturgy with Chinese customs and language. More recently I received an email from a pastor in Nepal asking for prayer because Hindu authorities were upset with a Christian church building they were erecting, most likely in western style. These forms can antagonize non-Christian believers.[1]

1. Cooper, "Learning from Persecuted Believers," 6–7.

Architecture and its influence on a community is a powerful purveyor of beliefs and culture. As Loré observed, the foreign look of Christianity in many places around the world makes its symbols—its architecture—an easy target for nefarious action.

All throughout Asia Minor, the monumental architectural structures speak as much about the gods and goddesses worshiped as they do about the worshiper's identity. As Christianity grew in the first four centuries of its history, we see how faith was expressed as much in the lives of believers as in the places they gathered. Over time, especially the Roman Empire's transition from paganism to Byzantine Christendom, Christian architecture and liturgy adopted familiar forms of imperial and religious opulence. Charles Freeman describes this opulence at the Church of St. John Lateran in Rome, founded in AD 324:

> Around 500 pounds weight of [gold] were needed at a cost of some 36,000 solidi. This sum, which might be translated into approximately £60 million today, could have fed about 12,000 poor for a year (according to calculations from Dominic Janes *God and Gold in Late Antiquity*). Another 22,200 solidi worth of silver (3,700 lbs.) was required for light fittings and another 400 pounds of gold for fifty gold vessels.[2]

The unintended consequence of such opulence ultimately resulted in Christianity becoming a target for nefarious actions due to its association with the Byzantine Empire.

So, it is fitting that we focus on places of worship after discussing places of peace. There is a marked transition from one to the other as the focal point of Christian gatherings took on the architecture of the past. In this chapter, we'll draw attention to the way that early Christians adapted the places of worship for their purposes. What we'll see is that as architecture becomes more elaborate so do liturgical practices, and so does its association with imperial power and spiritual authority. Sardis provides two fascinating examples: the Temple of Artemis and the monumental synagogue. Ultimately, the challenge for contemporary missions is reproducibility. Complex and culturally representative architecture and liturgies present issues that might lead as much to persecution as to an inability to reproduce.

2. Freeman "Emperor's State of Grace," 19.

THE CHRISTIAN USE OF RELIGIOUS SPACE

When Christianity took root as the imperial religion of the Roman Empire in the fourth century, which gradually became the Byzantine Empire after Constantine's move of the capital to Byzantium in AD 330, it redefined and repurposed space. The architectural legacy of Roman religion, once dedicated to a pantheon of gods and goddesses, suffered through destruction in the worst case and re-consecration in the best. The church, as it emerged from the margins, began to deconsecrate temple precincts and spaces and imbue them with new purpose or destroy them out of fear of demonic presence. Indeed, we see such destruction allegedly alluded to in the Theodosian Code, a set of imperial legislation wrongly used to justify the demolition of sacred pagan sites. David Hunt notes that the Christian use of the laws, "Reflects a contemporary world in which the destruction of paganism has been advancing apace (at least since the last quarter of the fourth century) at the hands of missionary bishops, fanatical monks and pious individuals, a process which laws have been powerless to control."[3] This wasn't just a pragmatic shift to demonstrate Christianity's dominance over the spiritual realm. It was deeply theological and an abhorrently misinformed missiology emanating from a profound belief in the continuing presence of malevolent beings haunting pagan sites.[4] As Daniel Hays points out, such an animistic worldview presents itself in the numerous apotropaic Christian graffiti found on walls, porticoes, and door jambs of temples throughout the empire (Figure 7.1, 2).[5]

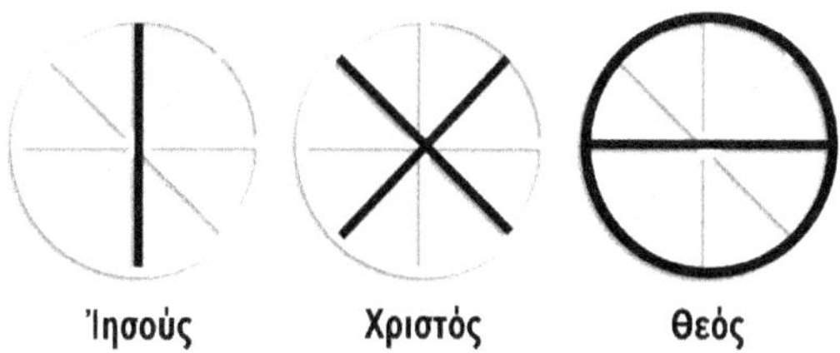

Figure 7.2: IXΘ monogram (a.k.a. Christogram and *ichthys* wheel).

While this animistic worldview appears to be a prominent practice in Christianity from the fourth century on, it is all together unclear if it

3. Hunt, "Christianising the Roman Empire," 157.
4. Saradi-Mendelovici, "Christian Attitudes."
5. Hays, *Ichthus Christogram.*

were or how it was present earlier. No doubt, there is a clear demonology beginning in the New Testament era which certainly is influenced by Jewish and pagan demonology. However, the New Testament claims that authority over the demonic is by the name of Jesus rather than an amulet, chant, or other mechanistic means (e.g., see Matt 10:1).

In the late second to third century, Tertullian conveys an awareness that demons freely roamed the earth and were not restricted to temples:

> And of course so pernicious an influence as this is not shut up nor limited within the boundaries of shrines and temples: [the demon] roams abroad, it flies through the air, and all the while is free and unchecked. So that nobody can doubt that our very homes lie open to these diabolical spirits, who beset their human prey with their fantasies not only in their chapels but also in their chambers.[6]

Yet, he allows for Christians to enter temples and other pagan sites without threat of the demonic attack as long as they did not participate in activities associated with them.[7] For Tertullian and others (e.g., Hippolytus, Cyril of Jerusalem, Basil), Christians renounced such demonic influence at their baptism, an act of renunciation they claimed dated to the apostles.[8] Even so, Christians were not permitted to participate in funerary rites, sacrificial meals, or any other form of Roman worship. After all, Tertullian writes, "'Not that an idol is anything,' as the apostle says . . . we cannot partake of God's feast and the feast of devils."[9]

Earlier in the second century, Justin clearly distinguishes the use of amulets by pagans from the Christian practice of exorcising demons. Similarly, Origen makes the same distinction, and Tertullian plainly states that it is by the name of Christ that demons are expelled.[10] Yet, as Hays comments,

> It is interesting to note that alongside the various forms and features of the cross, the acrostic word ΙΧΘΥC was also often used for individual protection. It was written on amulets or on doorways (entrances have special religious significance), where it appears to serve a similar function—to keep demonic forces away (prophylactic) or to drive them away (apotropaic) from

6. Tertullian, *Treatise on the Soul* 46 (*ANF* 3:225).

7. Tertullian, *On the Shows* 8 (*ANF* 3:82–83).

8. Proctor, *Demonic Bodies*, 152–56.

9. Tertullian, *On the Shows* 13 (*ANF* 3:85).

10. Proctor, *Demonic Bodies*, 109.

> someone's residence or business. Different types of crosses and other related symbols were used in these "magic formula" [for] apotropaic purposes on doorframes and on amulets that people wore. This included equilateral crosses as well as Tau-Rho Staurograms and Chi-Rho Christograms and the word ΙΧΘΥC.[11]

What seems to be occurring in later Christianity is precisely what we see in the early Christianity of Corinth. Cultural influences and past religious experiences, including animistic practices, slipped into the church. While no doubt innocent, the long-term impact on Christianity can be observed in the continued use of various icons, amulets, crosses, and signs as protective objects ostensibly restricting demonic influence (Figure 7.3). As Ildar Garipzanov notes, in a climate of spiritual authority, "Early Christian signs were bound to acquire apotropaic properties."[12]

Bayliss's Typology—Repurposing Pagan Space

Marking the architecture of temples across Asia Minor, we see various apotropaic graffiti clearly dating the practice to the fourth century and beyond. Richard Bayliss notes, "The position of crosses, usually adjacent to the temple doorways, appears to highlight their apotropaic function for keeping banished demons from re-entering the structure."[13] Their appearance seems to correspond with the various means by which Christians began to use pagan religious spaces. In his research on the subject, Bayliss identifies three distinct ways temples were repurposed into churches in the fourth to sixth centuries.[14] These categories—temple-church, temenos-church, and temple-spolia-church—help us see how early Christians reimagined sacred space to embody their purposes. Such reimagining appears to parallel a progressive superstition connecting temples with demonic inhabitation. Asia Minor, a region dense with both classical temples and early Christian witness, offers some of the best examples of this architectural and theological transformation.

11. Hays, *Ichthus Christogram*, 61.

12. Garipzanov, *Graphic Signs of Authority*, 20.

13. Bayliss, *Provincial Cilicia*, 13.

14. Bayliss notes, "While the historical evidence shows that cult activities in city temples had in most places ceased by the end of the 4th century, the conversion of standing temples into church was not at all widespread until the late 5th century and was most common in the 6th century, when the significance of pagan monuments in society had sufficiently waned" (Bayliss, "From Temple to Church," 16).

The first and most direct method of repurposing was the temple-church—the transformation of the temple itself into a functioning church. In Asia Minor, this form is clearly attested. In Ephesos, the Temple of Serapis, the Egyptian god of healing, was reused as a church by the fourth century.[15] While it is popular to identify the Church of St. Mary as the site of the third ecumenical council in AD 431—where Mary was affirmed as *Theotokos*—the date of the Serapis temple-church more closely aligns with the council, if indeed it was not held in an altogether different space. The reuse of this particular temple would have communicated a potent theological statement: the triumph of Christ as divine healer over the healing gods of the empire (Figure 7.4).

At Miletos, the Temple of Dionysos presents another example of a temple-church. An early Christian *ambo*—used for reading Scripture—is clearly visible among the ruins, while scattered lintel blocks marked with crosses reinforce the Christian transformation of the space to the Church of St. Michael (Figure 7.5). Similarly, the Temple of Apollo at Didyma was adapted for Christian use. When first excavated in the late nineteenth century, a church was found constructed in the *cella* of the temple. An apse was inserted into the interior staircase, and the presence of numerous Christograms, a *staurogram* in the *cella*, and columns carved with crosses all signal the building's new purpose (Figure 7.6). Here, the architectural stones of the pagan past were not erased, but reframed—used to proclaim Jesus Christ God in the very heart of a former cultic site dedicated to prophecy.

The second type of transformation involved building within the temenos, the sacred precinct of the temple, rather than converting the temple structure itself. In Ephesos, the Church of St. Mary—dated to AD 474—was built in the southern hall of the Olympeion temenos.[16] Though long associated with the council of AD 431 as noted, its construction came decades later, making it unlikely as the council's actual location (Figure 7.7). Still, its placement within the temple grounds of Olympian Zeus reflects a conscious decision to reclaim imperial religious space for Christian worship.

Sardis offers another compelling example. There, within the massive temple complex dedicated to Artemis, a small Byzantine-period church was constructed (Figure 7.8). Though modest in size, its location within

15. Bayliss, *Provincial Cilicia*, 125.

16. Bayliss, *Provincial Cilicia*, 54.

the temenos of one of Asia Minor's most important temples speaks volumes. Bayliss posits that some sort of deconsecration ritual would have been performed as indicated by the number of apotropaic graffiti (crosses and Christograms) on the eastern entrance to the temple. He notes,

> This common practice was an exercise in protection, and many statues of gods and pagan dignitaries were modified in the same way. There was nothing at all conciliatory about these acts. Christians were not attempting to appropriate or assimilate the gods and emperors by giving them Christian "badges." They were branding them as pagan and employing the cross in order to exorcise all that was evil about the statues and the building.[17]

In these first two examples, Christians didn't need to destroy the past—they simply reconsecrated it to serve their purposes. However, in the third and perhaps most symbolically rich category, the temple-spolia-church shows clear indications that pagan architectural elements—columns, capitals, marble—were taken from temples and reused in the construction of churches elsewhere. In these cases, the temples were either razed for such purpose or they had been abandoned and deteriorated. Not exclusively a practice for Christian churches after Constantine, stone and marble from abandoned temples were often used for houses and public buildings.[18] Nevertheless, back in Ephesos, the Church of St. John, believed to mark the burial site of the beloved disciple, stands as a powerful example (Figure 7.9). Marble from the Artemision was transported nearly seven hundred meters uphill for the church's construction. Some of the columns bear inscriptions indicating who was responsible for repurposing the materials or donating funding for their repurposing. One capital, conspicuously marked with a cross, remains at the Artemision—a visible witness to its transformation from imperial cult to Christian proclamation (Figure 7.10).

Consequences of Reimagined Space

Bayliss's typology helps us recognize that these weren't just building projects. They were theological declarations: Christianity was superior to pagan religion. Repurposed religious spaces communicated, not just a change in architecture but a new social imagination where Christian

17. Bayliss, *Provincial Cilicia*, 60.

18. Saradi-Mendolovici, "Christian Attitudes," 52.

identity reinterpreted Rome's religious architecture. In fact, we might imagine that numerous pagan worshipers converted to Christianity and naturally adapted their space if not also their religious practices to their new faith. Yet, as we consider such adaptation, a caution must also accompany any modern attempt to follow late antique Christianity in repurposing space. Along with adapting the architecture of Asia Minor, the church ultimately added rituals and liturgy that resembled former religious practices which contributed to an unnecessary burden on Christian life. We've already observed the emergence and use of apotropaic symbols, a practice completely foreign to the New Testament. Corresponding to their use and the use of monumental architecture was the natural development of liturgy to match Christianity's new-found spiritual authority over the lives of those in the Byzantine Empire. As history demonstrates, such authority was as much a feature of political hegemony as it was one of theological hegemony.

Additionally, due to its position of power, two unintended consequences confronted Christianity: it became a target of Byzantium's enemies, and Christian leaders became jealous of each other. First, even though the empire took on a Christian identity, its neighbors continued in pagan practices. While Christianity spread throughout the ancient world and had taken root in many places, once the empire declared its allegiance to the sign of Jesus Christ (*chi-rho*) and used that sign to conquer, Christianity emerged, not only as a political power but a military weapon. Outside of the empire, Christians were assumed to align with Byzantium. Philip Jenkins describes the issue:

> Once Rome became Christian, the link with that foreign government made life difficult for Christians living under the rule of the rival superpower of the time. (From the third century through the seventh, Persia was ruled by the powerful Sassanian dynasty.) The Persians responded by executing hundreds of bishops and clergy in a persecution at least as murderous as anything ever inflicted by pagan Rome: in the fourth century, the Persians killed sixteen thousand Christian believers in a forty-year period.[19]

When the Persians finally invaded, deep into Palestine and Asia Minor, church buildings were soft targets for plunder and their unsuspecting congregants for persecution. Andrew Walls summarizes, "Anything

19. Jenkins, *Lost History of Christianity*, 57.

so appealing to the Roman state as Christianity had now become could hardly appeal to Rome's perennial enemy."[20] Even in Jerusalem, the Persian sack of the city in AD 614 emboldened the Jews, who were allied with the Sasanians, to murder tens of thousands of Christians.[21]

Second, leading up to Constantine's legalization of Christianity, architecture factored prominently in the life of the church. Even a century prior, Clement of Alexandria spoke about "going to church," a dramatic shift in the Christian conception of *ekklēsia*.[22] Eusebius portrays the impact of this shift to buildings as church:

> How could one describe those mass meetings, the enormous gatherings in every city, and the remarkable congregations in places of worship? No longer satisfied with the old buildings, they raised from the foundations in all the cities churches spacious in plan. These things went forward with the times and expanded at a daily increasing rate, so that no envy stopped them nor could any evil spirit bewitch them or check them by means of human schemes, as long as the divine and heavenly hand sheltered and protected its own people, as being worthy. But increasing freedom transformed our character to arrogance and sloth; we began envying and abusing each other, cutting our own throats, as occasion offered, with weapons of sharp-edged words; rulers hurled themselves at rulers and laymen waged party fights against laymen, and unspeakable hypocrisy and dissimulation were carried to the limit of wickedness. At last, while the gatherings were still crowded, divine judgement, with its wonted mercy, gently and gradually began to order things its own way, and with the Christians in the army the persecution began.[23]

These two unintended consequences resulted in the church becoming a political pawn as well as target, and its leaders becoming greedy and powerful. Clearly, it seems, the human penchant for power and wealth did not discriminate then as it does not discriminate now. Nevertheless, the destruction of buildings during the Byzantine–Sasanian War of the seventh century does help us identify which of them might have been Christian, and Sardis provides a stunning example.

20. Walls, "Eusebius Tries Again," 108.

21. Jenkins, *Lost History of Christianity*, 102.

22. Clement of Alexandria, *Paedagogus* 3.11.

23. Eusebius, *History of the Church* 8.1.5.

BACKGROUND OF SARDIS

Nestled in the heart of ancient Lydia, Sardis was more than just a city of gold—it was a symbol of both affluence and pride. As the capital of the once-powerful Lydian Empire (seventh to sixth century BC), the Sardis emerging at the turn of the millennium embodied the fusion of Hellenistic urban sophistication and Roman imperial integration. It was indeed a city where the grandeur of its gymnasium and temple complex stood in stark contrast to the solemn faith of its early Christian community. The archaeological remains of Sardis, especially the partially restored synagogue and monumental Artemis temple, testify to a complex civic identity—ethnically diverse, religiously pluralistic, and economically strategic. Yet, as Rev 3:1–6 so poignantly reveals, Sardis was also a city haunted by an illusion of vitality. According to Jesus, the church there had a reputation of being alive, but was spiritually dead. And, once again, we see Jesus' intimate knowledge of the city, both culturally and spiritually.

Six hundred years after Jesus' letter to the church, the Persians under the Sasanian dynasty penetrated deeply into Asia Minor and by AD 615 they arrived in Sardis. Clive Foss explains some of the evidence:

> The sequence of the coins is uninterrupted until it comes to a sudden end with the issues of 615/6. After that, there is a gap lasting into the reign of Constans II (640–68). The coins do not speak in isolation, but form part of an archaeological context. The end of their sequence coincides with and provides a date for extensive traces of burning and destruction, which ruined both the gymnasium complex and a late antique mansion south of the highway. In other parts of the site, the sequence of coins stops with equal suddenness, even where the traces of destruction are not evident. At the temple, for example, a hoard of 216 copper coins, the latest of 615, was hidden in a sack under a block of marble and never recovered.[24]

Along with the disappearance of the numismatic record, Foss points to the burning of buildings, concluding that all the evidence points to an act of war, namely, the invasion of the Persians in what has become known as the Byzantine–Sasanian War.[25] Among the war ruins of devastation lay the "synagogue," the largest Jewish gathering space excavated

24. Foss, "Persians in Asia Minor," 737.

25. Greatrex and Lieu, *Roman Eastern Frontier*, 302; cf Magness, "Date."

in the Roman Empire. Steven Fine likens it as second to the Herodian Temple in Jerusalem in archaeological significance.[26]

As we have seen, the Persians reacted violently against Christians as they were indistinguishable from the Byzantine Empire. Yet, their relationships with the Jews appeared more conciliatory. Indeed, the Persian campaign throughout Palestine included a combined force with the Jews who were seeking liberation from their Christian oppressors.[27] So, it makes little sense that the Persians would destroy a Jewish gathering place and far more sense if that gathering place were actually that of Christians. Indeed, one might imagine that by the seventh century the grand synagogue and its congregants switched their faith to Christianity while maintaining a loose identity with their religious heritage. In fact, the archaeological evidence points to such a conversion.

THE SARDIS SYNAGOGUE

There might not be a more intriguing place of repurposed spaces for a Christian gathering than in Sardis. We've already observed the use of the Temple of Artemis as an example of temenos-church. Yet, using Bayliss's typology, the Sardis synagogue provides an example of temple-church, albeit we see many examples of *spolia* in use in this space. The synagogue of Sardis (ca. fourth century), located adjacent to the Roman bath-gymnasium, is a large basilica-style hall of ostensible Jewish worship that could accommodate a thousand people (Figures 7.11, 12). In fact, it is the largest so-called synagogue ever excavated in the Roman world.[28] Considerations for its surroundings, inscriptions, mosaics, graffiti, and *spolia* have raised the question of its potential multipurpose function. Adding to such an inference, we know from Melito, bishop of Sardis in the second century, that Christians and Jews observed Passover on the same day (the so-called Quartodeciman controversy).[29] So, assuming some amiability between Christians and Jews (at least liturgically), it might not surprise us that we would find Christian references in the structure.

26. Fine, "Synagogues as Foci," 97–98.

27. Greatrex and Lieu, *Roman Eastern Frontier*, 191.

28. I deliberately use "so-called" as we know the more common word for a Jewish gathering space is *proseuchē*, and *synagōgē* has quite an extended lexical range as we observed in chapter 6.

29. Melito of Sardis, *On Pascha*.

The existing building shows evidence of three stages, while a previous stage predating the other three has not been excavated. That early phase appears to have been connected to the adjacent bath gymnasium, perhaps classrooms or other such functional spaces concomitant with the activities of the site. The first stage of the existing building was most likely the space for the elders (*gymnasiarchs*) of the adjacent gymnasium. The second stage renovation in the third century occurs during a financial crisis in Sardis and might answer the question as to how the Jews of the city acquired the building. The final stage renovation occurred in the fourth century.[30]

Minor modifications of the interior are attested by several inscriptions of mostly Greek names including God-reverers (*theosebes*).[31] Along with what appears to be *spolia* functioning as liturgical pieces near the apse, a central position is highlighted at the center of Bay 4 (Figure 7.13). We know that in synagogues this would be the *bima*. In a Byzantine-period church, this would be an *ambo*. The area is surrounded by what would have been four thin columns. The mosaic on the floor, however, provides a clue. John Kroll translates it as "Vow of Samoé, Priest and Teacher of Wisdom" and maintains that the space was distinctly Jewish.[32] While Samoé is a translation of the Hebrew *Shamu'a*, it does not necessarily mean that Samoé held a position as a Jewish priest, although this could be likely.[33] Yet, if we consider the inscription of this individual as a "teacher of wisdom" it doesn't seem to fit the Jewish function of the *bima* where the Torah was recited but not explicated. In this case, I suggest that the feature located in the center of Bay 4 at least functioned as an *ambo* during Christian use (Figure 7.14). Thus, at some point in the fourth century, the building became the site of a Christian gathering. The fact that inscriptions dating prior to its Christian use remained indicates the conversion of and continuity with the Jewish community.

By the seventh century, a climate of anti-Christian animosity had been instilled in the Persians as we've seen. Thus, it's no wonder that when they saw such a grand facade as the Sardis sanctuary they would naturally

30. Bonz, "Differing Approaches."

31. Recall that *theosebes* is mistranslated as God-fearer and associated with Luke's God-fearers in Acts. See chapter 2.

32. Kroll, "Greek Inscriptions," 10, 17.

33. After AD 70, Judaism's rabbis appear to have gained increased prominence, though scholars question whether they achieved broad or immediate authority. The issues of priests outside of Jerusalem is discussed in McDowell et al., *Diversity and Rabbinization*.

react with violence and destruction. The archaeological evidence, as we will see, supports the view that by the fourth or fifth century, the original synagogue underwent repurposing: Christian dedicatory inscriptions and mosaic decorations featuring crosses, graffiti, and use of pagan *spolia* suggest a clear reappropriation of the structure for Christian worship or other para-ecclesial use. In a religious landscape where architecture conveyed communal identity and theological allegiance, such visible Christianization would have rendered the building a target for invading Persian forces seeking to undermine Byzantine spiritual authority.[34]

History tells us that the Sasanians, particularly under Khosrow II during the climactic 602–628 war with Byzantium, systematically targeted Christian religious structures, most famously razing the Church of the Holy Sepulcher in Jerusalem in AD 614 and looting prominent churches across the Levant. These actions were strategic: by attacking sacred sites, the Sasanians undermined Byzantine ideological and theological legitimacy. If the Sardis structure had, by this time, ceased to function as a Jewish synagogue and instead served as a visible symbol of Christian religious life—especially within a city so deeply embedded in the Greco-Roman and Byzantine civic-religious system—then its destruction was consistent with broader Sasanian war aims. It represented, not an assault on Judaism but a tactical blow against Byzantine imperial Christianity.

This interpretation also aligns with the broader late antique phenomenon of sacred space transformation. As Christian hegemony expanded in the fourth century, it was common for Jewish and pagan buildings to be converted for Christian use. The Sardis site likely reflected this pattern, embodying a layered identity that, by the seventh century, was predominantly Christian in both function and symbolism. Thus, when the Sasanians reached Sardis—a rare incursion deep into Western Asia Minor—the destruction of such a structure was not indiscriminate. Rather, it was a deliberate act against a building that had come to represent Byzantine religious dominance. Interpreting the event this way moves the conversation away from assumptions of Persian anti-Semitism and situates it firmly within the geopolitical and theological logic of late antique warfare.

34. See Fisher, *Rome, Persia, and Arabia.*

CHRISTIANITY IN THE SYNAGOGUE

While the Persian destruction of the space provides a compelling argument for its Christian function, there are two additional architectural features of the building that must be considered: the peacock mosaic and the Regina inscription. When weighed next to the *ambo* and Samoé inscription as well as the Christogram in the forecourt (Figure 7.15), the evidence for the synagogue's purpose as a church becomes increasingly persuasive suggesting a Christian reappropriation of the space securely by the early seventh century if not before—a conclusion further supported by the integration of Christian iconography and liturgical architecture inconsistent with continued Jewish use. So, let's take a brief look at the peacock mosaic and Regina inscription.

Peacock Mosaic

Near the apse of the synagogue was a seven-and-a-half-meter-wide dedicatory mosaic now removed (Figures 7.16, 17). At the center of the mosaic stands a large golden krater featuring a fluted bowl, a high flaring rim, and elegantly recurved volute handles. From the vessel, vines with tendrils and pointed red and black leaves extend across the white background. Originally, two peacocks flanked the krater, while an inscribed wreath commemorates the generosity of its patrons, the brothers Stratonikianos and Synphoros.[35] Around the edges are nine equal-armed (equal-lateral) crosses providing clear reference to the Christian provenance of the mosaic. Perhaps most striking, however, is the presence of the peacocks, ubiquitous in the art of the period.

The peacock, while aesthetically striking, carried deep symbolic resonance across the ancient world, eventually becoming a complex image of eschatological hope. Originating in India, where it was believed to protect against poison and symbolized royal authority,[36] the bird traveled westward through Persian royal courts before arriving in the Aegean world. As Juan Antonio Álvarez-Pedrosa argues, its migration was likely diplomatic, entering Achaemenid royal parks as early as the sixth century BC.[37] Among the Greeks, the peacock acquired dual associations—ad-

35. Rautman, "Color-Inlaid 'Champlevé' Reliefs," 104.

36. See Álvarez-Pedrosa, "Peacock's Arrival in Greece," 327 and the discussion of *Rigveda* 1.191.14 and *Mahabharata* 12.120.1–9.

37. Álvarez-Pedrosa, "Peacock's Arrival in Greece," 328.

mired for its beauty and exoticism, yet also marked by suspicion due to its perceived connection to Medism and Persian decadence.[38] Despite these political connotations, the bird was integrated into philosophical and religious traditions, particularly in connection with Pythagorean notions of the transmigration of souls.[39]

In the Roman period, the peacock became firmly linked to the goddess Juno and the imperial cult. Its frequent appearance on coins celebrating the *apotheosis* of empresses such as Faustina the Elder and Julia Domna—sometimes even bearing the soul of the deified empress to heaven—underscored its symbolic function as a mediator between earthly and divine realms.[40] The bird's resplendent tail, often compared to the starry vault of heaven, further reinforced its celestial associations. It is no coincidence that early Christian iconography, seeking visual language to express the promise of eternal life, appropriated the peacock for its funerary art. Augustine's assertion that peacock flesh resisted decay[41] offered a theological rationale for its use reinforcing the bird's emerging status as a symbol of incorruptibility and resurrection.

Christian art in catacombs and on sarcophagi often depicted paired peacocks flanking a kantharos or fountain—motifs that evoked paradise and eucharistic abundance. Vasilkov Ya notes that this imagery frequently included loaves, grapes, and chalices, integrating the peacock into the theological vision of communion with Christ in the life to come.[42] In Byzantine contexts, these associations were expanded further. As Henry Maguire observes, peacocks featured prominently in floor mosaics and domes, symbolizing not only the diversity of divine creation but also the hope of transformation through the resurrection.[43] Brooke Shilling similarly affirms the bird's role as a visual shorthand for eternal life, often depicted at fountains referencing the waters of paradise.[44]

While peacocks are less prominent in Jewish visual culture, their presence in two notable synagogue contexts—Priene and Sardis—invites further reflection. At Priene, a relief shows two peacocks flanking a menorah (Figure 7.18), while at Sardis, as we've seen, the mosaic depicts

38. Álvarez-Pedrosa, "Peacock's Arrival in Greece," 332.
39. Álvarez-Pedrosa, "Peacock's Arrival in Greece," 334–36.
40. Toynbee, *Animals in Roman Life*, 251–52.
41. Augustine, *City of God* 21.4.
42. Ya, "Peacock as the Bird," 85.
43. Maguire, *Earth and Ocean*, 36–39.
44. Shilling, "Many-Eyed Archangels," 353.

peacocks situated near a fountain (Figure 7.17). The spatial and iconographic parallels with Christian funerary mosaics, as we see across North Africa, suggests an appropriation of not only architecture but of art as well. As Waida observes, the peacock's consistent association with immortality across Greco-Roman, Christian, and Eastern traditions reflects its enduring theological potency.[45] When interpreted in this broader symbolic and historical framework, the presence of peacocks at Sardis becomes more than decorative—it signals a theological statement consonant with early Christian understandings of paradise and the life to come.

Regina Inscription

Next, we turn to the Regina inscription located in Bay 7 of the main hall of the structure (Figure 7.19). The inscription is a three-line Greek dedication carved into fragments of four white marble revetment panels. The fragmented Greek text reads,

[.... .....]C ΜΕΤΑ ΤΗC CΥΜΒΙΟΥ ΜΟΥ ΡΗΓΕΙΝΗC ΚΑΙ ΤΩΝ ΤΕΚΝΩΝ ΗΜΩΝ ΥΠΕΡ
2 [ΕΥΧΗC ΑΠΕΔ]ΩΚΑ ΕΚ ΤΩΝ ΔΩΡΕΩΝ ΤΟΥ ΠΑΝΤΟΚΡΑΤΟΡΟC $\overline{\Theta\Upsilon}$ CΚΟΥΤΛΩCΙΝ ΠΑCΑΝ [ΤΟΥ ΔΙΑΧΩΡΟ]
Υ ΚΑΙ ΤΗΝ ΖΩΓΡΑΦΙΑΝ

The preserved portion of the text records that a donor, alongside his wife Regina and their children, fulfilled a vow by dedicating the wall revetment and accompanying painting in a particular architectural space—likely a bay or assembly area—within the synagogue. The gift is explicitly attributed to the blessings received "from the gifts of the Almighty of God" (ΕΚ ΤΩΝ ΔΩΡΕΩΝ ΤΟΥ ΠΑΝΤΟΚΡΑΤΟΡΟC $\overline{\Theta\Upsilon}$) and reflects both the familial context of the donation and the donor's gratitude. The dimensions of the inscribed section are approximately .4 meters in height and 2.1 meters in preserved width, with letter height at .06 meters. The inscription dates no earlier than the last quarter of the fourth century AD. The donor's naming of his wife, inclusion of children, and reference to divine gifts situate this as an *ex voto* expression, perhaps due to a miracle or answered prayer, offering insight into the personal and theological dimensions of benefaction in the Sardis religious community. Two aspects of the inscription should draw our attention: ΠΑΝΤΟΚΡΑΤΟΡΟC

45. Waida, "Birds," 948–49.

(*pantokratoros*) and $\overline{\Theta\Upsilon}$. The presence of the *pantokratoros* inscription in the Sardis synagogue finds compelling resonance in the earliest Christian literature, indicating a shared theological vocabulary that may suggest overlapping sacred space or, at minimum, a conceptual continuity between Jewish and Christian expressions of monotheism. The term *pantokrator*—rendered in Greek as παντοκρατωρ, "Almighty" or "All-powerful"—functions in these expressions as a doxological identifier of God's sovereign and creative authority, and its recurrence reinforces the theological centrality of divine omnipotence in both Jewish and Christian liturgical and theological discourse of the first and second centuries.

In 1 Clement, written from the Roman church to the Corinthians in the late first century (ca. 70–90), the authors reference God twice as ο παντοκρατωρ θεος (*ho pantokratōp theos*), both in doxological praise[46] and in a theological argument for justification by faith.[47] Notably, 1 Clement 56, which quotes directly from the LXX version of Job 5:17,[48] reflects a continuity not only with the LXX tradition but also with the Regina inscription at the synagogue in Sardis. In each of these occurrences, the epithet does not serve a merely descriptive function; it denotes the God who is not only transcendent and sovereign, but who also acts justly and redemptively in the world. This theological framing anticipates the possible overlap between synagogue and ecclesial contexts in diaspora communities like Sardis.

The Didache, another late-first or early-second-century Christian text, offers further liturgical insight. In the eucharistic prayer of chapter 10, the phrase δεσποτα παντοκρατορ (*despota pantokrator*, "Master Almighty")[49] appears within a thanksgiving for both physical and spiritual sustenance. This invocation places the term within a distinctively Christian ritual setting, yet it preserves the Jewish theological meaning of divine omnipotence. The use of *pantokrator* here affirms the continuity of worship rooted in Jewish monotheism while simultaneously reorienting it around the person and work of Jesus Christ.

By the mid-second century, the term appears with philosophical and apologetic depth in the Epistle to Diognetus (ca. 160–181). The anonymous author describes God as both παντοκρατωρ (*pantokrator*) and

46. 1 Clem. 2.
47. 1 Clem. 32.
48. 1 Clem. 56.
49. Didache 10.

παντοκτιστης (*pantoktistēs*, "Almighty and All-Creator"),[50] emphasizing God's transcendence and sovereignty as foundational to the Christian claim of divine self-revelation in the incarnate *Logos*. This deliberate coupling of *pantokrator* with creative agency reflects an evolving Christian apologetic that remains anchored in Jewish conceptual frameworks while increasingly engaging Greco-Roman intellectual currents.

Perhaps most significantly for the Sardis context, Melito of Sardis—writing in the latter half of the second century—employs the same epithet ο παντοκρατωρ θεος in a doxology that universalizes the presence of God through Christ across the inhabited world. That Melito, a local Christian leader, would employ the same theological language inscribed in the synagogue's walls suggests not merely coincidence but a potential theological inheritance on the part of the donor.[51] Whether as shared space, repurposed venue, or conceptual overlap, the recurrence of *pantokrator* signals an intertextual and intercommunal dialogue in which early Christians at Sardis situated their christological convictions within the broader discourse of divine omnipotence familiar to their Jewish counterparts.

Alongside of the ΠΑΝΤΟΚΡΑΤΟΡΟC is the *nomen sacrum* $\overline{\Theta\Upsilon}$. A *nomen sacrum* in this contracted form with the characteristic horizontal line above the letters is the first and last letter of the genitive declension for God (θεου). The presence of this and other *nomina sacra* in early-Christian manuscripts provide the confidence for papyrologists to conclude that they do indeed derive from a Christian source.[52] In fact, Larry Hurtado asserts that it is,

> more likely that the specific practice originated among early Christian circles. As we have seen, there is no direct precedent in general Greek or Latin abbreviation practices or in Jewish scribal traditions for the pattern of words or the precise mechanics of how these words are treated. So it looks like we are dealing with a Christian scribal innovation.[53]

Regarding the *nomen sacrum* $\overline{\Theta\Upsilon}$, it appears in multiple instances in New Testament papyrus codices. Consider, for example, 𝔓45 of the Chester Beatty collection where we find thirteen instances of $\overline{\Theta\Upsilon}$. Fredrick

50. Diogn. 7 (*ANF* 1:27).

51. Melito of Sardis, *On Pascha*, 45.295.

52. Hurtado, *Earliest Christian Artifacts*, 96.

53. Hurtado, *Earliest Christian Artifacts*, 111.

Kenyon places a date of this codex to the first half of the third century. Also known as P. Chester Beatty I, 𝔓45 was found in Egypt containing the four canonical Gospels and Acts. Originally containing 220 leaves, the writing appears on both recto and verso. Folio 13 of 𝔓45 is a fragment of Luke 12:18–37 and line 22 reads, θησαυριζων εαυτωι και μη εις ΘΥ πλουτων (*thēsaourizōn eautōi kai mē eis theou ploutōn*, Luke 12:21), while line 32 reads την βασιλειαν του ΘΥ (*tēn basileian tou theou*, Luke 12:31). Additionally, folio 29, line 40 from Barnabas and Paul's first missionary journey reads εξηλθεν παραδοθεις τηι χαριτι του ΘΥ (*eksēlthen tēi chariti tou theou*, Acts 14:26). In the context of Luke 12 and Acts 14 in 𝔓45, all instances of ΘΥ must be translated as the genitive of *theos* (i.e., *theou*).

Importantly, Hurtado notes that the occurrences of *nomina sacra* was not limited to NT manuscripts. He writes, "*Nomina sacra* forms are also often found later on Christian icons, and sometimes on other Christian objects."[54] As it appears, when ΘΥ is used in the NT papyri it is always the genitive form of *theos*. Its appearance in the Sardis synagogue provides clear indication that a Christian contributed to the building's grandeur and leads to the conclusion that the so-called synagogue served as a gathering place for Christians. Indeed, when taken together with the definite article as we find in the Regina inscription, ΤΟΥ ΠΑΝΤΟΚΡΑΤΟΡΟC ΘΥ is an explicit reference to Jesus Christ.[55]

FROM ARCHAEOLOGICAL TO MISSIOLOGICAL APPLICATION

Christianity has always been at its best when it adapts space—physical, social, and spiritual—for the sake of mission, just as we've seen in Sardis. As the early church transformed temples and synagogues into places of worship due to the numbers of people converting, we are called to inhabit the public square with theological imagination. The archaeological past shows us how. Ultimately, we must consider that architecture is a powerful purveyor of worldview. It begs the question about what our church buildings communicate regarding our beliefs and priorities. As noted above, architecture connects a people's identity with space and, consequently, when that space conflates with other aspects of a culture

54. Hurtado, *Earliest Christian Artifacts*, 96.

55. Hays, *Ichthus Christogram*, 161.

(religious, political, intellectual), it provides a commanding symbol answering the question of who we are.

Too often, we assume that architecture is neutral—as if the church can adopt any form so long as its content is correct. But history teaches otherwise. The form we choose inevitably shapes the meaning we communicate. When we mimic the structures of celebrity culture, consumerism, nationalism, or therapeutic religion, we risk muting the gospel we intend to proclaim. Indeed, Asia Minor was a proving ground for the gospel. The church there faced a seductive array of religious, political, and philosophical alternatives, many of which shared surface-level similarities with Christian belief as we've seen. What set the church apart was not simply what it said but how it lived. In a world awash in options—ancient or modern—perhaps we need to recover this insight. Ecclesiology is not a footnote to theology; it is theology embodied. And in missiology, it is theology on display. So, let us not merely ask what the church teaches, but also how it lives, because in a pluralistic world, form reflects fidelity.

There are at least two implications for the Christian use of architecture coming out of this study. First, when Christianity aligns with a state or a culture, it might become a target by opposition forces. In modern times, we saw this with the rise of communism and the systematic destruction of churches by atheistic states. We saw this in Loré's research on the persecuted church as well. Second, when Christianity is seen as a representative of a government, then its symbols, namely church buildings, become targets of destruction as Christianity is perceived as an agent of the foreign state or culture. We saw this, for example, in Japan and China who perceived Christianity as European imperialism.[56] These implications should raise a strategic concern. When Western forms of church are used in missionary efforts, they risk being perceived as foreign and targets of persecution.

Ecclesial Safeguard: A Diagnostic Tool

God can and does use a wide range of contemporary ecclesial forms—from high production worship environments to multisite strategies and digital outreach. As we engage in the difficult and necessary work of adaptive ecclesiology, we must recognize that we walk a narrow line between faithful adaptation and functional syncretism. What begins as

56. Jenkins, *Lost History of Christianity*, 210, 255.

cultural engagement can, if left unexamined, become cultural captivity. So, the goal of safeguarding our ecclesiology is not to condemn form but to cultivate *awareness* of the human penchant to forget its meaning.

The following diagnostic tool (Table 7.1) is intended to help us self-evaluate. Are we adapting to culture in ways that remain faithful to the NT witness? Or are we becoming captive to cultural forms, pragmatically chasing influence or numbers at the expense of theological clarity and ecclesial integrity? The line between relevance and compromise is rarely clear, but we must be brave enough to ask the question and humble enough to recalibrate.

Ancient Cultic Form	**Analogous Contemporary Form**	**Syncretistic Risk**	**Missiological Corrective**
Theatrical rituals of Dionysos near temples/theaters	Stage-driven worship with light shows and performance bands	Worship becomes spectacle; congregants become passive observers	Return to participatory, dialogical gatherings centered on the Word and mutual edification
Oracle priests (Apollo); hierophants (Dionysos)	Charismatic "prophets" delivering ecstatic messages	Authority shifts from Scripture to private revelation	Anchor prophecy in communal discernment, submission to Scripture, and accountability
Imperial priesthoods or civic patrons with cultic honors	CEO-style, senior pastor culture	Leadership is sacralized; charisma replaces character	Cultivate teacher-models who form disciples through relational, ethical mentoring
Temple-centric worship (e.g., *neokoros* cities)	Church building as house of God	God's presence localized to buildings; spiritual geography conflated	Reassert the body of believers as the temple (1 Cor 3:16); focus on "sentness" not site
Mystery cult initiations (e.g., Isis, Mithras)	Ritualistic observance of communion/ baptism	Practices lose meaning; seen as magical or salvific acts	Recover communal teaching around meaning; practice identity in everyday life contexts

Ancient Cultic Form	Analogous Contemporary Form	Syncretistic Risk	Missiological Corrective
Mystery religions with progressive initiation (e.g., Eleusinian rites)	Spiritual elitism through "inner circle" discipleship	Fosters exclusivity, secret knowledge, hierarchy of holiness	Emphasize open instruction, transparency, and accessible formation for all believers
Imperial cult branding (e.g., coins with emperors and gods)	Branded churches with slogans, merchandise, and franchises	Church becomes a consumer brand; commodification of mission	Recover identity as family on mission, not a product; lean into relational networks over replication
Civil religion of Rome (e.g., worship of Roma, Athena, emperor feasts)	Nationalism-infused liturgies (e.g., flag ceremonies, military honors)	Fusion of kingdom of God with kingdom of Caesar	Center the liturgy on Christ's kingdom and its Christocentric ethic
Divine emperors, untouchable high priests	Leader immunity and moral exceptionalism	Undermines accountability; spiritual abuse enabled	Practice mutual submission, elder plurality, and visible, humble leadership
Oracular or symbolic riddles in cult temples	Reduced exposition in favor of inspirational content	Formation becomes emotional, not intellectual or moral (behavior)	Re-embrace instructional, dialogical teaching rooted in Scripture and community context

Table 7.1: A diagnostic tool for church formation

Through the centuries, Christians have taken different positions on the use of pagan space. From the power encounters we read about in Boniface's mission to Germany to the conversion of space for Christian use in England, the one constant has been the importance of space. For example, writing instructions to Mellitus, abbot to the Gauls, who was on his way to join Augustine of Canterbury in England, Pope Gregory stated,

> That the temples of the idols in that nation ought not to be destroyed; but let the idols that are in them be destroyed; let holy

> water be made and sprinkled in the said temples, let altars be erected and relics placed. For if those temples are well built, it is requisite that they be converted from the worship of devils to the service of the true God; that the nation, seeing that their temples are not destroyed, may remove error from their hearts, and knowing and adoring the true God, may the more familiarly resort to the places to which they have been accustomed.[57]

It is no surprise, then, that as Christianity spread across the Roman Empire, it did more than change hearts—it redefined space. The architectural legacy of Roman religion, once dedicated to a pantheon of gods, took on a new identity. The church, as it emerged from the margins, began to repurpose temple space—places previously reserved for empire and cult—and imbued them with new meaning in Christ. This wasn't just a practical shift; it was deeply theological. Occasionally, we see these shifts occur in the early centuries of the faith. For example, the Montanists, as we'll see in next chapter, though ultimately deemed heretical, served to challenge an early church shift toward rigid institutionalization. They elevated the role of laypeople, honored the presence of the Spirit, and emphasized the priesthood of all believers—insights that Tertullian, their most prominent adherent, championed with clarity and passion. In this way, God used their fervor to reawaken the church to realities it was at risk of forgetting.

57. Bede, *Ecclesiastical History*, 30.

Chapter 8

Gateway to Accommodation: Philadelphia

In a recent conversation with an Algerian Christian leader, I wasn't at all surprised to learn that a growing Christian movement in his country had been co-opted by Jehovah's Witnesses. I was in North Africa at the time exploring the potential for our next archaeological-missiological research project when I learned of this familiar tactic. Over the years that I've been involved in missions, many people have testified to situations where unsuspecting new believers were led astray by various aberrant Christian groups who arrived on the heels of legitimate evangelistic efforts. Algeria was simply another instance of what frequently happens when church-planting movements focus on evangelistic breadth and ignore the need for theological depth.

Interestingly enough, in the second century a new religious movement (NRM) emerges in North Africa all the way from Asia Minor. In the region of Phrygia, where Laodicea, Hierapolis, and Colossae are located and where Philadelphia sits as a gateway from Lydia to Phrygia, this movement appears espousing the belief that the Paraclete—John's word for the Holy Spirit—revealed the will of the Father through a new revelation. It became known as New Prophecy and ultimately spread throughout the Roman Empire. We see it in Gaul, Rome, and Carthage through the testimonies of Irenaeus and Tertullian, in the third century. The movement endures until the sixth century, so it outlasts many modern Christian NRMs. Its history even surpasses large NRMs such as the Jehovah's Witnesses or Mormons. Its beginning is connected with John's

Revelation and the church of Philadelphia as the founder, Montanus, believed that the New Jerusalem would be located somewhere near that gateway city.

Montanus, so we learn, was a new believer when he aspired to lead others in his version of the Christian faith.[1] He came naturally from a pagan background where he apparently had been a priest of either Cybele or Dionysos, perhaps both as it was common to serve multiple gods and/or goddesses. The details of his conversion are foggy, but his prophetic ministry was accompanied by ecstatic experiences and trances where he believed he was the mouthpiece of God revealing a new prophecy for his time.[2] While there seems to be some hint of a proper Christology, he is novel in his eschatology and charisma. Later, he and his cohort are declared heretics, but not before influencing Christianity throughout the empire. Even so, their impact was felt for hundreds of years and probably accommodated Christianity, if not outright syncretized it, with folk beliefs.

Located on the border of Lydia and Phrygia, Philadelphia was literally an open door for the exchange and flow of all sorts of cultural particularities from politics to religion. Indeed, such an open door compelled William Ramsay to label Philadelphia as the missionary city. Ramsay did not intend such a moniker in a Christian sense, although it certainly included the idea. Rather, Philadelphia was a gateway city from where the exchange of ideas and trade passed easily into and out of the interior of Asia Minor.[3] Such a city provided fertile soil for the birth of a NRM like the New Prophecy. However, like Thyatira, Philadelphia presents an archaeological challenge as there is little evidence to work with. Nevertheless, let's explore its characteristics through the literary, numismatic, and epigraphic records we do possess.

THE GATEWAY CITY

Philadelphia, founded during the Attalid dynasty of the Pergamene kingdom, occupies a unique place in the cultural and religious topography of Asia Minor. Established in the second century BC, its name—meaning

1. Citing an anonymous source, Eusebius relates that Montanus had an "unquenchable desire for leadership" (Eusebius, *History of the Church* 5.16–17).

2. Tabbernee, "Montanist Oracles Reexamined," 322.

3. Ramsay, *Seven Churches of Asia*, 391–400; cf Calder, "Philadelphia and Montanus," 327.

"brotherly love"—was attributed to the close bond between King Eumenes II and his brother Attalos II, who would later succeed him.[4] The legacy of this fraternal affection was etched not only into the city's moniker but into its cultural memory and religious heritage. The epithet *Kathegemon* (the leader) associated with the god Dionysos found in local inscriptions and civic dedications suggests a sustained connection to the cultic institutions of Pergamon, where the god likewise held a central role. Philadelphia thus functioned as a satellite of Attalid influence, even as it later negotiated its identity under Roman hegemony.

Geographically, Philadelphia was situated on the *Katakekaumene*—literally, the "burned land"—a region shaped by ancient volcanic activity. Its ashen soil proved especially fertile for viticulture, a fact that did not escape the economic designs of the imperial administration. During the reign of Domitian (r. 81–96), a controversial decree was issued, ordering the destruction of half the vineyards across Asia Minor in an attempt to stabilize the wine market and revive failing agricultural sectors elsewhere.[5] Characteristically, the Philadelphians resisted the edict. Their refusal to comply reflects both the centrality of viticulture to the local economy and a spirit of civic autonomy that would continue to define the city's posture in relation to imperial power.

Known in antiquity as "Little Athens," Philadelphia's urban landscape bore witness to its deep religious commitments.[6] The moniker is well-earned; the city's wealth of temples and cultic activity rivaled those of more prominent Hellenistic centers. In the numismatic corpus, three goddesses are uniquely portrayed within temple structures: Artemis—by far the most represented—appears in both dipteral and tripteral temples,[7] including those dedicated to Artemis *Anaitis*, reflecting a syncretism with Persian mother-goddess traditions. Tyche, the personification of fortune and civic well-being, is depicted within a peripteral temple, while Aphrodite, emblematic of beauty and fecundity, appears in both peripteral and dipteral structures. More on this momentarily.

The architectural iconography on coins extends to the imperial cult as well. Following the grant of *neokoros* status under Caracalla (r.

4. Hemer, *Seven Churches of Asia*, 155.

5. Hemer, *Seven Churches of Asia*, 158.

6. Fant and Reddish, *Guide to Biblical Sites*, 300–302.

7. Dipteral temple is an architectural style with a double row of columns surrounding four sides of the inner sanctum (cella). The tripteral has a triple column style whereas the perpteral is a single column surrounding the temple.

198–217), Philadelphia erected a dipteral temple in honor of the emperor, a clear indicator of the city's integration into Rome's religious and political fabric. The appearance of this temple on coinage not only commemorated the imperial benefaction but also reaffirmed Philadelphia's reputation as a city where civic piety and architectural grandeur coalesced in service of both the gods and the emperor.

Philadelphia exemplifies the kind of religious and cultural hybridity that marked many cities of Roman Asia. Its deep Attalid roots, agricultural resilience, and cultic diversity positioned it as a vital node in the broader narrative of accommodation, resistance, and identity formation in the imperial world. So, in this place, it is of little wonder that a new religious movement would emerge. Yet, in the first century, the church arises as one of the few which Jesus commends.

WHAT JESUS KNEW ABOUT THE CITY

The message to the church in Philadelphia, recorded in Rev 3:7–13, is distinct among the seven addressed communities of Asia Minor along with Smyrna. Whereas five other cities receive rebuke or warning, Philadelphia and Smyrna receive unqualified commendation. The words of Christ to Philadelphia, spoken "through the one who is holy and true" (Rev. 3:7), reflect a profound awareness of the city's historical resilience, sociopolitical pressures, and religious landscape. Embedded in this short letter is an acknowledgment of the city's precarious power, its faithful endurance, and its contested religious identity. What Jesus knew about Philadelphia reveals both divine insight into the city's present condition and eschatological promises tied to its future.

First, Jesus affirms, "Behold, I have set before you an open door, which no one is able to shut" (Rev 3:8). While the precise referent of the "open door" remains ambiguous, it likely connotes evangelistic opportunity. The metaphor aligns with Pauline usage (1 Cor 16:9; 2 Cor 2:12; Col 4:3), where an "open door" often signals divine initiative in gospel proclamation.[8] If so, this may indicate that, despite limited power, the Philadelphian church was strategically situated for missional engagement—perhaps along the imperial mail route that connected the city to Sardis, Pergamon, Laodicea, and beyond. The description that they have "little power" suggests a minority status, possibly numerical or social. In

8. Hemer, *Seven Churches of Asia*, 155.

a city known for its architectural and religious grandeur, such weakness stands in contrast to the civic prominence of pagan and imperial cults in the Little Athens of Asia Minor. And yet, in that vulnerability, they have "kept my word and not denied my name" (Rev 3:8); a striking testimony of faithfulness amid pressure.

The mention of opposition from "those of the synagogue of Satan, who say they are Jews and are not, but lie" (Rev 3:9; cf. Rev 2:9) reveals a contested religious environment. These are likely Jews who accommodated to the civic cult or collaborated with imperial structures to secure their protected status within the Roman legal system (see chapter 2). Their apparent hostility toward the Christian community points to the fracturing of Jewish–Christian relations in the late first century—a reality corroborated by the broader context of John's Apocalypse.[9] That Philadelphia is singled out as having such a synagogue implies the visibility, and perhaps vulnerability, of the early Christian community.

Jesus commends the believers for their patient endurance (Rev 3:10), a trait that echoes the city's own history of perseverance. After the catastrophic AD 17 earthquake, Philadelphia like Sardis suffered significant damage.[10] Tiberius offered financial relief and tax exemption, yet the trauma of seismic instability endured. Against this backdrop, Jesus' promise, "I will make him a pillar in the temple of my God" (Rev 3:12) takes on layered significance. The metaphor of a "pillar" is both architectural and symbolic. In a city where tremors drove citizens to dwell in temporary shelters outside the city walls, the promise of immovability—of never needing to "go out"—was a profound assurance of stability and belonging.

Moreover, the promise of a new name—"the name of my God," "the name of the city of my God, the new Jerusalem," and "my own new name" (Rev 3:12)—likely echoes Philadelphia's historical renaming. After the AD 17 earthquake, the city was briefly renamed *Neocaesarea* in honor of Tiberius, a reflection of civic gratitude and imperial patronage. Later, it bore the name *Flavia* under Vespasian.[11] In this political context, names were symbolic of loyalty, favor, and identity as much for people as for cities. Jesus subverts that imperial logic by bestowing a divine name, signaling a new eschatological citizenship far superior to any imperial affiliation. Finally, the reference to the church's "crown" (Rev 3:11) suggests

9. Hemer, *Seven Churches of Asia*, 160.

10. Hemer, *Seven Churches of Asia*, 156.

11. Ramsay, *Seven Churches of Asia*, 398.

a reward already in their possession—an image consistent with athletic or civic crowns awarded for victory or service. In a city renowned for its sacred games and religious festivals, the metaphor would not be lost on local believers. Their faithfulness amid adversity is not merely to be commended; it is to be crowned.

Taken together, these affirmations and promises demonstrate that Jesus knew Philadelphia, not merely as a geographic location, but as a community of fragile strength, faithful witness, and enduring hope. He saw their missional potential ("an open door"), their marginalization ("little power"), their conflict ("synagogue of Satan"), and their resilience ("a pillar in the temple of my God"). Each element of the letter reveals Jesus' intimate knowledge of the city's sociopolitical and religious realities reinterpreted in light of God's kingdom. Such a letter provided the "marching orders" for a new religious movement that would emerge on the scene a few decades later: Montanism.[12] We'll address this after we consider the religious landscape of pagan Philadelphia.

GODS AND GODDESSES OF PHILADELPHIA

In examining the religious landscape of Philadelphia, the epigraphic and numismatic records provide invaluable insight into the cultic environment that shaped civic and religious identity. Colin Hemer argues persuasively that Dionysos was Philadelphia's patron deity.[13] The numismatic record supports this view, with Dionysos appearing no fewer than fourteen times from the reign of Trajan (AD 98–117) to Decius (AD 249–251). This frequency positions him among the most attested deities in Philadelphia, although William Tabbernee suggests Zeus Helios may have also fulfilled a patronal role, appearing eleven times over the same period.[14]

Philadelphia's prominence as a center for the Dionysian cult is underscored by the convergence of textual and material culture. As the god of wine, ecstatic ritual, and theatrical performance, Dionysos finds natural expression in a region rich with vineyards and Hellenistic dramatic tradition. The identification of "Dionysos Kathegemon" in the numismatic record of Philadelphia situates the god within a broader

12. Calder, "Philadelphia and Montanus," 327.

13. Hemer, *Seven Churches of Asia*, 158.

14. Tabbernee, *Asia Minor and Cyprus*, 284.

Pergamene religious orbit. As the god of the Pergamene royal family, the epithet echoes the prominence of Dionysian worship in Philadelphia and the city's connection with Pergamon where Dionysos's temple was situated beside the Greek theater—the steepest in the empire (Figures 8.1 and 8.2). Such a placement was not incidental; Dionysian sanctuaries were commonly located near theaters due to the god's association with drama and performance.

A yet unexcavated temple near Philadelphia's own theater has been conjectured to be a temple to Artemis or Meter Phileis (a local Anatolian mother goddess), but the stronger correlation between Dionysian cultic activity and theaters—paired with the agricultural reality of vineyards—makes it more plausible that this was a Dionysian temple. However, further excavation is needed before a determination can be accurately posited.

Numismatic Testimony

Nevertheless, the iconography of Dionysos on coinage from this period further attests to his prominence. Early imperial coins depict the god leaning on a thyrsus, holding a cantharus in his right hand, with a panther at his feet—classical symbols of Dionysian revelry and excess (Figure 8.3). Later representations render him as an infant, perhaps reflecting the syncretic tendency to conflate Dionysos with other deities associated with birth and renewal. Alongside Dionysos, Cybele also appears with notable frequency beginning with the reign of Trajan. Typically rendered in a turreted crown, Cybele is seated with a patera in her right hand and a tympanum in her left, flanked by lions—a motif that resonates with her role as a guardian of city and nature (Figure 8.4). Other deities featured in Philadelphia's numismatic landscape include Artemis (forty-five times), Tyche (twenty-eight times), Aphrodite (twenty-two times), Nike (fourteen times), Helios (seven times), and others such as Pan (twenty times), Hermes (eleven times), Apollo (ten times), and Heracles (seven times). Even less prominent deities—such as Hecate, Hygieia, and Sabathikos—find occasional representation, illustrating the city's broad polytheistic spectrum.

The elevation of Philadelphia to *neokoros* status under Caracalla further confirms the city's religious vitality and imperial favor (Figure

8.5).[15] As discussed previously, the title signified the city's right to host an imperial cult temple bolstering its civic prestige. In the numismatic record, this elevation is confirmed through inscriptions and architectural iconography that celebrate the city as temple-warden with a dipteral temple.

With coins also bearing images of temples, an image of the landscape of the city justifies the spectacular epithet of "Little Athens." During the reign of Antonius Pius and again during the reign of Marcus Aurelius, the temple of Artemis was depicted as dipteral. A second coin during Antonius's reign depicts a tripteral—a triple row of columns—for Artemis *Anaitis*, a syncretized form of the Greek goddess with a Near Eastern goddess, *Anaitis*, associated with fertility and war. The numismatic records depict the temple of Aphrodite as dipteral during the reign of Septimus Severus. In total, the coins record temples for Artemis and Artemis *Anaitis*, Tyche, Aphrodite, Nike, and Helios along with the temple of the *sebastos* cult. With perhaps as many as seven temples, Philadelphia would have been a stunning site.

Epigraphic Witness: Dionysos and Ritual Functionaries

The epigraphic record, though limited due to overbuilding in modern Alaşehir, offers compelling glimpses into Philadelphia's civic religion. An inscription honors Aurelius Artemon, described as *hierophantes* (revealer of sacred objects) of Dionysos *Kathegemon* and secretary of sacred contests in honor of Zeus and Helios. As the inscription notes, "The greatest Council and the most brilliant People (*demos*) who oversee a temple (*neokoros*)" chose to honor him, pointing to a strong institutional link between the Dionysian cult and civic administration.[16]

Another fragmented inscription commemorates the dedication of an altar by Eutyches, a hierophant, and Hermippos, the *archiboukolos* (chief-cowherd) of a Dionysian *speira* (company). This ritual leadership suggests that Dionysian worship in Philadelphia was both corporately organized and socially stratified. As the inscription reads, "They set it up from their own resources," underscoring the importance of personal patronage in religious expressions.Yet another example reiterates the religious and civic nature of Dionysos *Kathegemon*. Philip Harland translates

15. Ramsay, *Seven Churches of Asia*, 399.

16. See Harland, "Honors by Civic Institutions."

the inscription found on a white marble slab with what appears to be a dancing man wearing a hairy costume, something symbolic of Bacchic mysteries. It reads,

> Some groups or civic institutions (?) . . . honoured T. Aelius Glykon Papias Antonianus, son of T. Aelius Glykon Papias—his father being high-priest and financial auditor of the sacred Council—the initiate (*mystes*) according to the decision (*diataxis*). The initiates who are gathered around Dionysos Kathegemon ("Dionysos the Leader") have supervised the setting up of the monument.[17]

Other Deities in the Epigraphic Record

Though sparse, other inscriptions illuminate the complex religious pluralism of Philadelphia. A richly detailed inscription, likely associated with a household cult, references altars to Zeus Eumenes—perhaps a reference to King Eumenes II who the Attalid Kingdom worshiped as a god—and Hestia, along with numerous divine personifications such as Eudaimonia, Ploutos, Arete, Hygieia, Agathe Tyche, and Nike. It also delineates ethical boundaries within ritual space, explicitly forbidding spellwork, sexual impropriety, and social division—a pagan moral rigor often overlooked by Christian scholars but certainly reflecting the ethical nature of religious expression at this time period. The gods "watch over these things . . . and will not tolerate those who transgress," reminding us of the moral and ritual demands placed upon participants.[18]

Another inscription from the *synodos* of Zeus Hypsistos outlines detailed rules for ritual meals, association hierarchy, and behavior demonstrating that Philadelphia's religiosity extended into private religious associations with formalized leadership and disciplinary structures. The inscription provides a real sense of the moral rigor related to worship in Philadelphia

> For good fortune! The law which those belonging to the synod (*synodos*) of Zeus Hypsistos ("Highest") devised jointly to be binding. Acting in the prescribed manner, they first chose for themselves Petesouchos the son of Teephbennis as their leader (*hegoumenos*), a learned man, worthy of the place and of the banqueting hall (*andron*), for a year from the month and day

17. Harland, "Honors for an Initiate."

18. See Harland, "Divine Instructions."

> written above. You shall arrange one banquet a month in the sanctuary of Zeus for all the contributors, at which they should in a common banqueting hall pour libations, pray, and perform the other customary rites on behalf of the god and lord, the king. Further everyone must obey the leader and his assistant in matters concerning the association (*koinon*) and they shall be present for all occasions that have been prescribed for them, at meetings (*synlogous*), gatherings (*synagoga*), and outings (*apodemia*). It is not lawful for any one of them to . . . (unknown verb), or to establish factions, or to depart from the brotherhood (*phratra*) of the leader to join another brotherhood, or for men to argue about one another's genealogies at the banquet (*symposion*) or to abuse one another verbally at the banquet, or to chatter or to indict or accuse another, or to resign for the course of the year, or to be absent from the banquet, or . . . or to steal the wife of another member, or to obstruct the leader (?) . . . public . . . at the marriages and . . . each shall contribute their dues (?) . . . and if any of them becomes a father (?), he shall receive (?).[19]

Finally, fragmentary inscriptions referencing Sabathikos (or Sabbatistes) point to localized or syncretistic divine figures whose origins and associations remain debated; figures which are perhaps of Jewish origin giving credence to Jesus' assertion of a synagogue of Satan with Jews who are not truly Jewish. These inscriptions invite further investigation into the permeability of religious categories and the role of non-canonical deities in civic religion. In all, the epigraphic testimony of Philadelphia depicts religious practices—ritual and behavioral expectations on adherents—that read remarkably similar to emerging ritual and behavioral expectations in Christian worship.

The numismatic and epigraphic records converge to present Philadelphia as a vibrant religious center marked by diversity, civic ritual, and imperial entanglement. Dionysos, whether as *Kathegemon* or as a symbol of ecstatic expression, occupied a privileged place in this milieu anchored in both architectural space and civic memory. As with much of Asia Minor, Philadelphia exemplifies the title of this chapter, "Gateway to Accommodation," where imperial identity, local cults, and economic vitality, even household codes, fused into a public theology that undergirded civic life. To be Philadelphian was, in many ways, to participate in the liturgical rhythms of these gods. In such a context, a new religious

19. See Harland, "Regulations of an Association."

movement that adopted similar forms—ritual leaders, sacred geography, ecstatic prophecy, moral rigor—would be easily assimilated into the broader religious landscape. Christian distinctiveness would be lost. Its gospel blurred. This, it appears, is precisely what began to happen with the *kataphrygians*, otherwise known as Montanists, in the middle of the second century.

THE FERTILE SOIL OF ACCOMMODATION

The shape of Christianity in Phrygia and Lydia may well be as complex and variegated as the pantheon of deities worshiped in the region. As Stephen Mitchell has observed, Christianity appears to have taken root most deeply in the rural hinterlands, where an abundance of funerary inscriptions attest to a robust, if localized, Christian presence.[20] These epitaphs frequently contain distinctly Christian references to God, ecclesiastical offices such as *presbyteros*, and formulaic appeals that reveal theological convictions and communal belonging. The phenomenon has been aptly termed *phanero*-Christianity, an open and public declaration of Christian identity. Mitchell comments,

> Christian gravestones from the largely rural interior regions used a range of devices to signal the religious identity of their owners—the use of the cross, the Christogram or other symbols, including the fish; the naming of clergy: deacons, priests, church leaders or bishops; adjuring protection for their graves from interference by the use of formulae that were almost exclusively Christian: εσται αυτωι προς τον θεον δωσει λογον τωι θεωι τον θεον σοι μη αδικησεις; or, quite simply, by declaring the members of the family to be Christians, or to be members of the community of "the faithful" (*pistoi*). "Coming out" as Christian was normal in Phrygia, but taboo in the cities of the coastal regions.[21]

The obvious question arises: Why was such open Christian identification normalized in Phrygia, while remaining a social liability in other parts of Asia Minor where persecution becomes severe? Part of the answer lies in the accommodation—if not outright syncretism—between

20. Mitchell, "Epigraphic Display."

21. Mitchell, "Epigraphic Display," 281.

Christianity and local religious traditions.[22] The porous religious boundaries in rural Anatolia allowed for considerable fluidity in belief and practice as Christians navigated a landscape saturated with folk religion, magical invocation, intermediary spirits, and ecstatic experiences. Paul Hiebert refers to such a landscape as having a mechanistic worldview in search for the cause of various effects through ritual efficacy.[23]

One revealing example comes from a fragmentary inscription in Laodicea *Catacecaumene*, located in Lycaonia. The text begins with a clear theistic declaration: πρωτον μεν υμνησω θεον τον παντει ορωντα δευτερον υμνησω πρωτον αγγελον, ος (*prōton men umnēsō theon ton pantei orōnta deuteron umnēsō proōton angelon, os*). Mitchell suggests that the "first angel" (πρωτον αγγελον, *prōton angelon*) may be a veiled reference to Christ. If so, this interpretation suggests a heterodox Christology more aligned with the angelic Christology critiqued in Paul's letter to the Colossians than with orthodox formulations. The inscription is ambiguous at best, but if read christologically, it reflects a theological deviation that likely resonated with what Paul identified as the Colossian heresy—a fusion of Christian language with local spiritual cosmologies.

Clinton Arnold provides another compelling example of such syncretism by citing a tomb inscription from the necropolis at Hierapolis:

> I adjure you by God who created the earth and the heavens.
> I adjure you by the angels, Cherubim, the harmony above.
> [I adjure you] by Michael, Raphael, Abrasax . . .
> That I might be averted from injury![24]

Arnold remarks,

> This text, in particular, illustrates calling on angels for help and deliverance and thereby provides us with insight into "worship of angels" in Col 2:18. If this text belonged to a Jew, which is quite possible, because of the predominance of Jewish names and themes, it is surprising to see that the pagan god, Abrasax, is invoked alongside Michael and themes [of the] creator God.[25]

Earlier, in his formative study on the Colossian heresy, Arnold notes that "their folk religion roots provided a belief structure that some of them considered compatible with Christianity: One must call on intermediary

22. We will explore this more in depth in the next chapter.

23. Hiebert et al., *Understanding Folk Religion*.

24. Arnold, *Colossians*, 110.

25. Arnold, *Colossians*, 110.

spirits and angels for protection."[26] This religious logic—characteristic of Phrygian spiritual consciousness—blurred the lines between orthodox Christianity and local religious tradition. It is precisely in this context that Paul inserts his high christological hymn in Col 1:15–20, a theological corrective to intermediary worship and cosmic pluralism:

> He is the image [lit. *eikon*, statue] of the invisible God, the firstborn of all creation. For by him all things were created, in heaven and on earth, visible and invisible, whether thrones or dominions or rulers or authorities—all things were created through him and for him . . . that in everything he might be preeminent. For in him all the fullness of God was pleased to dwell.

Paul's insistence that Christ is both creator and sustainer of all things directly confronts the belief that angels or intermediary beings must be invoked for cosmic protection or spiritual favor; another example of a polemical parallel.

Despite this theological tension, an accommodating form of Christianity "flourishes" in the region. As Robert Parker notes, while "other newly imported cults are all but invisible, as are Mysteries," Christianity seems to endure and even expand.[27] Yet, the precise theological contours of that Christianity remain elusive. It was, at minimum, simpler and more adaptable than the elaborate pagan cults marked by costly rituals, public festivals, and monumental temples. The comparatively stripped-down nature of Christian worship likely proved attractive in agricultural settings where economic means and architectural grandeur were limited. Thus, Phrygian Christianity occupied a liminal space: distinct, but not always doctrinally pure; visible, but not always institutionally structured. It was Christianity rooted in vernacular theology, shaped by animistic pragmatism, and sustained through religious familiarity. Such a form of faith may not easily conform to later orthodox categories, but it underscores the complex processes of religious identity formation in the early Christian centuries.

26. Arnold, *Colossian Syncretism*, 246.

27. Parker, *Religion in Roman Phrygia*, 141.

MONTANUS AND THE OVER-CONTEXTUALIZATION OF CHRISTIANITY

In the religiously fluid and syncretistic landscape of second-century Lydia and Phrygia, Montanus emerged as a uniquely provocative figure whose affinity for the book of Revelation and especially the church of Philadelphia is well-attested. William Calder enumerates the connection points with Jesus' letter: 1) strict faithfulness to Jesus during persecution; 2) descent of the New Jerusalem in the region; and 3) announcement of a great persecution. He concludes,

> If the Philadelphian Letter shows that, at the end of the first century, Philadelphian Christianity was similar in an important respect to that of the sect which afterwards originated there, it is equally clear that, when Montanism was formulated in the middle of the second century, this Philadelphian movement was certain to regard the Philadelphian Letter as its charter and marching orders.[28]

A self-proclaimed Christian prophet, Montanus announced that the Paraclete—the promised Holy Spirit of John's Gospel—was speaking anew through him and two women, Priscilla and Maximilla. In a prophetic voice, Montanus declared, "I am the Lord God, the Almighty, dwelling among humans" (see Table 8.1).[29] Their movement, self-identified as the "New Prophecy," combined eschatological imminence, moral rigor, and ecstatic gifts. On the surface, none of these themes were alien to apostolic Christianity. After all, Pentecost had inaugurated the age of the Spirit, the early church lived in expectant hope of Christ's return, and the Pauline corpus frequently exhorted believers to holiness and self-control. Yet, it was not just the form of Montanus's proclamation that set his movement apart, it was its claim that his content was a new revelation. In the words of Calder, the oracles of Montanus and his prophets were "the completion of Old Testament and New Testament revelation."[30] Such a declaration, nonetheless, is portrayed by a careful study of the known Montanist oracles. Yet, for a movement which held John's Revelation so high, there is no mention of the prophecy John is told to remind the churches: "You must again prophesy about the many peoples and nations and languages

28. Calder, "Philadelphia and Montanus," 327.

29. McGinn, "'Montanist' Oracles," 129.

30. Calder, "Philadelphia and Montanus," 323.

and kings" (Rev 10:11)—a clear reference to the worship of Jesus found throughout the apocalypse (Rev 5:9; 7:9; 14:6; 15:4).

Prophet	**Oracle**	**Source**
Montanus	"I am the Lord God, the Almighty dwelling in man."	Epiphanius, *Panarion* 48.11
	"Neither angel nor envoy, but I the Lord God the Father have come."	Epiphanius, *Panarion* 48.11
	"Behold, man is like a lyre, and I flit about like a plectron; man sleeps, and I awaken him; behold, it is the Lord who changes the hearts of men and gives men a heart."	Epiphanius, *Panarion* 48.4
	"Why do you call the more excellent man saved? For the just, he says, will shine a hundred times brighter than the sun, and the little ones among you who are saved will shine a hundred times brighter than the moon."	Epiphanius, *Panarion* 48.10
Maximilla	"I am pursued like a wolf from the sheep. I am not a wolf. I am word, and spirit, and power."	Eusebius, *Ecclesiastical History* 5.16.17
	"After me there will no longer be a prophet, but the end."	Epiphanius, *Panarion* 48.2.4
	"Hear not me but Christ."	Epiphanius, *Panarion* 48.12.4
	"The Lord has sent me as partisan, revealer, and interpreter of this suffering, covenant, and promise. I am compelled to come to understand the knowledge of God whether I want to or not."	Epiphanius, *Panarion* 48.13.1
Priscilla	"They are flesh, and they hate the flesh."	Tertullian, *Resurrection of the Flesh* 11.2
	"For purification produces harmony, and they see visions, and when they turn their faces downward they also hear salutary voices, as clear as they are secret."	Tertullian, *Exhortation to Chastity* 10.5
Quintilla (or Priscilla)	"Having assumed the form of a woman, Christ came to me in a bright robe and put wisdom in me, and revealed to me that this place is holy, and that it is here [Pepouza] that Jerusalem will descend from heaven."	Epiphanius, *Panarion* 49.1

Prophet	Oracle	Source
Unidentified Prophet(s)	"The church can pardon sin, but I will not do it, lest they also commit other offences."	Tertullian, *On Modesty* 21.7
	"It is good for you to be publicly exposed. For he who is not exposed among men is exposed in the Lord. Do not be disturbed; righteousness brings you before the public. Why are you disturbed when you are receiving praise? There is opportunity when you are observed by men."	Tertullian, *Concerning Flight* 9.4
	"Wish not to choose to die in your beds, nor in miscarriages and mild and mild fevers, but in martyrdom, that he who has suffered for you may be glorified."	Tertullian, *Concerning Flight* 9.4

Table 8.1: Authentic Montanist oracles[31]

Montanus's method of prophecy, expressed in ecstatic experiences and trance, bore uncanny resemblance to the cultic traditions embedded in the Phrygian religious world. The Dionysian and Cybelian cults, widespread throughout the region, practiced divine possession, frenzied worship, and ritual ecstasy. In such a context, Calder notes, "There was undoubtedly an element which appealed to a population which had been devoted for centuries to the orgiastic cult of Phrygia."[32] Eusebius, citing Miltiades's anti-Monatist polemic, claims that the Monatists practiced prophecy like no other mentioned in the Old or New Testaments: "But the pseudo-prophet speaks in a state of unnatural ecstasy, after which all restraint is thrown to the winds. He begins with voluntary ignorance and ends in involuntary madness."[33] Further tying Montanus and his prophetesses to Philadelphia, Miltiades notes that Montanus claimed himself, along with Maximilla and Priscilla, as successors to Quadratus and Ammia of Philadelphia. Of Ammia, we know little other than a comparison of her to the daughters of Philip, as well as Agabus, Judas, and Silas. Quadratus, on the other hand, lived in the second century as a contemporary of Ignatius and Polycarp. As with Ammia, he was compared to the daughters of Philip and other recognized prophets as having the same prophetic gift. Eusebius places him alongside the evangelists who built upon the foundations of the apostles by "sowing the saving seed of

31. Adapted from Heine, *Montanist Oracles and Testimonia*, 2–7.

32. Calder, "Philadelphia and Montanus," 328.

33. Eusebius, *History of the Church* 5.17.

the Kingdom of Heaven."[34] Yet, Miltiades clearly draws the distinction between the ministry of Ammia and Quadratus, and that of Montanus, Maximilla, and Priscilla, "But [Montanus's followers] cannot point to a single one of the prophets under either the Old Covenant or New who was moved by the Spirit in this way."[35]

The New Prophecy likewise incorporated a clerical hierarchy and sacred geography—including the expectation that the New Jerusalem announced by Christ to the church in Philadelphia (Rev 3:12) would descend in Pepouza—and unique rites such as "baptism by blood," the tattooing of infants and the newly baptized, and eucharistic celebrations involving bread and water or cheese.[36] These ritual patterns mirrored rather than subverted the religious conventions of Phrygia. Scholars have long speculated about Montanus's religious background, suggesting that he may have previously served as a priest of Cybele or Apollo. While that hypothesis remains inconclusive, the syncretistic impulse in the movement is difficult to deny. As William Tabbernee concludes, "Regardless of whether Montanus had really been a priest of Apollo/Cybele, as claimed by some late opponents of Montanism, the role of prophetic oracles in the lives of ordinary people engaged in the cult of Apollo/Cybele cannot but have affected the nature of prophesying within the 'New Prophecy.'"[37] Indeed, the transposition of ecstatic forms onto Christian content constitutes a reintroduction of ritual models laden with pagan meaning. In this way, the New Prophecy repeated the same theological danger Paul addressed in Corinth: the conflation of Christian worship with pagan form. To partake of the Lord's Supper "in an unworthy manner" was not merely an issue of personal introspection, but one of sacramental confusion—"You cannot drink the cup of the Lord and the cup of demons" Paul would exclaim (1 Cor 10:21).

So, I suggest, Montanism must be situated within the broader pattern of religious accommodation that characterized the rural Christianities of Phrygia and Lydia. As noted previously, these were regions where Christianity flourished not by disengaging from local culture, but by embedding itself in it. For instance, Calder notes, "The social picture which the [Montanist] inscriptions present, as Ramsay has pointed out, is one of orderly development, and of good feeling and accommodation between

34. Eusebius, *History of the Church* 3.37.

35. Eusebius, *History of the Church* 5.17.

36. Tabbernee, *Fake Prophecy*, 116–17, 350–66.

37. Tabbernee, "Asia Minor and Cyprus," 315.

Christians and their pagan neighbors."[38] Indeed, grave inscriptions bear witness to a *phanero*-Christianity—open declarations of Christian identity through symbols, clergy titles, and appeals to divine judgment. Yet, this openness was possible in part because of Christianity's syncretic engagement with indigenous religious forms. In such a context, Montanus's turn toward ecstatic prophecy and eschatological exclusivity was not anomalous but culturally resonant.[39]

The New Prophecy asserted itself not only through charismatic practice but through rigorous moral demands not altogether unlike what we encounter in the epigraphic record above. Montanists rejected second marriages, refused absolution for the lapsed, and demanded unflinching fidelity to the Spirit's voice as mediated through their prophets. Their rigorous asceticism gave birth to movements like the Novatians and, later, the Donatists of North Africa, both of which emphasized the purity of the church and the inadmissibility of compromise. In this regard, Montanism, or some form of it, might be considered less a heresy of doctrine and more a rupture over ecclesial authority and sacramental discipline.[40]

Tertullian, the North African theologian from Carthage and Montanism's most articulate advocate, saw in the New Prophecy a revival of apostolic power. He praised its eschatological urgency, its charismatic energy, and its spiritual elitism. For Tertullian, *Ecclesia spiritus per spiritalem hominem non ecclesia numerus episcoporum*—the church of the Spirit was constituted not by the number of bishops, but by those who possessed the Spirit.[41] In this, Montanism constituted an anti-institutional response to an increasingly structured monarchical episcopal church. As Rex Butler observes, "Montanists viewed their religious context as a Christian community replete with ecclesiastical hierarchy yet devoid of prophecy. In response, they cast themselves in the role of new prophets who would reinvigorate apocalyptic expectation."[42] Eventually, he adds, "episcopal stability rendered prophecy superfluous to ecclesiastical ministry."[43]

38. Calder, "Philadelphia and Montanus," 316.

39. Cf. Parker, *Religion in Roman Phrygia*, 223–26.

40. Although there is evidence that later iterations of it were aberrant and most likely some form of modalism. The fact that Tertullian becomes an adherent lends weight to the notion that some forms of Montanism maintained orthodoxy.

41. Tertullian, *On Modesty* 21.17.

42. Butler, *New Prophecy*, 35.

43. Butler, *New Prophecy*, 38.

Philadelphia, within this Phrygian matrix, provides fertile soil for understanding Montanism's appeal. The city had already demonstrated a penchant for resistance—refusing the imperial edict of Domitian to burn its vineyards—and an aversion to centralized authority. Moreover, Philadelphia became known for its martyrs. Alongside Polycarp of Smyrna, eleven Christians from Philadelphia were executed—an event recorded in the *Martyrdom of Polycarp*: "So it befell the blessed Polycarp, who having with those from Philadelphia suffered martyrdom in Smyrna—twelve in all—is especially remembered more than the others by all men . . . whose martyrdom all desire to imitate."[44] That we know so little about the Philadelphian martyrs may itself indicate that they were Montanists—devout, marginalized, and uncompromising. A letter from the churches in Gaul describing the martyrdom of Attalos of Pergamon and others was addressed, not to Smyrna but to the church in Phrygia, suggesting the presence of a spiritually vibrant and martyr-honoring community in the Western empire—likely Montanist. That being said, Montanism does seem to take hold in Thyatira and possibly Smyrna. If the martyrdom accounts of Karpos and Papylus in Pergamon are accurate, then it seems plausible that they also were Montanists.[45]

The prominence of martyrdom in Montanist theology is attested not only in literature but also in epigraphic remains. Tabbernee alleges that a third century inscription from Carthage found at the *basilica majorum* testifies to the presence of Montanism in North Africa. The inscription honors Saturus, Saturninus, Revocatus, Secundulus, Felicitas, and Perpetua who were martyred in the amphitheater on the March 7, AD 205. Most recognizable among the names are Felicitas and Perpetua. Perpetua's visionary experiences leading up to her martyrdom have given rise to the suggestion that she and the others were a part of the Montanist community, had pro-Montanist sympathies, or, at minimum, the editor of the *Passion of the Holy Martyrs Perpetua and Felicitas* had pro-Montanist tendencies.[46] An early-fourth-century inscription honors Gennadeios, a shepherd (*poimenon*) of sheep who suffered death because of the holy Scriptures.[47] Tabbernee relates that Calder believed this inscription to be Montanist as the name Gennadeios is absent from Christian

44. Ehrman, "Martyrdom of St. Polycarp," 19.1.

45. Tabbernee, *Montanist Inscriptions and Testimonia*, 136–41.

46. Tabbernee, *Montanist Inscriptions and Testimonia*, 105–17.

47. Tabbernee, *Montanist Inscriptions and Testimonia*, 333.

martyrologies.[48] However, he concludes, "It is unlikely that Gennadeios was a Montanist, but the possibility that he was should not be ruled out."[49] Whatever the case, both of these accounts testify to the fact that Christians, whether Montanists or sympathizers, willingly suffered martyrdom.

Jerome, writing in the fourth century, claimed that Montanus had mutilated himself, possibly indicating a priestly service to Cybele.[50] In the fifth century, Michael the Syrian recounts that John of Ephesos exhumed the bodies of Montanus and "his two women" in Pepouza, and burned their bones—a symbolic annihilation of memory and power. Notably, gold plates were found on their mouths. While such plates were used in elite pagan burials to signify eternal life, in this context they may have indicated a prophetic office—*chrysostomoi*, "golden mouths." A similar practice was found in a first-century BC grave in Greece, where a woman presumed to be a priestess of Apollo—the god of prophecy—was interred with a gold mouthpiece near a sanctuary of the prophetic god.[51] If such practices echo in Montanism, they underscore the religious continuities that bound pagan and Christian experience in the region.

By the fourth century, streams of Montanism appear to have shifted toward modalistic theology embracing the "doctrine of Sabellius." Nevertheless, their ecclesiology remained distinct: they privileged the Phrygian church as primary, structured their hierarchy with a "patriarch" above bishops and stewards, and continued to forbid second marriages and deny reentry to the lapsed. As late as the Constantinian period, Montanist presence was still visible in inscriptions across the region. Their prophetic movement—infused with rigor, ecstatic vision, and apocalyptic hope—serves as both a mirror and a critique of early Christian institutional development. In the end, Montanism was an over-contextualized movement. Born in a region saturated with divine ecstasy, prophetic oracles, and religious improvisation, it adopted indigenous forms into a new expression of charismatic Christianity. Whether viewed as heretical, schismatic, or heroic, the New Prophecy reminds us that form matters as much as content, and that faith, when shaped by culture, must be continually reformed by the gospel.

48. Tabbernee, *Montanist Inscriptions and Testimonia*, 334.

49. Tabbernee, *Montanist Inscriptions and Testimonia*, 334.

50. Jerome, *Epistle 41* (*NPNF*^{2} 6:55–56).

51. Kontogianni, "Skeleton of Ancient Woman."

FROM ARCHAEOLOGICAL TO MISSIOLOGICAL

If there are core missiological principles that we find in the archaeological record, however loosely connected with Philadelphia, they are these: leadership matters and cultural context matters. First, leadership matters. Montanus is a cautionary tale of a recent believer ascending to leadership before he is properly grounded (cf. 1 Tim 3:6). Similar to the anecdote at the beginning of this chapter, instances of new believers being thrust into leadership dot the landscape of CPMs and DMMs around the world. The insatiable appetite for fast growth driven by an eschatological vision focused on finishing the task results more often than not in movements which are a mile wide and an inch deep. Church movements in China testify to how a shallowness of theology spawns aberrant forms of Christianity like the Church of Almighty God which believes Jesus has reincarnated as a woman.[52] Movements such as this are often left unreported in the statistics. At the same time, aberrant movements do not always emerge overnight. It was one hundred years after Paul's mission in Asia Minor when Montanus arrives on the scene. Even though we might want to believe that such a movement will not result from our efforts, Montanism reminds us that it could take a generation unless a solid theological and missiological foundation are laid and reinforced through the years.

Second, cultural context matters. The rural environment where Montanism flourished provides an example of the importance for theological safeguards erected to ensure that an animistic worldview does not creep into Christianity. Such folk traditions as the evil eye, use of amulets, magical incantations for healing are an ever-present challenge where the veil between the seen and unseen is thin. Rural communities tend to be mechanistic as they see undesired effects—death, famine, plague, crop failure, natural disaster—and seek a cause that can be mitigated through divine intervention if the rituals are properly performed. Mitchell describes this reality:

> They were prosperous peasants in a rich and fertile region. Their agricultural way of life was displayed explicitly on their gravestones, which were decorated with all the tools and equipment required for cereal-growing, animal husbandry and viticulture; and by the pagan dedications, mostly of the second and third centuries, set up in local shrines of Zeus, of Mother Goddesses,

52. Introvigne, *Church of Almighty God.*

> and other deities, who here were pre-eminently concerned with the success of the harvest and the health of their livestock.[53]

In spite of the scant archaeological record in Philadelphia, its topology—viticulture, volcanic soil, gateway to and from Phrygia—and moniker as Little Athens helps tell a story of over-contextualization manifested in accommodation to religious practices and eventually to syncretism. There is no doubt that Christians from Philadelphia suffered under the persecution of Domitian. Jesus tells us there were faithful followers. Yet with the rich soil of religious pluralism and an environment where everything in life blended together, it is no real surprise that Christianity conformed to the status quo. Could it be that the evangelism efforts were sloppy or discipleship was poor? Whatever the case, Philadelphia was a gateway to Pergamon and we've seen that Christianity strangely disappears from that imperial city. How and why is a mystery that still merits exploration.

53. Mitchell, *Rise of the Church*, 40.

Chapter 9

Avoiding Spiritual Complacency: Laodicea

I suspect that when Christians hear the name of the city, they immediately recall the church that Jesus wanted to spit out of his mouth. N. T. Wright and Michael Bird are correct when they suggest that Jesus' letter to the church in that city is the most well-known.[1] Perhaps famous for all the wrong reasons, it provides an example of a complacent church. And, Revelation's first commentator would agree. In the third century, Bishop Victorinus described the church as a group of people who held positions of status in the city, even spoke about Scripture, but did little to demonstrate their knowledge.[2]

No doubt that such a description might be applied to various churches throughout history. Certainly today, data on the Western church indicates an enduring complacency. For example, in 2018, Barna Group reported that 51 percent of American Christians have never heard of the Great Commission and 25 percent do not know what it means.[3] This is more understandable once we learn that according to a 2022 Lifeway Research study, 62 percent of Christians have not shared their faith with a friend or family member and 70 percent have not shared with a stranger in the past six months. Not surprisingly, 43 percent are either unprepared to put into words the essentials of the gospel or do not know

1. Wright and Bird, *New Testament*, 1507.
2. Cooper, *Faithful Witness*, 27.
3. Barna, "51% of Churchgoers."

where to begin. It all makes sense when Lifeway revealed that 70 percent of Christians have not been trained to tell others about Christ.[4]

While the ability or desire to share one's faith might be one indicator of complacency, the increasing numbers of Christians who do not hold to what Barna Group defines as a "biblical worldview" is certainly another. In 2017, Barna Group shocked American Christians with the announcement that their study discovered only 17 percent of Americans who regularly attend church and consider faith important truly hold a "biblical worldview."[5] They revealed that Christians are just as likely to be influenced by new spiritualities, secularism, postmodernism, and Marxism as they are by the Bible.[6] Indeed, the rise of so-called conversions to cultural Christianity influenced by secularism, materialism, and even atheism testifies to the conflation of a Christian ethos with the values of competing worldviews. Instead of representing a vibrant faith with followers prepared to die for the name of Christ, Western Christianity has become a pragmatic faith prepared to capitalize on social and economic benefits. Reflecting on prominent cultural icons like Elon Musk, Jordan Peterson, and Richard Dawkins, who all claim some affinity with the spirit of Christianity, Alan Noble observes,

> What these arguments have in common is the recognition that Christianity is tangibly good for the human person and society. It improves our sex lives, mental health, and social networks, and it gives us a stability, order, and foundation for liberty and justice that the contemporary secular world can't replicate. These are powerful reasons to become a Christian and encourage the spread of at least a superficially Christian culture—one that assumes the ethos of Christianity even if it doesn't accept the orthodoxy of Christianity. After all, the data seems clear: A more Christian culture would produce more human flourishing. But is this awareness of Christianity's measurable benefits a threat to authentic faith or an opportunity for the gospel?[7]

The answer to Noble's question lies in the ability of the existing church to rise above its current complacency. So, let's consider the rest of the story of the church in Laodicea. We'll see that the church took

4. Lifeway Research, *Evangelism Explosion Study*.

5. I use "biblical worldview" in quotation marks as it raises the question of which worldview is biblical. Instead, I often discuss a biblically informed worldview since there are multiple understandings of what can be considered "biblical."

6. Barna, "Competing Worldviews."

7. Noble, "Let the Cultural Christians."

the words of Jesus seriously and moved from an apathetic expression of faith to a passionate force impacting every segment of the community. It is a beautiful story about a church's return to vibrancy, and also one that serves as a warning for global church-planting efforts which follow a Western model.

BACKGROUND

Named after Laodike, the wife of the Seleucid ruler Antiochus II, Laodicea was constructed around 260 BC upon of an earlier settlement known as the city of Zeus—Diospolis.[8] Indeed, on the eastern city gate entrance leading to the colonnaded Syrian road (Figure 9.1), a Greek dedicatory inscription honors *Zeus Megistos Soter*, that is, Zeus the Great Savior, as the city's patron deity. Archaeological material establishes a continuous occupation of the region from 5500 BC to the seventh century AD. The city became a part of the Roman Empire in the second century BC (see Map 9.1).

As a prominent city of the Lycus Valley, it was known for a robust textile-manufacturing and banking industry.[9] At some level, its wealth eventually secured its independence from the Roman Empire's vast coffers as it refused Nero's gesture to help reconstruct the city after the earthquake of AD 60.[10] As discussed in chapter 3, a medical school was established in the Lycus Valley characterized by a strong focus on anatomical study. The school remained active under the direction of Alexander Philalethes, whose student Demosthenes went on to gain particular recognition for his work in ophthalmology.[11] Within sight of the city to the south and southeast are the snow-capped mountains (Figure 9.2, Salbakos and Cadmus) which supplied streams of cold water throughout the year thanks to the Roman aqueduct system. To the city's north, about six miles away and within visual sight, lies the white travertine hot springs of Hierapolis (Figure 9.3).

Located at a crossroad of commerce connecting Western, Central, and Southern Asia Minor, Laodicea represented many different cultures and corresponding religious beliefs. The citizenry comprised Macedonians, Seleucids, Pergamenes, Romans, and Jews among others. Colossal

8. Pliny the Elder, *Natural Histories* 5.105:300–301.

9. Cicero, *Letters to Friends* 68.5. See Yamauchi, *New Testament Cities*, 137.

10. Tacitus, *Annals* 14.27.1:151.

11. Smith, *Dictionary*, 991; cf. Galen, *Hygiene* 13.

bath houses at the eastern and western entrances reduced the transmission of disease from commercial travel (Figure 9.4). Two theaters on the north side of the city indicate a vital artistic community. The restored western theater currently under excavation seats an estimated eight thousand people (Figure 9.5). Still to be excavated, the northern theater on the east side of the city has an estimated capacity of twelve thousand people (Figure 9.6).

The sports complex to the south of the city, one of the largest in the Roman Empire with a capacity of more than twenty thousand (Figure 9.7), is adjacent to an agora, bath complex, and *bouleuterion*, all testifying to an active civic life.[12] Temples dotting the landscape of the city were dedicated to gods, goddesses, and emperors. Temple A on the north side of the colonnaded Syrian road might have been dedicated to Apollo, Artemis, and Aphrodite, if not to Zeus (Figure 9.8). The capitals of the columns bear the telltale relief of the beehive or egg associated with Artemis (Figure 9.9).

After a failed attempt for a bid to be the site of an imperial temple in AD 25, Laodicea eventually achieved the status as *neokoros*[13] under Emperor Commodus (AD 177–192) in the late second century AD. Many emperors were honored in Laodicea: Vespasian with a sports stadium; Domitian with a dedicatory inscription on the Syrian and Ephesian gates; Trajan with a fountain commemorating his victory over the Dacians (Figure 9.10); Hadrian with a bath-gymnasium complex; Commodus and eventually Caracalla and the cult of the *sebastos*; and Diocletian with two columns celebrating the twentieth year of his reign.

Historiographic, epigraphic, and *graffito* evidence testify to the existence of a Jewish community in Laodicea leading up to the first century AD. No architectural evidence of a synagogue has surfaced to date. Mark Wilson suggests an estimated male Jewish population of 7,500 based upon records of the temple tax, while Ulrich Huttner estimated 10,000.[14] Whatever the case, Laodicea boasted a sizeable Jewish population. It is quite possible that this Jewish community converted to Christianity as we see in other communities in the book of Acts. The *graffito* of a menorah, shofar, palm branch, and cross located on the south side of the Syrian road across from Temple A might testify to Christianity emerging from

12. Şimşek, "Archaeological Site of Laodikeia."

13. Laodicea identified as *neokoros* (ΛΑΟΔΙΚΕΩΝ ΝΕΩΚΟΡΩΝ) in the numismatic record during the reign of Elagabalus (AD 218–222).

14. Wilson, *Biblical Turkey*, 243; Huttner, *Early Christianity*, 71.

Judaism as the cross protrudes from the center candle possibly indicating that Christ is the glory of God (Figure 9.11). Steven Fine refers to this as visual supersessionism.[15] Yet, set in the context of the book of Revelation, it is more likely a reference to Laodicea as one of the seven churches whose lampstands Christ walked among (Rev 1:20).

LAODICEA AND THE NEW TESTAMENT

Christianity arrives in Laodicea near the middle of the first century. The missionary endeavors of Paul and his associates began in the region in the late 40s with Paul leaving the area known as Roman Asia (in Asia Minor) in the mid 50s.[16] Paul and Timothy testify to the Colossians learning the gospel from Epaphras (Col 1:7).[17] Presumably, Epaphras continued the work throughout the Lycus Valley in both Laodicea and Hierapolis (Col 4:13). In spite of Colossians receiving the only extant apostolic letter to a church in the Lycus Valley, it is the church in Laodicea which garners most of the attention of early Christianity as evidenced in the archaeological record.[18] In AD 60, Laodicea, Hierapolis, and Colossae were devastated by an earthquake.[19] An inscription honoring the repairer of a bath house at Colossae suggests the city began rebuilding in the late first century to early second century.[20] Numismatic artifacts show that Colossae does not fully recover for another one hundred years. In the meantime, Laodicea, refusing the aid of the Roman Empire, reconstructed and continued as a significant city in the valley.[21] Whether or not the oracles predicted earthquakes or they simply testified to the seismic events, there is no doubt of their occurrence:

15. Fine, "Synagogues," 117.

16. Cooper, *Ephesiology*.

17. It is also plausible that Timothy visited at least Colossae if not also Laodicea and Hierapolis. As a possible pattern, other letters to the saints in different cities coauthored by Timothy had been visited by Timothy (namely Philippi, Thessalonica, and Corinth).

18. Laodicea is mentioned in the NT in Col 2:1; 4:13–16; Rev 1:11; 3:14–22. Even though we have no record that Paul had visited Laodicea (Col 2:1), he did write a letter to the church which is no longer extant (Col 4:16). Some have mistakenly argued that Ephesians is the missing letter to Laodicea (see Witherington, *Letters*, 53). A plausible case might be made that Paul visited the area due to his eye disease.

19. Tacitus, *Annals* 14.27.1.

20. Cadwallader, "Honouring the Repairer," 152.

21. Huttner, *Early Christianity*, 100–103; cf. Witherington, *Letters*, 69.

> Wretched Laodicea, thee sometime; Shall earthquake lay low, casting headlong down, But thou, a city firmly set, again; Shalt stand.[22]

While, as noted below, a letter to the church is included in Revelation, Paul also wrote to the community and expected the letter to be read by the Colossians (Col 4:16). The lost letter to the Laodiceans must have been written before AD 60 while Paul was imprisoned in Ephesos (Col 4:10). Some have argued that Ephesians is actually the lost letter to the Laodiceans as early manuscripts do not include the destination "in Ephesos" (Eph 1:1).[23] In the second century, Marcion claimed the Ephesian letter is addressed to the saints in Laodicea.[24] Whatever the case, Paul tells us that a church met in the house of Nympha (Col 4:15). The verse could also infer another meeting place where other *adelphoi* gathered. All that being said, the letter to the Colossians was as much for the saints in that city as it was for the saints ten miles away in Laodicea and sixteen miles away in Hierapolis.

Material Culture Illumines the Biblical Text

For many, the church of Laodicea symbolized qualities and behaviors unbecoming of those called saints. As mentioned, Victorinus in the third century AD, writing the first commentary on Revelation, described them as dignified people who read Scripture but did nothing to enact it.[25] Perhaps reserving his harshest letter until the end, Jesus offers no praise for the church as he did for six others in Asia Minor (see Table 1.1). Instead, he warns the angel of the church using explicit language that connected with the culture:

> And to the angel of the church in Laodicea write: "The words of the Amen, the faithful and true witness, the beginning of God's creation. 'I know your works: you are neither cold nor hot. Would that you were either cold or hot! So, because you are lukewarm, and neither hot nor cold, I will spit you out of my mouth. For you say, I am rich, I have prospered, and I need nothing, not realizing that you are wretched, pitiable, poor, blind, and naked. I counsel you to buy from me gold refined

22. Terry, *Sibylline Oracles* 4.135–140:105.
23. See Witherington, *Letters*, 326.
24. Metzger, *Textual Commentary*, 601.
25. Cooper, *Faithful Witness*, 21.

> by fire, so that you may be rich, and white garments so that you may clothe yourself and the shame of your nakedness may not be seen, and salve to anoint your eyes, so that you may see. Those whom I love, I reprove and discipline, so be zealous and repent. Behold, I stand at the door and knock. If anyone hears my voice and opens the door, I will come in to him and eat with him, and he with me. The one who conquers, I will grant him to sit with me on my throne, as I also conquered and sat down with my Father on his throne. He who has an ear, let him hear what the Spirit says to the churches.'" (Rev 3:14–22)

There can be no mistake in the language Jesus uses to communicate with the church. He connected with the Laodiceans in a manner representing someone who knew them intimately. He understood their culture, their geography, and their history. He begins the letter with what many assume to be clear reference to their water. Whether or not the reference addresses the hydrological situation of the city is debated.[26] The city's location between the hot springs of Hierapolis (Figure 9.3) and the cold springs of Mount Cadmus (Figure 9.2) might not be in view. Instead, the dining reference in Rev 3:20 provides a better context. Craig Koester effectively argues that the reference is to lukewarm wine when the dining custom in Greek cultures was to serve it either cold or hot depending on the season.[27] Whatever the case, it is clear that Jesus is not pleased with the Laodiceans' apathetic posture about their faith: "So, because you are lukewarm, and neither hot nor cold, I will spit you out of my mouth" (Rev 3:16).

Their wealth produced from banking and textiles created an independence even from Rome as they refused Nero's help after the earthquake of AD 60: "For you say, 'I am rich, I have prospered, and I need nothing'" (Rev 3:17). Such wealth made it easy for them to purchase gold just as the Jews did to pay the temple tax to Jerusalem. Jesus says, "I counsel you to buy from me gold refined by fire, so that you may be rich" (Rev 3:18a). Dotting the landscape of Laodicea, now mostly in museums, were statues (*eikon*) of naked gods and goddess fashioned from white marble (Figure 9.12). So, his words are poignant: "And white garments so that you may clothe yourself and the shame of your nakedness may not be seen" (Rev 3:18b). Finally, aware of the medical school with a specialty

26. Wilson, "Did the Laodiceans."

27. Koester "Message to Laodicea"; cf. Cadwallader and Harrison, "Perspectives," 32–36.

in the anatomy of the eye and eye diseases, Jesus connects with them saying, "And salve to anoint your eyes, so that you may see" (Rev 3:18c).[28]

However, this is not the complete story of early Christianity in Laodicea. As we might imagine, Jesus' letter captured the attention of a people who held social status yet were apathetic to their faith. He promises that if they conquer, they, too, will sit on a throne even more prominent than those of the many emperors honored throughout the city. Only they need to hear what the Spirit is saying to the churches. And we begin to see their repentance and return of zeal in the architectural record.

THE ARCHITECTURAL RECORD OF CHRISTIANITY

Excavation of Laodicea began in full force in 2002. This is not to suggest that there were not others who attempted an excavation prior. Indeed, a Canadian excavation began in 1961 while an Italian one conducted a topographical and archaeological survey in 1993. Today, a team from Pamukkale University and the Municipality of Denizli work year-round at this tentative UNESCO World Heritage site. Their findings described by lead archaeologist Celal Şimşek are impressive:

> The structures of Laodikeia have a special importance because of their monumental scale and elegant ornamentation. In comparison with the nearby World Heritage Site of Hierapolis (Pamukkale), located ten kilometres north of Laodikeia, the theatres, baths and streets of Laodikeia are much more monumental. No similar ancient city has four monumental baths. Laodikeia has the biggest stadium in Anatolia and is the only city with two theatres. Laodikeia has a special significance and sacredness for the Christian world because of its churches. One of these, the Laodikeia Church, is dated back to the fourth century CE. Laodikeia is as important as Ephesos with her expansion and monumental structures. Laodikeia has more buildings and bigger buildings than Athens Acropolis, which is the one of the most important place [*sic*] for World Cultural Heritage.[29]

As Şimşek alludes, the site of Laodicea holds a unique place in the historical development of Christianity in Asia Minor. Among the

28. Luke the beloved physician, interestingly enough, greets the church in Colossae (Col 4:14), making it plausible that: 1) he studied at the medical school in the Lycus Valley; or 2) he traveled with Paul due to his eye disease (Acts 9:18; Gal 4:15, 6:11). Luke's profession is only mentioned in Colossians.

29. Şimşek, "Archaeological Site of Laodikea," 10.

impressive late-first to second-century discoveries is what is believed to be a house church (*oikos ekklēsia*, Figure 9.13). Walking south from the north theater along the marble road, one is met with an impressive architectural feature in the form of a peristyle home. Radiating from the main courtyard are a number of rooms including two apsidal halls (west and north of the main entrance on the west side of the road) and smaller rooms accessible from the shallow colonnaded water feature presumed to reflect the heat of the sun away from the home (Figure 9.14).

The apsidal hall is a common architectural feature in homes of affluent families. Often used as a reception hall, dining hall, or even a lecture hall, the apse provided an ideal space for the projection of one's voice, display of an object of worship, or the entertaining of guests and clients.[30] Both apsidal halls of the house are of particular interest as they included a raised pulpit space differentiating the apse area from the rest of the hall, a feature which became popular in churches (Figure 9.15). These apsidal halls could easily accommodate one hundred people challenging the notion of the small house church.

Marking the entrance to the house from the road leading north to the theater and south to Temple A is an eight-spoked wheel incised into the marble (Figure 9.16). The eight-spoked wheel is a common feature on marble roads throughout Asia Minor. Wilson has argued that the wheel is an ancient game board.[31] However, their frequency and location along the Harbor Road in Ephesos as well as at numerous sacred places across the empire suggest something else. Tuomas Rasimus effectively argues that early Christians employed the symbol as a monogram for Ιησους Χριστος Θεος (ΙΧΘ, see Figures 9.17). According to Rasimus, the monogram ultimately evolved into the symbol of the fish and the acrostic ΙΧΘΥΣ (or ΙΧΘΥC) representing Jesus Christ, God's Son, Savior.[32] Appropriately, at the entrance of the residence near the north theater appears ΙΧΘ standing at the door of a late first- to second-century house church, perhaps an allusion to Rev 3:20—"Behold, I [Jesus Christ, God] stand at the door and knock, if anyone hears my voice and opens the door, I will come in to him and eat with him [in the apsidal hall], and he with Me."

30. See Yegül and Favro, *Roman Architecture and Urbanism*, 696–703.

31. Wilson, *Biblical Turkey*, 216.

32. Rasimus, "Revisiting the Ichthys," 342; cf. Hurtado, *Earliest Christian Artifacts*, 135–54.

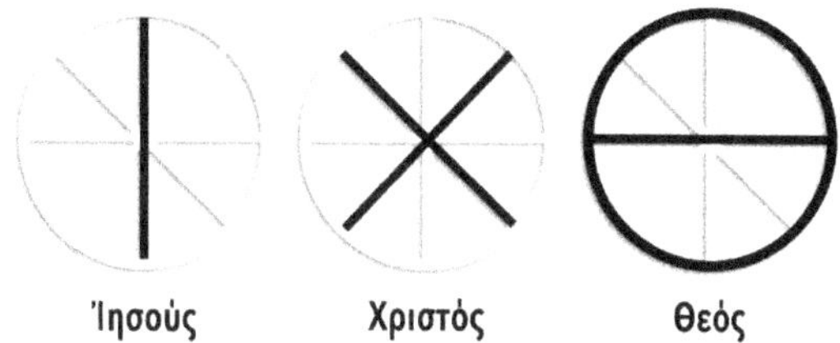

Figure 9.17: IXΘ monogram (a.k.a. Christogram and *ichthys* wheel). Author's recreation.

There is little doubt that the architectural and archaeological records testify to the Christian impact in the city. One testimony of the impact is observed as you walk west from the Syrian Gate toward Temple A. Strewn along the Syrian Road are broken columns and capitals, some with the relief of crosses perhaps marking the location of Christian businesses (Figure 9.18). No doubt that their style reflected the legalization of Christianity in the fourth century. Yet, these Christian symbols were quite prevalent. Arriving at the eight-thousand-seat western theater (Figure 9.5), we were privileged to meet with one of the archaeologists completing the excavation of this magnificent Greco-Roman style structure embedded in the hillside. He was particularly excited to show us the capitals of columns recently excavated from the theater that also included reliefs of crosses. Although not yet published, the archaeologist indicated that the theater had been used as a place of Christian gathering.

Several other buildings utilized as churches have also been excavated. Some are obviously house churches; others are clearly dedicated buildings used for Christian worship (Figure 9.19). Consequently, the architectural record demonstrates that the Laodicean saints grew significantly to be a transformative force in the city, if not the entire region. Indeed, as the lead archaeologist of Laodicea states, the city became a pilgrimage site whose church "is one of the oldest sacred places of the Christian world."[33] He continues,

> Excavations have revealed that a part of some large houses was used as a church, evidencing Christianity's early tradition of house churches. Many churches were unearthed in the city as well. Moreover, the Laodikeia church was discovered in 2010 and fully excavated and restored in the two excavation seasons that followed. The Laodikeia Church has a distinctive place in Christian history. The church was built at the time of

33. Şimşek, "Archaeological Site of Laodikeia," 9.

> Constantine the Great and provides a unique example with its basilican plan, mosaics, opus sectile pavements, frescos and dedicatory inscription.[34]

FROM ARCHAEOLOGY TO APPLICATION

What does this mean for the Christianity of the twenty-first century? For the house church movement, it means that we should not think of *oikos* as a monolithic and normative form for the *ekklēsia*. Instead, the house church served a purpose at a particular point in history. In the first century, the *oikos* provided a place of gathering that was relatively secure from social and religious persecution. As observed in Laodicea, the *oikos* was more than simply the home of a family. It also provided the economic, social, and spiritual well-being of a web of relationships that were common in the patron–client system of the Roman Empire (see Philemon). Out of such a network, the community transformed from the domain of darkness to the kingdom of light (Col 1:13).

Symbols of crosses, the christogram, possibly a literal *ichthys* along the western wall of the Laodicea Church (Figure 9.20) testify to the depth of impact of Christianity on the city. Yet, it demonstrated not only the impact, but also the commitment of the saints to Jesus Christ—God's Son and Savior. Equally as important are the clear signs of Christian space. From house churches to the use of the theater and dedicated buildings to places of business marked by crosses, what we learn is that the Christians adapted to the needs of the community. In essence, they utilized the space around them to regularly gather together. As Huttner concludes, "Besides the Jewish synagogues in the Lycus Valley, several models were therefore available to serve as a precedent for the formation of the Christian congregations."[35] The congregation had examples in the private home with apsidal halls, theater, *bouleuterion*, and even the pagan temple when its material was used as *spolia*. However, L. Michael White challenges us to keep in mind the irony of sacred space: "It is perhaps ironic, then, that a religious movement that began by challenging the very notion of the gods who resided in the pagan temples should over time come to adopt a form of pagan public architecture as its standard for church building."[36]

Along with the adaptation of space came the creation of rituals and traditions commensurate with White's observation. The beautiful

34. Şimşek, "Archaeological Site of Laodikeia," 9.

35. Huttner, *Early Christianity*, 31.

36. White, *Texts and Monuments*, 31.

baptistry at the Laodicea church is a clear architectural confirmation of the development of ritual (Figure 9.21). The same cross-shaped style baptistry found its way into the Church of Mary (Figure 9.23) and the Church of John, both in Ephesos. The ongoing development of rituals tempt some to believe that Christian ecclesiology had not fully formed in the first century. However, to suggest some need for Christian maturation in ritual evolution privileges one time period over another. First-century Christianity had all it needed to be a fully formed ecclesial and theological expression reminiscent of philosophical schools (*hairesis*) and guilds or associations (*collegia*) that required *metanoia* for membership as opposed to religious cults which voluntarily poured out libations to whichever god or goddess one might appease in order to meet a need.

Just as architecture is fluid, so also language is fluid. It would not be long until the *ekklēsia* evolved from an identity as the people of God, the body of Christ, to a location. Architecture is here to blame in part. The *space* for gathering took on the moniker intended for God's people. By the third century, Christians began to "go to church." Clement of Alexandria (AD 150–220) hints at this change: "Women and men should *go to church* decently attired, with natural step, clinging to silence, possessing genuine love, being pure in body and pure in heart, and fit to offer prayers to God."[37] If we did not know any better, we might think that Clement is describing early, twentieth-century Western Christianity.

Yet, the same is true of the twenty-first-century church. We still "go to church." We continue to speak of multiple churches in our communities: First Methodist Church, Second Baptist Church, Third Reformed Church, and so on. Christianity has become so fragmented over the centuries that the word "church" has lost its meaning.[38] So, if Laodicea offers us any hope, it is this: a church once threatened to be vomited out of Jesus' mouth for its complacency repented and became zealous to such an extent that it left an archaeological record that testifies to its faithfulness during the tumultuous first three centuries marked by the birth of Christ. That is a church we might consider emulating in all its simplicity and adaptability.

Additionally, there is a caution that we must heed. Along with numerical increase comes the search for means to manage the increases. As noted, we see this in the archaeological record as spaces for Christian gathering are eventually called "church." At the same time, the development

37. Clement of Alexandria, *Paedagogus* 3.11 (emphasis added).

38. See Korner, *Origin and Meaning*.

of ritual and tradition often conflate influences of the religious and even secular culture with Christianity. In the Laodicea Church, the *pastophoria* housed sacred items similar to the *pastophoria* of the pagan temple. Likewise, the apse area took on the look of the *bouleuterion*, where prominent members of society ruled the assembly (Figures 9.23 and 9.24). Over time, the saints in Laodicea were governed by formal positions of authority that were foreign to the first-century church. As observed in the fourth century at the regional Council of Laodicea,[39] where leaders from many Asian provinces gathered, some canons seemed remarkably out of touch with the NT. Consider the following:

> Canon 20: It is not right for a deacon to sit in the presence of a presbyter, unless he be bidden by the presbyter to sit down. Likewise the deacons shall have worship of the subdeacons and all the [inferior] clergy.
>
> Canon 21: The subdeacons have no right to a place in the Diaconicum, nor to touch the Lord's vessels.
>
> Canon 22: The subdeacon has no right to wear an orarium, nor to leave the doors.
>
> Canon 24: No one of the priesthood, from presbyters to deacons, and so on in the ecclesiastical order to subdeacons, readers, singers, exorcists, door-keepers, or any of the class of the Ascetics, ought to enter a tavern.
>
> Canon 28: It is not permitted to hold love feasts, as they are called, in the Lord's Houses, or Churches, nor to eat and to spread couches in the house of God.[40]

The regional council also provides a clear indication of a move toward the language of membership, demonstrated not only by interdictions but also requirements. For example:

> Canon 9: The members of the Church are not allowed to meet in the cemeteries, nor attend the so-called martyries of any of the heretics, for prayer or service; but such as so do, if they be communicants, shall be excommunicated for a time; but if they repent and confess that they have sinned they shall be received.

39. Several canons address the relationship between Christians and Jews. Keir Hammer and Michele Murray argue that these canons provide literary evidence for religious fellowship between the two groups. This, they contend, is the backdrop for the Sardis synagogue and the Jewish and Christian shops along its north exterior wall (see Hammer and Murray, "Acquaintances, Supporters, and Competitors").

40. *Synod of Laodicea* 20–22, 24, 28 (*NPNF*[2] 14:140, 144, 148).

Canon 10: The members of the Church shall not indiscriminately marry their children to heretics.

Canon 19: After the sermons of the Bishops, the prayer for the catechumens is to be made first by itself; and after the catechumens have gone out, the prayer for those who are under penance; and, after these have passed under the hand [of the Bishop] and departed, there should then be offered the three prayers of the faithful, the first to be said entirely in silence, the second and third aloud, and then the [kiss of] peace is to be given. And, after the presbyters have given the [kiss of] peace to the Bishop, then the laity are to give it [to one another], and so the Holy Oblation is to be completed. And it is lawful to the priesthood alone to go to the Altar and [there] communicate.

Canon 46: They who are to be baptized must learn the faith [Creed] by heart, and recite it to the bishop, or to the presbyters, on the fifth day of the week.

Canon 48: They who are baptized must after Baptism be anointed with the heavenly chrism, and be partakers of the Kingdom of Christ.[41]

Lessons from Laodicea	
Missiological Application	**Missiological Caution**
• The house church provides an example of the adaptive nature of the Christian gathering. • Christians were comfortable using public space for gathering (e.g., Western theater). • Allegiance marked the early Christians as shown by the Christogram. • Growth demands structure and the church adapted from leadership models in the culture. • Christianity permeated every aspect of society—business, religious, arts—and demonstrated is transformative impact. • Care must be given to ensuring adapted forms are infused with Christian meaning.	• The house church is not a normative model as the early church employed many spaces for gathering. • Dedicated buildings as space for gatherings do not appear until late third or early fourth century. • Membership marked the later Christians as shown by the canons of the regional council. • Growth demands structure and the church must guard against hegemonic leadership forms. • Ministry began to focus on a growing hierarchy of clergy—clergy were not permitted to attend the theater and assumed a political status by election. • Adaptation of cultural forms can result in over-contextualization or syncretism.

Table 9.1: Lessons from Laodicea

41. *Synod of Laodicea* 9–10, 19, 46, 48 (*NPNF*[2] 14:129, 136, 154).

*

The saints of Laodicea span seven centuries of Christianity. Their first two centuries were founded on instructions from Paul, Timothy, and Epaphras, *and* Jesus. The saints seemed to heed the loving discipline of Christ and returned to the zealous ways as the archaeological record unearthed. Yet, as they experienced their new-found freedom beginning with the reign of Constantine, two things occurred, one negative and one positive. First, their numerical increase created new forms of being the church. Certainly, they emerged out of the culture and naturally took on qualities of the culture. Yet they began to distance themselves from previous generations and expressed influences from the once pagan cults surrounding them.[42] Second, their numerical increase placed them in a position of influence in the city. The church and the bishop assumed an authority equal to the aristocrats and political powers. This resulted in their responsibility growing from the care for the spiritual needs of their flock to their involvement in the secular affairs of the city.[43] Such influence is desperately needed for the reputation of the church today. However, it must be measured and constrained by leadership expectations in the NT.

42. See Arnold, *Colossian Syncretism*.

43. Ceylan, "Episkopeia in Asia Minor," 171.

Chapter 10

Mind the Gap

Sir William M. Ramsay (1851–1939) might be the quintessential Renaissance man. Academically, he was trained as a Latin scholar. However, he is perhaps most well-known for his contribution to the areas of NT studies and biblical archaeology. In 1885, he became Oxford's first professor of archaeology until he took a post as a Latin professor the following year at his alma mater, the University of Aberdeen. It was his first trip to Anatolia in 1879 that would forever structure the trajectory of his scholarly contribution. In subsequent years, his archaeological work helped shape the future of NT studies in ways that often go unnoticed, especially by missiologists. It was largely Ramsay's study of the book of Acts and the corresponding cities mentioned by Luke that the whole direction of Lukan scholarship shifted away from the Tübingen higher criticism to the view that Luke was a first-rate historian. His archaeological pursuits validated Luke's narrative of the travels of Paul and no doubt prompted Ramsay to write, "If we want to understand the Ancients, especially the Greeks, we must breathe the same air as they did and saturate ourselves with the same scenery and the same nature that [shaped] them."[1] Ramsay's interdisciplinary approach integrated archaeology, history, geography, and NT studies. His biographer notes,

> He always insisted upon originality in research and firsthand acquaintance with the facts. Throughout his life he had little time for those who would assume the position of authorities on the history and geography of Asia Minor or the missionary travels

1. Ramsay, *Historical Geography*, 52.

> of the Apostle Paul without having a firsthand acquaintance with the facts of the matter.[2]

Ramsay and those who followed him demonstrate the importance of archaeology for the study of the biblical record. Indeed, Jonathan Reed correctly asserts, "Archaeology is imperative for the study of the New Testament. There is no chance of understanding Jesus or Paul, Peter or Mary, [James or Timothy,] without understanding their world. And there is no way to reconstruct that world without archaeology."[3] And the same is true for any attempt to reconstruct the missionary engagement of first-century Christians. If we are going to understand the manner in which the gospel was shared, disciples were formed, leaders were developed, and the early church grew we must "breathe the same air" as the first missionaries. Failing to do so will inevitably lead to strategy bias, as contemporary principles and methods of church planting require a historical foundation rooted in the biblical text and illuminated by the archaeological record.

Yet, this raises an obvious question: How does archaeology inform missiology? Equally important is the opposite of that question: How does missiology inform archaeology? At first glance, these questions seem to pit one discipline against the other. Naturally the archaeologist might declare that there is no relationship. The mere fact that we have no volume addressing these questions testifies to the lack of relevance. The missiologist might agree with this point and argue that the written record is sufficient in the formation of contemporary missions practices. Both have their arguments. Archaeology in relationship to the biblical world of the Near and Middle East has been the purview of biblical theologians and apologists. Missiologists have largely ignored the discipline, perhaps due in part to a lack of interest or unawareness, which I can attest to, of the interesting if not vital gaps archaeology fills in our understanding of the impact of the Christian mission and the development of adaptive structures, corporate practices, and contextual theologies.

The gap between the literary record of the Bible and material culture that archaeology fills reveals a richness and depth to understanding the dynamics of communication and architectural space as they intersect with the interpretation of the NT movement. As CPM practitioners, church planters, and researchers appeal to the NT record, it is imperative that

2. Gasque, *Sir William Ramsay*, 20.

3. Reed, *What Archaeology Reveals*, 2. Brackets are my addition.

their strategies and methodologies are grounded as they rapidly spread Christianity around the globe. That can only happen as missiologists focus more attention on the ways in which material remains enlighten our understanding of the first-century record. Our final chapter hopes to inspire missiologists to consider the importance of an interdisciplinary approach that includes history and archaeology in our examination of the early-Christian movement so that we avoid anachronistic assumptions evident in some contemporary missions methodologies. Let's now turn our attention to the often contentious relationship between CPM, and legacy and traditional churches.[4]

DEFINING CONTEMPORARY CPM

Church planting movements (CPM) are reported to be growing at an unprecedented rate around the world.[5] Since David Garrison first drew our attention to CPM and the 200 movements he tracked, these so-called rapid, multiplicative, and indigenous church movements have cascaded to more than 1,020 in 2021.[6] Garrison defined CPM as "a rapid multiplication of indigenous churches planting churches that sweeps through a people group or population segment."[7] Further clarifying CPM in his extensive study of global movements, Justin Long notes that movements are "rapidly multiplying groups that have surpassed four generations of church planting in multiple streams."[8] Furthermore, he suggests that "each of these falls into general size categories of 'small' (around 1,000 members), 'medium' (some thousands to tens of thousands), or 'large' (over 100,000 to some millions)."[9] Altogether, they constitute around 1 percent of the global Christian population.[10] Interestingly, Warrick Farah, among others like Dave Coles and Stan Parks, observes that 80 to 90 percent of CPMs are initiated by near-culture missionaries rather

4. Arlund and Farah, "Discussing and Catalyzing Movements"; Rhodes, "Advancing Conversations."

5. Long, "How Movements Count."

6. Garrison, *Church Planting Movements*; Garrison, *Inside Church Planting Movements*; Long, "How Movements Count," 68.

7. Garrison, "10 FAQs," 9.

8. Long, "How Movements Count," 68.

9. Long, "How Movements Count," 75.

10. Long, "1% of the World."

than expat missionaries.[11] Indeed, CPM is celebrated as a key missionary strategy for the global growth of Christianity, while it has also become both a buzz word and target for proponents and critics of this latest missiological trend.[12]

In his 2012 book, *Church Planting Movements: How God is Redeeming a Lost World*, Garrison observed that CPMs share ten universal characteristics: 1) extraordinary prayer; 2) abundant evangelism; 3) intentional planting of reproducing churches; 4) the authority of God's word; 5) local leadership; 6) lay leadership; 7) house churches; 8) churches planting churches; 9) rapid reproduction; and 10) healthy churches. In his response to Jackson Wu's critique of CPM's ostensible biblical eisegesis, Garrison lays out examples of each of these characteristics and argues that CPM is consistent with what we find in the teaching and practice in the NT.[13] Herein lies the challenge that missiologists often confront when attempting to support a contemporary strategy with biblical language. While Garrison and other CPM researchers rely on ethnographic research methods such as interviews, participant observations, and phenomenology, if not careful, either a bias can influence a researcher's interpretation of phenomena or the phenomena can be generalized to strategies developed for a broader application. In both instances, biased interpretations and generalized strategy development might justify themselves by using biblical language. In such instances, anachronisms emerge as we'll see.[14]

DEFINING LEGACY AND TRADITIONAL CHURCHES

Stephen Gray and Franklin Dumond defined a legacy church as one which has progressively lost its ability to reach its community effectively.[15] The

11. Farah, "Homophilous Unit Paradox," 71; cf. Coles and Parks, "Movement Servants." This fact goes unnoticed in Rhodes, *No Shortcut to Success*.

12. "Trend" is the proper word here. Any claim by CPM practitioners that the observable sociological phenomena describing movements as biblical simply cannot be supported. This does not mean that they are unbiblical, and we might correctly assert that they are consistent with observations in the NT record. Indeed, I have repeatedly suggested throughout this book that observable sociological phenomena in the NT and archaeological record are demonstrable. However, such phenomena are qualitatively different from the phenomena we observe today even though we might suggest general principles such as prayer, evangelism, discipleship, fellowship, church leadership, etc.

13. Wu "Influence of Culture"; Garrison, "Planting Movements Are Consistent."

14. See Garrison and my conversation about the misuse of his phenomenological research by CPM practitioners: Cooper and Garrison, "Church Planting Movements."

15. Gray and Dumon, *Legacy Churches*.

Protestant version of traditional churches might be defined as those who hold to some form of sixteenth-century ecclesiology whether Reformed, Free, Lutheran, or others associated with the Reformation. Additionally, upon entering the church, one is immediately familiar with the architecture and order of service, albeit recognizing modern attempts to adapt liturgical style and music. Both legacy and traditional churches share a common focus on various marks of the church and Protestant forms will differentiate themselves from Roman Catholic, Orthodox, or Coptic, even Anglican, expressions of traditional high church. In the United States, legacy churches are closing at an unprecedented rate. A recent report indicates that as many as fifteen thousand will close in 2025.[16]

In both high and low church traditions, we observe ecclesial forms which might have begun as adapting to various cultural forms as we have seen in the archaeological record with the church adapting temples and synagogues as well as philosophical schools. A modern example is the suburban Chicago church Willow Creek which in the 1980s met in a movie theater. However, no matter if one is from a high or low church tradition, they both have become captive to their particular ecclesial forms and look at them in some monolithic manner as prescriptive across cultures. So, it is of no surprise as one travels the world that you might join a congregation in a remote village which looks strangely familiar with one's home church. While some might point to this as a testimony to the oneness of the body of Christ, others look at this as a sign of colonialism.

ANACHRONISTIC LANGUAGE IN CONTEMPORARY ECCLESIOLOGIES

Organizations such as E3, East West, International Mission Board, and networks like No Place Left, Big Life, and 2414 encourage the use of CPM strategies including Four-Fields Training, Obedience Based Discipleship, and concise gospel presentations like Three Circles which are simple, "biblical," and reproducible. Some missionaries use Four-Fields as a method of CPM while others use it as a filter to find the most productive "disciples" who can rapidly multiply indigenous churches. Among the catchwords and phrases being used by CPM practitioners and researchers are terms such as *oikos*, "person of peace," "unreached people groups," "gen map," "simple and reproducible," and "discovery Bible study."

16. Contreras, "15,000 Churches."

Other organizations like Radius International, Exponential, Radical, 9Marks, and CrossCon promote traditional Protestant ecclesiologies which have customarily included evangelism, discipleship, and preaching as primary activities of church planters leading to the gathering of believers on Sunday (in most contexts) to focus on various "marks" of the church such as outlined by 9Marks's Mark Dever:

1. Expository preaching
2. Gospel doctrine
3. A biblical understanding of conversion and evangelism
4. Biblical church membership
5. Biblical church discipline
6. A biblical concern for discipleship and growth
7. Biblical church leadership
8. A biblical understanding of the practice of prayer
9. A biblical understanding and practice of missions[17]

In both CPM and traditional churches, language expressing church-planting strategies or ecclesiology is often presented as biblical and therefore represents principles that can be prescriptively applied cross-culturally. However, after looking through a missiological lens at archaeological evidence for the NT movement in first-century Asia Minor, I've arrived at the conclusion that some of the language we use for CPM and traditional churches is anachronistic and misleading. The danger of codifying such language as biblical is that these largely Western strategies become misguided neo-colonial efforts. Here are four examples: *oikos*, person of peace, marks of the church, and theological education.

Oikos and Person of Peace

In my observations of "house churches" in Southeast Asia and the Arabian Peninsula, there is a clear departure from the first-century archaeological record. Contemporary "house churches" commonly resemble a traditional Western church only on a microscale. There are typically microphones and speakers, electric musical instruments like the guitar and piano, chairs lined across a room with a center aisle, religious art on

17. Dever, *Nine Marks*.

the walls, a pulpit and podium, overhead projector, and more. While this might very well be an adaptation of the idea of "house church," we must be careful not to assume that the early church practiced a fully developed liturgical form or that such forms were expected to emerge later.[18] In an extensive study of the Christian use of architecture, L. Michael White remarks, "By definition, then, a 'house church' did not entail alteration or architectural articulation of the space for specific religious functions. In the absence of a normative architectural definition or style, it remains indistinguishable from private or domestic building."[19] Whatever today's "house church" has become, it does not resemble the *oikos-ekklēsia* of the first Christians. In fact, it is more likely that the first-century house church resembles today's small group Bible study without all the pageantry of contemporary worship.

Additionally, *oikos*, often understood as "house church," does not necessarily mean that house church was *the* NT model as is often communicated in CPM literature. As we've seen, the spaces used by the early Christians appear to have varied from places of business, theaters, lecture halls, gymnasiums, dining areas, and residences of wealthy families. Nevertheless, in his phenomenological study of contemporary movements, Farah embraces a common anachronistic tendency in CPM thought—"The oikos is the basic unit of New Testament ecclesiology"[20]—and assumes that movements begin with *oikos* albeit a "contextually situated" one. I wasn't immune to such a view in *Ephesiology* where I argued that Ephesos had as many as 340 "house churches" by AD 67.[21] While it is very likely that the Ephesian-Christian population in the middle of the first century was quite sizable (I estimated 5,100), it is highly unlikely that they met in 340 houses.[22]

18. We have to reject any idea of the early church being a "primitive" church whose ecclesiology was not fully formed. Such a suggestion is elitist and misunderstands the full capacity of the body of Christ to function as Christ intended while adapting culturally appropriate forms. Rather, the complex liturgical development we observe beginning in the middle of the third century (if not earlier) must be regarded as extrabiblical but not unbiblical.

19. White, *Texts and Monuments*, 25.

20. Farah, "Homophilous Unit Paradox," 74. I am not suggesting that the contemporary use of *oikos* is inherently misaligned with the NT. Rather, the contemporary *oikos* is quite different from the NT *oikos*. So, to suggest an equivalence of the two understandings risks imposing CPM strategies onto the NT, resulting in an unwarranted codification of the strategy across cultures.

21. Cooper, *Ephesiology*, 28.

22. Cf. Farah, "Homophilous Unit Paradox," 73. In Farah's observation, the *oikos*

In any case, other missiologists have propagated the same idea about the house church being a central strategy in the early church. Ed Smither, for instance, taking his cue from Roger Gehring, states,

> House churches were also central to Paul's mission. A cursory reading of Acts and the Pauline epistles show that house churches were the most visible outcome of Paul's missionary labors. In addition to these homes being centers for fellowship, worship, and teaching, they were also places where leaders could be trained and set apart. Often, heads of houses provided hospitality and financial assistance for the community and became the natural leader for those that met in their homes. Gehring adds that "the house with its workshop and its network of relationships . . . offer[ed] natural evangelistic contacts and conversation opportunities." That is, the house church was also a center for mission.[23]

While there is little doubt that *oikos* factors prominently, but not exclusively, in the formation of *ekklēsia* in the NT, CPM practitioners and strategists take a slightly different posture. For them, the NT house church became a strategic location for evangelism of entire households. In 2018, Steve Smith, a leading CPM strategist, wrote an article with the provocative title "The Oikos Hammer." He notes,

> If Persons of Peace (POPs) are the gateways [to new communities], then the second principle is that movements expand as those POPs and the evangelists who reach them take the gospel to their households. Biblically, these households can include people from their biological, geographical, vocational and volitional worlds. The term the New Testament uses for this is *oikos*.[24]

Lamenting how some CPM strategists emphasize the person of peace (POP) while underemphasizing *oikos* evangelism, he declares, "From Creation to Consummation, God's promise and pattern is this: you will be saved, you and all your household."[25] This CPM strategy has

starting place isn't stagnate but multiples with those in its network. Yet, the NT idea of *oikos* constitutes an inherent network of family, servants, hired servants, and others who benefit from the benevolence of a patron. It was a socio-religious-economic system and remained the same when adapted by Christians.

23. Smither, *Mission*, 153–54.

24. Smith, "Oikos Hammer," 44.

25. Smith, "Oikos Hammer," 45.

garnered the attention, both positive and negative, of many exegetes. Nevertheless, it found its foundation on the idea expressed in two Gospels: Luke and Matthew. Two points need to be asserted.

First, Gehring's thoughtful exegetical work on the person-of-peace passage in Luke 10:1–12 indicates, among other things, an ambiguity surrounding the head of the household. Even so, he argues that household evangelism is a model practiced by Jesus and the early church. That said, Gehring adds that those Jesus sent two-by-two into various cities were not simply to find a person or house of peace. They were to live in the house as a base for their mission. Additionally, he correctly assumes that such a person or house of peace also accepts the message of the missionaries.[26] He notes, "Remaining in a house only makes sense if, beyond the initial confrontation with the salvation message, the messengers are allowed to stay to further nurture and establish a faith community."[27]

Second, often overlooked in the *oikos* conversation are the primary words used in the biblical text. If Luke 10:1–12 and Matt 10:5–15 provide the foundation for the CPM *oikos* strategy, then the word to be used is *oikia* rather than *oikos*. In Greek, *oikia* is literally the physical structure that we call a house whereas *oikos* encompasses all those associated with an estate of a household. For instance, in Luke's account, the messenger goes into a physical building (*oikia*) and announces peace to the entire household (*oikos*).[28] This nuance is important in understanding Luke's and Matthew's accounts of sending the disciples on mission. The *oikia* functioned as the base of operation for the missionary activities of the disciples. We do not have any hint that the person of peace continued the missionary endeavors alongside the disciples or after their departure.[29] Nor do the new disciples move immediately on to the next city as Gehring points out.[30] For CPM strategists to insist that a person of peace bears the ongoing responsibility for the mission in his city is a misreading

26. Gehring, *House Church and Mission*, 55–58.

27. Gehring, *House Church and Mission*, 58.

28. See Gehring for a contrasting view on the lack of distinction between *oikia* and *oikos* (Gehring, *House Church and Mission*, 7–8.

29. Steve Smith summarizes CPM thought on the person of peace: "Person of Peace searches have become the default strategy from most CPM strategists. Persons of Peace are the God-prepared doorways into new communities. Their hearts have been prepared for 1) the missionary, 2) the message, and 3) the mission to reach their household or circle of influence (Gk. *oikos*)." See Smith, "Oikos Hammer," 44.

30. Gehring, *House Church and Mission*, 58.

of both Luke and Matthew. Pure and simple, it is reading a contemporary missionary strategy back into the NT.

This is not to say that POP/*oikos* is a bad or an unbiblical strategy. The fact is, the strategy espoused by CPM practitioners is working as Long's data indicates.[31] It is simply not the same thing as we find in the Gospel record. In this sense then, to impose a CPM strategy onto that record is anachronistic and potentially reductionistic as the strategy ignores the multifaceted mission of the first centuries. In fact, a cursory study of Luke's account of the early mission reveals that the households who came to faith were often prominent members in the community: Dorcas (Acts 9:36–42); Cornelius (Acts 10:1–48); Lydia (Acts 16:13–15); the Philippian jailer (Acts 16:23–34); Titius Justus (Acts 18:7); Crispos and Sosthenes (Acts 18:8–16).[32] White posits, "In the first period (ca. 50–150 C.E.) assembly and worship (following the pattern of Acts) would have been held in the homes of wealthier members."[33] Such homes would have apsidal halls functioning as both a *triclinium* (dining room) and audience hall where Christians would gather much like we observed in Laodicea, for example (Rev 3:20).[34] This space could accommodate a hundred or more congregants. Yet, the *ekklēsia* was far broader than simply *oikia*/*oikos*.

Considering the adaptive nature of the *ekklēsia* as we see in the archaeological record, it seems missiologically irresponsible to reduce NT ecclesiology and evangelism to a single unit: *oikos*. Instead, the early *ekklēsia*'s use of space demonstrates a characteristic desire to engage people where they are. That is, Christians were in proximity to the other, something that the literary record also confirms (1 Cor 5:9–10).[35] Yes, they were certainly a part of an *oikos*, but they were members of multiple aspects of society: trade guilds, philosophical schools, political forums, synagogues, etc.[36] Michael Bird rightly notes, "Becoming Christian

31. Long, "1% of the World."

32. It is noteworthy to mention that while Paul does go from house to house in Ephesos (Acts 20:20), Luke does not mention any house that became a base of his mission in Acts 19. Instead, it was a *schole*. In many instances, Paul begins at a *synagoge* which served more as a place of peace. As noted in a previous chapter, these *synagogai* could be Jewish places of worship or trade guilds.

33. White, *Building God's House*, 19.

34. See chapter 9.

35. See also *Epistle to Diognetus* 4–6:137–47.

36. See Randy Hacker's excellent critique of the *oikos* idea from Gehring and Edward Adams in Hacker, *House Churches*.

in antiquity might have required one to be cut off from Greco-Roman cults, but it did not cut one off completely from Greco-Roman culture."[37] Granted, Smith expands the definition of *oikos* to include family, neighbors, coworkers, and others who share similar interests.[38] However, such an anachronistic reading of the Greco-Roman idea of *oikos* fails to understand that heads of households held social standing in a community and often fulfilled administrative duties such as the *episkopos*, a civic-leadership form Paul borrows for the church in Ephesos (1 Tim 3:1–7) and Philippi (Phil 1:1). Additionally, while people were members of families, such connections did not necessarily correspond to an *oikos*. They might have simply been a member of the *oikos* of a patron as a hired servant rather than a head of household as inferred in the household codes of the NT (Eph 5:21—6:9; Col 3:18—4:1; 1 Pet 3:1–7; Titus 2:1–10). In fact, it is safe to assume that more *members* of *oikos* came to Christ than heads of households simply due to the fact there were numerically more members of *oikos* than heads of *oikos*.

In summary, while contemporary CPMs are producing results, their missiological claims, especially regarding *oikos* as the normative model for ecclesiology and missions, are anachronistic and reductionistic. A historically and textually grounded view of the first-century *ekklēsia* reveals a far more complex and adaptive movement than the simplified "house church" strategy often promoted in CPM literature. The archaeological record should result in broadening our contemporary strategies to include the gathering of the people of God (*ekklēsia*), not only where we live (*oikia*) but also where we work and play. In other words, wherever people gather in our communities, there can also be the church. The NT and archaeological records do not constrain the *ekklēsia* to a particular location or space.

Marks of the Church

Similarly, anachronistic language often surrounds any conversation about the marks of a church. As is common, such marks often represent the best practices of a contemporary church and therefore reflect its culture more than what might be regarded as a first-century culture. In and of themselves, there is nothing wrong with nine marks of the church or nineteen

37. Bird, *Jesus Among the Gods*, intro.

38. Smith "Oikos Hammer," 47.

marks—Laodicea boasted 59 of them—until such marks become a codified expectation on churches around the world. In the traditional church model, such marks are assumed to be prescriptively biblical and therefore the missionary takes this ecclesial form as a contextless ecclesiology that can be contextualized in various cultures. Let's consider only a couple examples from the popular "9Marks."

First and understandably, we are hard pressed to find any hint of expository preaching in the archaeological record. Instead, the architecture of the early *ekklēsia* reveals evidence that Scripture was first read in community from the *ambo* or in an apsidal hall, often by the *presbyteros* or *epistates* (as we see in Justin Martyr's *First Apology*,) and discussed in a similar fashion as what we know occurred in philosophical schools.[39] Nevertheless, Dever argues that expository preaching is the most important mark of the church because, according to him, if you get this wrong you will only accidentally stumble onto the other marks and probably not understand them biblically. As expected, he contrasts expository preaching with topical preaching, asserting a preference for the former although recognizing that topical preaching should begin with a proper exposition of relevant passages.[40] According to Dever, the preacher stands in the place of God as he exposes God's word.[41] In the contemporary church, that place is usually behind a podium on a raised platform signifying the position and authority a pastor holds to deliver God's word to the people. Architecturally speaking, the podium and raised platform are absent from the archaeological record until the third century. Even then, the raised platform as we see in Priene, Miletos, and Sardis, is in the center of the building while the front of the space, often in an apse, was reserved for the community's leaders. It isn't until much later that the pastor takes his place in front of a congregation which no longer participates in the discussion about the apostles' teaching but becomes a spectator in its place.

Instead of constructing their own architectural space, early Christ followers adapted the space that was available to them. Yet, what seems clearly described in the literary record and visualized in the archaeological one is the community participation in the message that is inferred by early-Christian adaptation of architectural space. In other words, the regularly and apparently daily exhortation of the *ekklēsia* was a dialogue,

39. See chapter 5 and below.

40. Dever, *Nine Marks*, 47–48.

41. Dever, *Nine Marks*, 41.

not a monologue. And it is probably best described as topical, not expository. The architecture invited the community to do theology together in fellowship often around a meal in the *triclinium* of a guild, voluntary association, or the *oikos* of a wealthy patron, something resonant with Discovery Bible Study in CPM strategies. Eventually, the preacher's role not only became central but also prominent in the weekly gathering, as daily gatherings, including table fellowship, eventually fell out of favor. It is difficult to determine exactly when this takes place, but there is no doubt that it does, and the adoption of formal architectural space is partly to blame.[42] So, Allan Doig is spot on:

> What was about to change under Constantine was not related to the hidden nature of the Church, nor that the Church was going to rise out of poverty, but that it was about to emerge into the imperial realm, taking on official and imperial forms in its architecture and in the performance of its liturgy. Half a century before, c. 265, Paul of Samosata, Bishop of Antioch, was censured by his congregation because in both architecture and ritual he surrounded himself with the trappings of a Roman magistrate. He occupied a throne on a platform, and also had an audience chamber. At the time it caused outrage, but under Constantine it would become the norm. With changed social circumstances and official position, the Church would develop a monumental public architecture which would dominate the Western tradition for the next one and a half millennium.[43]

Second, evangelism's focus is the good news who is Jesus Christ. The Western church often expresses this message as the good news of salvation from one's guilt of sin satisfied by the propitiation of Christ (Heb 2:17). In the Western context, this makes perfect sense as the Western judicial system is based on the notion of guilt or innocence of wrong doing. While in the United States there is a presumption of innocence until proven guilty, such a belief has crept into the evangelical perception of the individual in relationship to sin.[44] Naturally as a corrective to such a presumption, guilt has been the predominant theme in Western evangelism and a biblical understanding of conversion and evangelism rightly appears among the nine marks. However, the graffiti we have examined in Asia Minor suggests a different approach. The gospel message appears

42. See chapter 8 above.

43. Doig, *Liturgy and Architecture*, 19.

44. Ligonier Ministries, "State of Theology."

to focus mostly on the ontological identity of Jesus Christ as God, *pantokratoros*, and *logos* in missiological parallelisms, a concept explained below, declaring Jesus as the superior God and philosophy. This should not imply an early monolithic evangelism. That is, we should not begin to develop an evangelistic strategy based on the observations in the archaeological record as this would be just as inappropriate as implying that our current strategies are the same as those in the NT. The best we can say is that evangelism strategies in the early church are different from today and were suited for a different context.

More could be mentioned regarding how the archaeological record clarifies the meaning of membership and leadership, but that will have to wait for another book. However, I'll conclude with reference to the final mark: a biblical understanding and practice of missions. This appears almost as an afterthought in Dever's nine marks as it was not included in the original edition. By the second edition, Dever acknowledges a challenge by John Piper to include missions among the marks but resists its inclusion by stating dismissively, "But we've decided not to [include missions]."[45] Now, most of us have written or said things that we later regret and, thankfully, Dever's latest edition corrected this oversight, otherwise one might be tempted to question 9Marks's commitment to expositional preaching.[46] After all, a good expositor of the Bible will certainly see missions as the central motif of the missionary God who makes the missional move to reveal himself to the world. Clearly, *Gods, Emperors, Philosophers, and a New Movement* has focused attention on the archaeological record proving this crucial point.

Granted, just as with CPM, the emphasis here should not be on the correctness of these marks of the church but rather their prescriptive imposition as a codified list for all times and places. What the archaeological record indicates is that such codified lists must be understood in historical context. So, Dever and others rightly identify their marks of the church as the perennial challenge for the Western church. While their nine marks can undoubtedly be affirmed by the Western church as addressing Western church issues, they should not be imposed colonially on churches in other contexts. These churches must develop their own marks to address their issues just as we observed in the marks of the Laodicea Church.[47]

45. Dever, *Nine Marks*, 26.

46. Dever, "Biblical Understanding and Practice."

47. See chapter 9 above. Cf. Stetzer, "9Marks Purists Should Know."

Theological Education

Another anachronistic tendency in contemporary CPM strategy surrounds the idea of education. Education, sometimes dismissed by CPM practitioners, was an important aspect of a city's well-being. Whether set in formal contexts like lecture halls in gymnasiums[48] and the barrel vault of a temple foundation, or informal contexts as an apprentice learned a trade, ancient education focused as much on character as it did on craft and content. It required a level of expertise and an ability to mentor (disciple) on the part of the teacher. Contrastingly, it is not uncommon to hear from CPM practitioners that education is less important than allowing the indigenous population to be led by the Holy Spirit in a discovery process as if the two thoughts were mutually exclusive. Indeed, the emphasis on rapid reproduction of churches tends to privilege the "go" above the "disciple" in one of Jesus' final commands (Matt 28:19).[49]

In his study of CPMs started by the International Mission Board of the Southern Baptist Convention (IMB), Todd Lafferty identifies a gap in the mission strategy: education. With an overemphasis on the roles of apostles and evangelists, Lafferty observed that while many churches were being planted, they were often abandoned—or left to the care of the Holy Spirit—for the sake of starting more churches.[50] In some cases, CPM strategy appears to ignore or is unaware of the fact that Paul often spent years in certain locations struggling for the maturity of the saints. When not on site, Paul wrote letters and sent emissaries. He even revisited new churches to strengthen and encourage them (Acts 18:23; Col 1:28–2:1).

With a focus on a Bible study method referred to as Discovery Bible Study (DBS), CPM places a high priority on helping new disciples rely on the Holy Spirit to reveal to them the meaning of Scripture largely without any need for historical context.[51] For example, Steve Smith and Ying Kai

48. Regarding Ephesos, Steven Friesen notes, "The Harbour gymnasium involved the city with an older urban ideal in which such a building, where physical and philosophical training were inseparable, functioned as a center of municipal cultural life." See Friesen, *Twice Neokoros*, 161.

49. See Blair and Cooper, "Do Not Make Disciples" which addresses the mistranslation of Matt 28:19 and the idea of discipling the nations as the thrust of Jesus' final command.

50. Lafferty, "Developing Pastors and Teachers."

51. Often an argument for the perspicuity of Scripture is put forward. Such a "doctrine" argues that Scripture is sufficiently clear, especially on issues of salvation, and therefore easily understood and applied by those who have faith no matter the context.

advocated for a six- to eighteen-month process of equipping new disciples to lead emerging churches.[52] No doubt concerned for the traditional seminary requiring the student to relocate and be taken out of ministry, Smith and Kai, along with many other CPM advocates, believe what John Massey observed: "Church Planting Movements strategy and T4T training is opposed to deep-level theological training for leaders because it allegedly slows down the movement and causes leaders to become (in what I have often heard from T4T proponents) 'disobedient and proud.'"[53]

Clearly, CPM strategists read contemporary educational models of seminary back into the educational systems of the first century. Assuming that the irrelevance of today's seminary is testament to the unimportance of formal theological education during the early missionary activities is misunderstanding first-century education. It would be no exaggeration to assert that education was discipleship as much for Greek philosophy as for the maturation of Christians. The archaeological record bears this out. For example, the second-century AD Library of Celsus (Figure 10.1) in Ephesos, which held as many as twelve thousand volumes, testifies that Greek learning focused on wisdom, virtue, intelligence, and knowledge; themes articulated throughout the NT.

Additionally, the archaeological record helps us see that the early *ekklēsia* looked more like a philosophical school than it did a religious cult.[54] The fresco paintings in the terrace houses of Ephesos attest to the influence of philosophers on the city. No doubt, the apsidal hall in Terrace House 2, Dwelling Unit 6 would have been used for educational purposes among other uses. Even the Roman bath houses served as places for education, offering students a cool environment in which to learn from philosophers. Curiously enough, the bath-gymnasium of Ephesos provides the backdrop to Paul's encouragement to Timothy: "For while bodily training is of some value, godliness is of value in every way as it holds promise for the present life and also the life to come" (1 Tim 4:8). It is plausible that the hall of Tyrannos was located in such a complex, although I believe there might be better options (Acts 19:9; see appendix 1).

Steve Mason notes that philosophical schools emulated characteristics concomitant to the social values of a community. Most often these included piety to the gods and care for people. Mason describes the intentionality of the philosophical schools in language reminiscent of the

52. Smith and Kai, *T4T*, 171.

53. Massey, "Theological Education," 9.

54. See Alexander "Paul."

ekklēsia: "Joining a philosophical school was not an abstract exercise or simply another activity such as music or farming; it often involved what Nock calls 'conversion': a radical break with one's previous way of living and the resolute adoption of a new path."[55] Such fanaticism did not bode well in an empire where allegiance to the emperor was paramount to what it meant to be a Roman citizen. Consequently, philosophical schools were "largely for slaves, freedmen, and women."[56] Indeed, the NT testifies to the same population—slaves, freedmen, women—converting to a new "philosophy" (i.e. Christianity) as well as to the desire for learning as discipleship. Conversion amounted to an identity shift for Christ followers and learning about what such a shift meant became vital to the Christian experience.

In this regard, Paul certainly took on the form of a philosopher in his travels which is clearly demonstrated while in Athens (Acts 17:22–31). His knowledge of *logos* in Ephesos was undoubtedly a subject of his teaching in the hall of Tyrannos (Acts 19:9–10). Ramsay described Paul as "educated in his thoughts and polished in his tone of courtesy, yet fiery and vehement in his temper, versatile and adaptable so that he moves at his ease in every class of society, the Socratic dialectician in the Athenian marketplace, the philosophical rhetorician in the Ephesian School of Tyrannus."[57]

Any formulation of a CPM strategy must properly emphasize the place of education for the well-being of the *ekklēsia*. This could very well begin with DBS as a form of basic discipleship, but it cannot remain there. Even the most well-intentioned interpreters of the Bible come across passages that, when read from their cultural lenses, can take on unintended meaning as we see, for instance, with Oneness Pentecostals in India who only baptize in Jesus' name since that is what Peter says in Acts 2:38. Without developing skills of biblical exegesis that are culturally appropriate, all sorts of wonky theology can emerge.[58]

Yet, something similar can be said about the traditional church. Much like the colonial forms of "church" propagated by traditional church-planting strategies, we see monolithic forms of seminary complete

55. Mason, "Philosophiai," 33.

56. Mason, "Philosophiai," 37. Considering the lexical range of *synagoge* to include philosophical schools (see chapter 5), Acts 6:9 and the *synagoge* of freedmen might be best understood in this sense. Rather than a gathering place of Jews who were freed from slavery, *synagoge* of freedmen might be a school.

57. Ramsay, *Teachings of Paul*, vi.

58. See Caldwell, *Bible in Culture*. And, yes, "wonky" is a *terminus technicus*.

with systematic theology which is often modeled after Western systems. Frequently, the theological issues of the Western world are exported across the globe as if Western theologians have arrived at some contextless theology which deserves to be contextualized to other countries. So, it is not unusual for me to encounter discussions of dispensationalism, creationism, Free Grace Theology, and complementarianism, four clearly Western theologies taught by missionaries, in the most remote places on the planet. Traditional church-planting strategies must permit theology to emerge from within the missions context as we see in the archaeological record. For instance, the declaration of "Jesus Christ God" we see with the Christogram emerges as a missiological parallelism to address the immediate issue of the Roman emperors as gods if not also the various other deities. The archaeological record demonstrates that instead of imposing theology on people, it emerges from the context of people.

MINDING THE GAP

Now, we move to wrapping up the volume. Perhaps appropriately so, this is a call to mind the gap. In the rich tapestry of Asia Minor's religious and cultural milieu, the early church faced a formidable challenge—how to faithfully embody Christ in a context saturated with temples, gods, and ritualized expressions of devotion. From Ephesos to Sardis, from Pergamon to Philadelphia, every city was a stage for divine pageantry. The architecture, the numismatic record, the epigraphic inscriptions, all testify to a society profoundly shaped by religious practice. Yet, within this context, the first-century Christian *ekklēsia* did not take its structural cues from the cults; at least not in the beginning. Instead, it adapted a form that stood in sharp contrast to temple-based religion: the philosophical school. While this might seem a subtle ecclesiological nuance, I believe it constitutes one of the most significant—and overlooked—missiological decisions of the early church. The choice of form mattered. It still does.

Form as a Missiological Strategy

We are accustomed to emphasizing the content of the Christian message—Christ crucified, risen, seated, and returning. But the form through which that message is embodied and practiced cannot be underestimated.

The *ekklēsia* is not merely a container for theology but a living expression of theology itself. The way the church organizes itself—its rhythms, structures, leadership, rituals, and architecture—communicates what it believes about God, humanity, and our mission. In this light, the early Christian preference for the philosophical school model over cultic or temple-based forms was more than a sociological inheritance; it was a deliberate theological move as well as a profoundly missiologically one.

In this sense, the philosophical school offered an environment characterized by dialogical teaching and fellowship, moral and character formation, voluntary association, and the pursuit of wisdom—an excellent definition of what it means to disciple. It was not centered around a sacred building or a ritual calendar. It had no sacrifices to offer. Its "liturgy," if we may call it that, was conversation and contemplation. It regularly met in homes or lecture halls. It easily moved between vocational and voluntary associations. Indeed, as Randy Hacker makes clear, "The church … met wherever it could."[59] Such a model stood in stark contrast to the ecstatic frenzy of Dionysian worship, the ritual sacrifice of Artemis, or the mystery cults of Cybele. Instead, this structure proved inherently resistant to religious syncretism—a problem that would go on to plague many of the earliest Christian communities (see 1 Cor 8–11).

In contrast, the philosophical-school model provided a form that was culturally legible, theologically safe, and architecturally diverse. Interestingly enough, the Jewish place of prayer shared similarities with the philosophical schools as well. The so-called synagogue emphasized practices that could be observed outside of the ritualistic temple: reading Scripture, teaching, prayer, and Jewish dietary laws. When Paul gathers the disciples in the *schole* of Tyrannos in Ephesos (Acts 19:9; appendix 1), he is not simply renting a lecture hall. He is adapting a form familiar to Greco-Roman culture that prioritized reasoned dialogue and pursuit of virtue over ritual spectacle. And it is in this environment that the gospel spreads "throughout all the residents of Asia" (Acts 19:10). Indeed, Loveday Alexander observes, "To the casual pagan observer the activities of the average synagogue or church would look more like the activities of a school than anything else."[60]

This form also allowed for the inclusion of women and slaves as co-participants, echoing the inclusivity of schools like the Pythagoreans

59. Hacker, *House Churches*, 60.

60. Alexander, "Paul," 60.

and Stoics. It was structured but not hierarchical. It was formative but not performative. Indeed, Pythagoras's biographers, Porphyry and Iamblichus, both writing in the third century AD, describe the gathering of disciples in ways that are remarkably similar to Acts 2:42–47. In both, we see a rhythm of shared meals, communal property, ethical instruction, and a commitment to mutual formation—an intentional way of life, not just a meeting. These schools were spaces where men and women, rich and poor, learned together in pursuit of the good, and where philosophy wasn't merely an idea but a way of being. When compared with the early-Christian community, the similarity is striking. This suggests that the earliest expressions of *ekklēsia* may have looked more like these philosophical communities than what we've come to know as the house church. And if that's true, then perhaps it's time to recover a model of missional engagement that prioritizes holistic formation and public witness over institutional replication (see Table 10.1). This model minimized the potential for ritual confusion. The absence of temple, priesthood (clericalism), or sacred geography meant that the Christian *ekklēsia* could not easily be mistaken for a new cult. It was something else entirely: a new movement formed around the God-man Jesus Christ, committed to love, truth, and transformation.

Pythagorean Element	**Source**	**Parallel in Acts 2**
Semicircles for public discourse	Porphyry, *Life of Pythagoras* 9	Devotion to the apostles' teaching
Ethical instruction for hearers and students	Iamblichus 18.81	Ethical formation through apostolic teaching
Shared property and communal meals	Iamblichus 18.81; 21.98	Acts 2:44–46
Vegetarian discipline	Porphyry, *Life of Pythagoras* 7	Asceticism and simplicity, implicit in Acts lifestyle
Equality in education for women and men	Porphyry, *Life of Pythagoras* 19–20	Echoes of Gal 3:28 and early-female discipleship
Devotion to philosophy as life formation	Porphyry, *Life of Pythagorus* 57 and Iamblichus, *Life of Pythagorus*, 34.189–193	Devotion to "the Way" (Acts 9:2; 24:14)

Table 10.1: *Ekklēsia* compared to philosophical school

The philosophical-school model gave early Christians a form of life that emphasized transformation over performance, dialogue over ecstasy, and instruction over initiation. It helped preserve their theological clarity amid cultural confusion. In this sense, Montanism serves as an object lesson (chapter 8). So does Corinth. So does the usurpation of temple space after the Christianization of the Roman Empire (chapter 7). Rather, the early *ekklēsia* in Asia Minor, when it held to the simplicity of the philosophical school model, serves as a hopeful witness to a form that fostered fidelity to the faith. In this manner, it provided a theological safeguard for the ongoing expansion of the movement across the empire. It also provided the space for early Christians to think about the manner in which God moved in their cities and how to best communicate his movement.

Missiological Parallelisms

Throughout this volume, I've drawn upon Colin Hemer's idea of polemical parallelism. Now, I wanted to introduce what A.K. Amberg and I call "missiological parallelism." While the idea in polemical parallelism of juxtaposing a biblical informed worldview against contemporary culture is retained, missiological parallelism goes a step further to the culturally appropriate declaration of Jesus Christ as superior. We define it in this way:

> A missiological parallelism is a literary, rhetorical, and missiological device in which a cultural or religious form mirrors a biblical narrative, image, or idea that subsequently both clarifies what God is doing within a culture and confronts the spiritual distortions within the form. These parallels can be identified by such literary genre as allegory, typology, metaphor, and analogy as well as observed in other particularities of cultural actors expressed in forms that juxtapose and clarify related or contrasted ideas. This engagement follows what Cooper calls missiological exegesis of culture through dialogue and observation, and missiological reflection by meaningful expressions of ideas developed in a hermeneutical community.[61]

In other words, missiological parallelism is a theological method that juxtaposes Christ with cultural narratives or practices to reveal both

61. Amberg and Cooper, "Revisiting Contextualization."

God's presence in culture and Christ's ultimate sufficiency as it engages people respectfully rather than dismissively.

Throughout this volume, we've seen how the archaeological record presents various aspects of culture in contradistinction to the Christian claims. Epigraphic evidence shows us how emperors were viewed as saviors and benefactors of communities. The monumental architecture of temples and ubiquitous statues of gods and goddesses believed to be imbued with power give us the picture of cultures animated with benevolent powers promising salvation, healing, and divine help. Against this backdrop, the Christian movement asserts claims that Jesus is a better philosophy (Jesus as the *logos* of God), a better healer (Jesus as the true physician), a better ruler (Jesus as the *pantokratoros* of God), and a better god (Jesus as God). These claims were not polemical ploys, nor were they redemptive analogies. They were claims of practical function and ontology. Jesus is not like these other things. He is far superior to them in every way.

When we speak of these claims as missiological parallelisms rather than polemical parallelisms, we recognize God's missionary activity in culture. We see his activity through the manner in which people, his image bearers, are creating meaning in order to understand the phenomena going on around them. Unsurprisingly, missionaries observe that people naturally have a penchant to philosophize about life and death, worship various objects to secure favor and well-being, seek restoration of health and fortune, and generally explain what is often unexplainable. When we view the human penchant toward these grand questions of meaning missiologically, we see God's work in preparing people to see him. Just as we observed with Theophilos, Luke communicates the truth about God in ways that are parallel to Theophilos's lived experience.[62] So, then, our missiological parallelisms also seek culturally meaningful expressions of God's work that help people make sense of the world around them.

Depth of Evangelistic Engagement

In such a context, graffiti in the archaeological record serve as declarative statements and demonstrate that the early *ekklēsia* called followers to acknowledge Jesus as Lord in opposition to the emperor. He alone is God juxtaposed to the *apotheosis* of emperors as well as the worship of

62. See chapter 3.

various religious cults. In many instances in Asia Minor, this idea found expression in the Christogram. The eight-spoked wheel afforded a simple manner in which Christians communicated their beliefs and perhaps even marked locations of Christian trade guilds, homes, and other places of gathering. The Christogram symbol became a marker of identity as it connoted an entire system of belief along with the expected behaviors. Jesus' superiority over the sundry intermediary figures of gods and goddesses clearly distinguishes him from other savior cults in Asia Minor. Indeed, as Bradley Bitner points out, the riot surrounding the worship of Artemis in Ephesos "was a conflict irrupting around the proclamation of the name of the Lord Jesus in first-century Ephesus."[63]

The early church's survival and growth prior to the Christianization of the empire were not merely due to its theological claims but also to the way it embodied those claims in daily life. By resisting the adoption of temple-based structures (see chapter 7) and instead rooting itself in the pedagogical, virtue-forming rhythm of the philosophical school, the church maintained its theological integrity in the face of overwhelming religious pluralism. And this has implications for our own time.

A MISSIOLOGICAL AND ECCLESIOLOGICAL PATH FORWARD

As a first principle, the adaptation of the philosophical school provides a strategic and safe model for engaging culture. That is not to say that everyone needs to become philosophical. Rather, the form of the school accompanied by the similarities with the simple practices of the early church lead me to the conclusion that it is a minimal starting point that reflects the intentions of the body of Christ.

A philosophical-school model is best positioned to consider the missiological parallelisms in a culture. In such a model, a community is as much about fellowship as it is about learning and engaging in missiological theology. If it has not been clear by now, a missiological parallelism is rooted in the theological insight of Justin Martyr's *logos spermatikos*. The missiological parallelism recognizes that elements of divine truth are often embedded in culture; however, it re-centers those elements around the fullness revealed in Jesus Christ. Therefore, as a missiological tool, the missiological parallelism affirms that God is already at work in every

63. Bitner "Acclaiming Artemis in Ephesus," 163.

culture, yet it disrupts incomplete or idolatrous expressions by offering a more compelling vision of Christ. It simultaneously critiques and redeems, dismantling false hopes while revealing Christ as the true and better expression. This approach allows the missionary-theologian to engage culture, not through wholesale rejection but through subversive reorientation—always pressing the questions: What is God doing and why is Jesus better? And what wonderful questions to consider in a community of learners, "be-ers," and doers who worship the true God, Savior, and Lord: genuinely *tou pantokratoros*.

A missiology that ignores cultural forms risks irrelevance. But a missiology that affirms culture uncritically risks syncretism. Missiological parallelisms thread the needle. They allow us to enter culture with both discernment and hope—recognizing *logos spermatikos* while declaring that now we see with unveiled faces (2 Cor 3:18). These parallels are theologically and missiologically strategic acts of redemptive engagement reframing familiar cultural narratives to make Christ known, not as one option among many but as the very image of the invisible God and therefore the better option. It affirms that traces of divine truth exist across cultures but re-centers them around the fullness found in Christ. As a tool of redemptive engagement, the missiological parallelism critiques false hopes while offering a clearer, truer vision of Jesus, not merely as an alternative but as the fulfillment of every cultural longing.[64]

As a point of clarification, I am not arguing that anachronistic language is wrong. It is simply confusing and potentially misleading. A natural tendency in interpretation is to take what we think we know about a word—*ekklēsia* or *synagōgē* for example—and impose its meaning back on the biblical text. Such eisegetical practices plague contemporary sermons as well as seminary lectures. Even more so, they plague our missions strategies, if not also our missiology. That being said, as a scholar, I must also be open to the way in which the archaeological record critiques my work. While *Ephesiology: A Study of the Ephesian Movement* relied primarily on the literary record, both biblical and historical, there was a glaring gap in the omission of the archaeological record. Over the past two years, I've attempted to fill that gap by breathing the air and observing the scenery of those first Christians. What I've discovered has ignited this research

64. Amberg and Cooper, "Revisiting Contextualization."

agenda focused on the intersection of missiology and archaeology. This agenda includes the material remains, architectural space, as well as epigraphical inscriptions that enrich our understanding of the first-century missionary efforts. In a very real sense, the agenda is a phenomenological approach to interpreting the archaeological record. Phenomenology is a hallmark of the research methodology for the missiologist. Observing the ancient space and ritual artifacts as well as reading historical accounts of the use of that space along with religious practices is vitally important for understanding the first-century cultures of Asia Minor just as it is for understanding a contemporary tribal culture. If we are to claim that our missions strategies are biblical, then it is incumbent upon us to take the time to consider how archaeology informs missiology and vice versa.

We need to remember that missiological research is generally a phenomenological exercise. That was Garrison's objective in his research of CPMs. Missiologists describe what they observe as occurring at a point in history. As sometimes happens, phenomenological studies by missiologists can become anachronistic when practitioners impose them on the NT. That is, when what we observe is understood in biblical terminology and forced back on the text, we risk propagating strategies only disguised as biblical. In a genuine desire to relate what is happening in the biblical text, our enthusiasm for our observations can translate into an unintentional bias based on presuppositions about what a movement should have looked like in the first century.

Nonetheless, our end game is not a movement; it is God's glorification by more people worshiping him. As a result, movement happens, and it's not contingent on the language we use for our missions strategies. Perhaps more importantly, movement happens in the context of relationships with the goal of not only more people worshiping Christ but also more people joining the community of Christ followers. The first-century *ekklēsia* was a single, united church focused on the well-being of the people in a city. No doubt that there were multiple spaces where they gathered like large lecture halls in Ephesos, trade guilds in Sardis, and theaters in Laodicea. But it was one *ekklēsia* that coalesced around Jesus, the anointed one, who is God, the head of the body. This community multiplied faithful people who shifted their allegiance away from gods, goddesses, emperors, and philosophers and took on a new identity who kept all that Christ commanded.

Returning to the starting point of the chapter, Ramsay retired from the academy in 1911, but he continued to write. Among his final volumes was *The Bearing of Recent Discovery on the Trustworthiness of the New Testament*, where he explored the impact of archaeological discoveries on the NT and argued for its historical reliability. Reflecting on his education, these words, written more than a hundred years ago, are *apropos* as a final thought for this chapter, if not the book:

> In my education, the sense of discovery was never quickened, and the power of perceiving truth was becoming atrophied. Scholarship had been a learning of opinions, and not a process of gaining real knowledge. One learned what others had thought, but not what truth was. [Professor Theodor] Benfey was a vivifying wind, to breathe life into dry bones, for he showed scholarship as discovery and not as a rehearsing of wise opinions.[65]

I hope we will continue to discover how the archaeological record of our past helps us understand our ancestors and inform our missiological practices.

65. Ramsay, *Bearing of Recent Discovery*, 13.

Appendix 1: Paul's Tyrannos

In November 2024, our research team walked down the sloped marble road from the *bouleuterion* in Ephesos to the *sebasteion*. The *sebasteion*—the location of the imperial cult—provided the city with its status of twice *neokoros* at the end of the first century AD. At one point in the city's glorious history, the vaulted arches raising the temple area for optimal visual effect was known as Domitian's Temple (Figure A1.1). A sixteen-foot marble statue of his image no doubt embellished his larger than life genius (Figure A1.2). Declaring himself the *Dominus et deus*[1] did not endear him to the Roman senate who issued a *damnatio memoriae* after his death. Subsequently, Domitian's name was erased from Rome's history. Suetonius writes, "[The senate] passed a decree that his inscriptions should everywhere be erased, and all record of him obliterated."[2] Evidence of such erasures litter the dedicatory inscriptions once proclaiming his prominence in the empire as well as the status of Ephesos as *neokoros* (Figure A1.3).

Levent Oral, the president of Tutku Educational Tours, arranged for us to meet archaeologist Cengiz Icten. Cengiz's long history in Ephesos dates back to 1969, and he was the perfect guide to help us understand the material culture in the form of inscribed marble slabs. Among other things, his continuous work on the archaeological site resulted in a re-dating of the occupancy of the city to the Neolithic times in the sixth millennium BC. Closed to the public, we received special permission to visit and explore the inscriptions on display along each side of the *cryptoporticos* at the inscription gallery beneath the *sebasteion*. Representing only a fraction of the four thousand or more inscriptions safely warehoused in the space, we were in search for an inscription of Tyrannos in hopes

1. Suetonius, *Lives of the Caesars* 2:8.13.2.
2. Suetonius, *Lives of the Caesars* 2:8.23.

that it might shed light on the allusive figure whose school functioned as a location for Paul's teaching in Ephesos (Acts 19:9–10).

Meticulously photographing each inscription and quickly scanning them for Tyrannos, I finally stumbled upon it with great excitement only to be disappointed as part of the inscription references emperor Antoninus (AD 138–161) and his adopted son Marcus Aurelius (AD 161–180), dates sufficiently outside of those the New Testament (NT) account would permit (Figure A1.4). I would have to wait for our next trip before accidentally finding the proper Tyrannos inscription.

READING THE STONES

As I was concluding the work on chapter 3, I had heard about another Theophilos inscription at the *prytaneion*, but this one was not accessible to the public. So, in March 2025, our Tutku guide, Sonat Fişek, secured permission for me to walk the grounds of the *prytaneion* to search for the inscription (Figure A1.5). Among the fragmentary remains in the ancient city's civic and religious heart, columns and lintel blocks served as archives documenting prominent figures (Figure A1.6). Photographing everything I could, I encountered inscriptions that, at first glance, appeared like just another honorific list. Yet, on closer inspection, they actually began to illuminate my understanding of the cultural and social networks intersecting with the NT account of Paul's ministry in Ephesos (Acts 18:18–20:1).

The columns tell the story about the lives of *prytanis*, *Kouretes*, priests, and cult attendants. They tell us something about their families and citizenship as well as the time period when they lived. Their location in the *prytaneion* tells us of their responsibilities as keepers of the sacred flame of the goddess Hestia, who symbolized the vitality and unity of the Ephesians (Figure A1.7). Piecing together the historical and archaeological puzzle, we also learn about their association with Artemis, whose statue (*eikón*) proudly stood on display among her adherents (Figure A1.8). And on that left Doric column, just above the ΕΥΜΕΝΗΣ ΘΕΟΦΙΛΟΥ and ΘΕΟΦΙΛΟΣ ΟΛΥΜΠΟΥ ΤΟΥ ΜΕΜΝΟΝΟΣ inscriptions I discussed in chapter 3, the name ΤΥΡΑΝΝΟΣ appears prominently as one of the pious *Kouretes* (Figure A1.9). Here is the reconstructed text from the inscription:

[ΕΠΙ ΠΥΡ]ΤΑΝΕΩΣ ΝΕΙΚΟΜΑΧΟΥ	During the prytany of Neikomachos
[ΤΟΥ ΘΕΟ]ΛΥΤΟΥ ΘΕΥΔΑ ΚΟΥΡΗΤΕΣ	son of Theolytos, Theuda, *Kouretes*
ΕΥΣΕΒΕΙΣ	the pious
ΑΠΟΛΛΩΝΙΟΣ ΜΗΝΟΦΑΝΤΟΥ	Apollonios, son of Menophantos
ΜΑΡΚΟΣ ΠΑΚΟΥΙΟΣ ΤΥΡΑΝΝΟΣ	Marcus Pacuvius Tyrannos
ΦΗΛΞ ΖΕΖΕΛΕΥΚΟΥ	Felix, son of Zezeleukos
ΤΙΒΕΡΙΟΣ ΚΛΑΥΔΙΟΣ ΟΥΕΣΠΑΣΙΑΝΟΣ	Tiberius Claudius Vespasianos
ΚΟΙΤΟΣ ΛΟΥΛΙΟΣ ΠΕΙΟΣ	Coitus Lulius Peius
ΠΟΗΛΙΟΣ ΚΑΡΒΙΛΙΟΣ ΤΥΡΑΝΝΙΟΝ	Poelius Carvilius Tyrannion
ΑΛΕΞΑΝΔΡΟΣ ΣΠΟΝΔΑΥΛΗΣ	Alexandros *Spondaules*

Table A1: Tyrannos inscription

DATING THE INSCRIPTION

The date of the inscription, during the tenure of the *prytanis* (president) *Neikomachos Theolytou*, falls within the reign of Emperor Claudius (r. AD 41–54). Based on Roman naming conventions, the appearance of Tiberius Claudius Vespasianos (line 7) suggests that this *Kouretes* had been granted Roman citizenship, reflected in the adoption of the imperial names "Tiberius Claudius." Colin Hemer concurs that the period of the column inscription must be during the Julio-Claudian dynasty although he dates this inscription during the reign of Tiberius.[3] However, during the reign of Claudius, whose full name was Tiberius Claudius Caesar Augustus Germanicus, Roman citizenship was extended to individuals in Ephesos. In many cases, such citizenship was demonstrated by an individual honoring the *praenomen* of the emperor. Thus, Tiberius Claudius Vespasianos became a Roman citizen sometime between AD 41 and 54. This allows us to securely date the inscription during Paul's work in Ephesos (Acts 18:19).

What stands out here is the *cognomen* Tyrannos, found not once but possibly twice (*Tyrannos* and the diminutive *Tyrannion*). This leads us to revisit Acts 19:9, where Paul is said to have taught daily in the hall of Tyrannos (εν τη σχολη Τυραννου). While scholars debate the existence and meaning of σχολη, Craig Keener appropriately surmises, "Whether Tyrannus's building was a school, lecture hall, or guildhall makes little

3. Hemer, *Seven Churches of Asia*, 234; cf. Knibbe, *Der Staatsmarkt*, 162.

difference in the end, as Paul does use it as a lecture hall and school. But Paul's use of it probably does match the building's usual function, increasing his status for using that particular site."[4]

While the name "Tyrannos" was not unknown in the Greco-Roman world, its occurrence in Ephesos during the early first century AD is rare—and therefore highly suggestive.[5] According to the Packard Humanities Institute database, which holds approximately 210,000 Greek inscriptions, the name *Tyrannos* appears fifty-nine times, with thirty-five of those from Asia Minor. When narrowed to Ephesos, just seven attestations remain—and most fall outside the time frame of Paul's ministry. A brief survey of these epigraphic entries underscores the rarity of this name within the correct social and chronological window:

1. Ephesos 242—list of donations by *prytanis*; AD 180/192 (too late)
2. Ephesos 267—dedication of a customs house; AD 54/59[6]
3. Ephesos 447—our inscription above; likely during Claudius's reign
4. Ephesos 457—*Kouretes* under *prytanis* Claudia Trophime; AD 92/93 (too late)
5. Ephesos 475—*Kouretes* under Quintus Cerrinius Cimber; AD 112/139 (too late)
6. Ephesos 558—list of priests; AD 180/192 (too late)
7. Ephesos 1423—honorary inscription by Publius Claudius Tyrannos; AD 165/180 (too late)

This makes Ephesos 447 the only known attestation of *Tyrannos* from the right social class, civic status, and time period to plausibly intersect with Luke's account of Paul's Ephesian ministry.[7] The presence of *Marcus Pacuvius Tyrannos* and *Poelius Carvilius Tyrannion* among the *Kouretes* places them within the Ephesian elite. This raises the strong possibility that Tyrannos was not an obscure figure or a tyrannical philosopher. Instead, in his role as *Kouretes*, he was someone intimately connected to the civic–religious framework of the city. The *Kouretes* functioned as the guardians of religious ritual in the Ephesian cult of Artemis. Their names

4. Keener, *Acts*, 2828.

5. Cf. Keener who states, "The name was unusually common in Ephesus" (Keener, *Acts*, 2829).

6. Social class unlikely; see Fairchild, *Christian Origins in Ephesus*, 36.

7. See Keener, *Acts*, 2827–38.

inscribed in the *prytaneion* emphasize their significance in the civic and religious order of the city. For Paul to have partnered or engaged with such individuals reveals a highly intentional strategy—one that inserted the early-Christian movement into the symbolic and structural heart of the city.

As already noted, Tyrannos's name appears above another list of *Kouretes* which includes the name *Theophilos*. Just below this list is the name *Trophimos* inscribed among the priests of Artemis. Hemer leaves open the possibility that this is the same Trophimos we meet in Acts 20:4; 21:29; and 2 Tim 4:20.[8] If so, it would be of little surprise that the Jews in Jerusalem would be upset with the accusation that Paul brought, not simply a Gentile into the temple but a former priest of Artemis. Whatever the case, the proximity of these names—on the same column, in the same civic space, and dated to the same period—is striking. It suggests a personal or institutional relationship between the three men. This proximity might help explain Luke's narrative silence about Tyrannos. If Theophilos of Ephesos is indeed the intended recipient of both Luke and Acts—as I've argued in chapter 3—then the absence of details about Tyrannos could be deliberate. Theophilos would not have needed an explanation; he would have known Tyrannos personally or at least by reputation.

RETHINKING THE "HALL OF TYRANNOS"

Acts 19:9 mentions the "hall of Tyrannos," which a later scribal note in Codex Bezae (a.k.a. the Western text) interpreted as a rented lecture space. Keener comments,

> Many scholars suggest that the Western text preserves a reliable tradition concerning when Paul used the lecture hall—namely, from 11:00 a.m. to 4:00 p.m. Although the Western text is often given to guesses (some more educated than others), this variant reading is both specific and plausible enough that it might reflect reliable tradition; if not, it is at least a reasonable guess from someone familiar with the arrangements of ancient schools.[9]

However, the civic status of Tyrannos in the *prytaneion* inscription suggests a more nuanced interpretation. Such a hall may have been an established venue of public instruction used for civic or religious teaching

8. Hemer, *Seven Churches of Asia*, 252.

9. Keener, *Acts*, 2829.

that was then repurposed by Tyrannos for philosophical or theological dialogue. Indeed, we have precedent for this in Ephesos: the so-called hall of Gaius the priest of Dionysos in Terrace House 2 (Figure A1.10) is an example of a religious leader owning or managing such space (see appendix 2).

If the inscription is indeed Luke's Tyrannos, Paul's strategic use of the *schole Tyrannou* was more than spatially convenient. It was symbolically charged. It placed the gospel proclamation at the intersection of education, religion, and civic identity—precisely the kind of location from which a new movement could spread to every resident of Asia with rapid influence (Acts 19:10, 20). As I explore further in *Ephesiology*, Paul's ministry was not peripheral to the social life of Ephesos. It was embedded in the civic, vocational, and religious structures, positioned at the nodes of power and cultural formation—what I've called "places of peace" in chapter 6.

The identification of *Ephesos 447* with the Tyrannos of Acts 19 adds weight to the growing body of evidence suggesting that early Christianity was not a marginal sect operating in secrecy. Rather, the church was a public, embedded movement—engaging city structures with wisdom and respect, recognizing the inherent dignity of all people made in the image of God. The *ekklēsia* did not retreat from civic life. It leaned into it—boldly and thoughtfully—but not as a political pawn. Instead, as a prophetic voice declaring Jesus Christ God, the *ekklēsia* did "Jesus-y" things: healed the sick, cared for the marginalized, and announced the kingdom of God.[10] And so, a tentmaker-philosopher from Tarsus stepped into a hall in Ephesos and began to turn Asia upside down.

10. And, yes, I'm using "Jesus-y" as a *terminus technicus* just as I used "wonky."

Appendix 2: Aphrodite in Ephesos?

TERRACE HOUSE 2 IN Ephesos provides an extraordinary glimpse into the social and religious life of one of the most important cities in the Greco-Roman world. Nestled on the southern slopes of the city near the Triodos (the intersection of three main streets), these seven peristyle houses reflect the wealth, sophistication, and religious diversity of the Ephesian elite.[1]

Within this remarkable complex, Dwelling Unit 6 is the peristyle home of Gaius Flavius Furius Aptus, a priest of Dionysos. His residence included a magnificent marble hall, peristyle forecourt, water features, statues, and frescos.[2] Among the impressive features of the home is the enormous barrel-vaulted apsidal hall—a space full of social and religious significance. Outside its entrance, two pedestals for statues bear inscriptions that offer insight into the intersection of religious devotion and syncretism, social identity and cultural dynamics.

While we are most familiar with Artemis of the Ephesians, these inscriptions point to the importance of Aphrodite in Ephesian life and highlight the challenges faced by the early-Christian church as it sought to navigate and engage the cultural paradigms of its day. By examining these inscriptions in their context, we begin to see how archaeology, history, and missiology intersect to illuminate the world of the New Testament (NT), especially Paul's concern for the dignity of the women of Ephesos.

1. See Zimmermann, "Archaeological Evidence."

2. See Thür, "Sacred Space for Dionysos."

APHRODITE'S ROLE IN EPHESUS

While Artemis reigned as the primary deity of Ephesos, Aphrodite's presence reflects the city's religious diversity and its embrace of sensual beauty, love, and fertility. As the patron goddess of courtesans (Gr. *hetaera*), Aphrodite was revered, not only for her divine beauty but also for her association with the art of social refinement and influence. While there is no denying acts of sexual service associated with courtesans, it's important to dispel the common misconception of Aphrodite as merely a "whore goddess" or a deity of prostitution. While she was certainly connected to sensuality and love, her domain extended far beyond physical desire. Aphrodite embodied ideals of beauty, attraction, fertility, and even political harmony, as seen in her role as a unifying figure in marriage and civic relationships (see chapter 2).

Her patronage of courtesans did not glorify immorality but rather it aligned with the Greco-Roman admiration for elegance, social influence, and the cultivation of relationships. Indeed, Plutarch describes a courtesan, Aspasia, from Ephesos who was admired as much for her beauty as her intellect:

> And so Aspasia, as some say, was held in high favour by Pericles [the Athenian military leader and statesman] because of her rare political wisdom. Socrates sometimes came to see her with his disciples, and his intimate friends brought their wives to her to hear her discourse.[3]

THE APSIDAL HALL AND ITS INSCRIPTIONS

The apsidal hall in Dwelling Unit 6 was likely a space of both social and religious significance and very likely the site of a religious guild as its owner was a priest of Dionysos. Apsidal halls, with their semicircular back walls, were multifunctional spaces commonly used as dining and entertainment areas, audience halls, or even lecture halls. They often served as venues for gatherings that blended intellectual discourse, guild meals, and religious rituals. The placement of two inscribed statue bases at the hall's entrance emphasize the importance of the space they framed, marking it as a site for both religious devotion and identity.[4] There is little

3. Plutarch, *Pericles* 24.
4. See Rathmayr, "Significance of Sculptures."

doubt that this space was used for cultic purposes: singing hymns, eating food sacrificed to gods and goddesses, etc.

The Left Pedestal: A Hymn to Aphrodite

Looking into the apsidal hall, the inscription on the left pedestal is highly stylized, with poetic language alluding to Aphrodite, the goddess of love, beauty, and sensuality. This hymn celebrates Aphrodite's divine lineage, mythological birth from the sea, and beauty, connecting her to the themes of love, refinement, and nature. The references to the sea and waves reflect her close association with maritime imagery as does her epithet "foam-born" (ΑΦΡΟΓΕΝΗΣ). The inscription serves as both a dedication to Aphrodite and an acknowledgment of her role as a central figure in Ephesian religious and cultural life, especially in a city where beauty and fertility were central to worship and social identity (Figure A2.1).

The Right Pedestal: Gaius Pericles and Cultural Honor

The inscription on the right pedestal appears to honor two individuals: Gaius and possibly his son, or perhaps a priest in the Aphrodite cult, Pericles, whose legacies are tied to both prosperity and religious devotion (Figure A2.2). The central message of the inscription describes them as protectors and very prosperous, with divine favor and blessings bestowed upon them. It references their influence and virtue both at home and abroad and emphasizes their mobility and influence. The honorees are praised for their hospitality, being described as both strangers (guests) and hosts of strangers, reflecting the Greek ideal of *xenia* (hospitality). The reference to goddesses—perhaps a poetic allusion to courtesans—are portrayed as eagerly bestowing blessings upon them, while revering and respecting "all things" about their character and actions. The reference to *Kythira* (ΚΥΘΗΡΗ) only solidifies the connection to Aphrodite.

Given the prominence of these inscriptions and their placement at the entrance to the hall, it is reasonable to suggest that Gaius and Pericles both served as priests in the cult of Aphrodite in the first century as well as the hosts of the social and religious gatherings conducted there. As wealthy Ephesian elites, they likely acted as patrons to the courtesans who played significant roles in such gatherings.[5] Yet, of special note, Gaius appears to blend his priestly duties for both Dionysos and Aphrodite, signaling the syncretism so common in the Greco-Roman world.

BROADER IMPLICATIONS

The inscriptions on the pedestals at the apsidal hall in Dwelling Unit 6 highlight the value of archaeology for understanding the cultural context of the NT. Inscriptions, artifacts, and architectural features provide tangible evidence of the pressures faced by early Christians as they navigated their pluralistic and often morally complex world. For example, the devotion to Aphrodite and the prominence of courtesans in Ephesos help set Paul's exhortations in 1 Tim 2:11–15 in their *Sitz im Leben*.[6] He was not propagating some first-century notion of complementarianism. Instead, he upheld the dignity and respect of women while condemning their exploitation by men frequenting places like Gaius's and Pericles's apsidal hall.

Understanding the cultural and historical background of the NT is essential for accurate interpretation. Paul's teachings on modesty, morality, and authority in 1 Tim 2:11–15 are best understood within the context of Ephesian society where figures like Aphrodite and courtesans shaped cultural norms, and in this case, the role of women. Considering the cultural and historical background prevents anachronistic readings of the text and helps readers discern Paul's original intent. After all, the biblical text cannot mean to us what it did not mean to the first readers.

The early church's response to cultural pressures offers a model for modern Christians. By rejecting the sensuality and immorality of their culture, the Ephesian church provides an example of what it looks like to elevate the position of women and emphasize the values of faith, love, and holiness. Similarly, modern believers can draw on a model for navigating cultural challenges while remaining faithful to biblical truth. The Ephesian church resoundingly rejected any association with Artemis, Dionysos, or Aphrodite as it worshiped the one true God who saves both men and women.

5. See Cooper, *Ephesiology*.

6. See Bird, *Jesus Among the Gods*.

CONCLUSION

The inscriptions outside the apsidal hall in Dwelling Unit 6 at Terrace House 2 offer a glimpse into the religious and social world of Ephesos. They reflect a household that sought to align itself with the divine, blending personal honor, civic identity, and religious devotion. At the same time, these inscriptions highlight the cultural challenges faced by the early church, as they sought to redefine societal norms in light of the worship of Jesus Christ.

Archaeology, combined with the biblical text, helps us better understand the NT world, bringing its teachings into sharper focus. By studying the cultural and historical background of Scripture, we gain not only a richer understanding of its message but also valuable lessons for living faithfully in a complex and often pluralistic world. A proper understanding of the world of the NT reduces the chance of anachronistic theological tripe that so often divides the body of Christ.

Glossary

Archisynagōgos (αρχισυναγωγος): "Ruler of the synagogue" or "head of a synagogue." This could refer to leaders of cult associations, Jewish leaders, or masters of trade guilds, not exclusively Jewish religious leaders.

Asiarchs: High-ranking provincial officials in Roman Asia, responsible for organizing imperial cult festivals. Mentioned in the context of Paul's ministry in Ephesos.

Asklepios: Greek god of healing, widely worshiped in Pergamon and referred to as "Soter" (Savior), creating a polemical parallel with Jesus Christ.

Attalid Dynasty: The ruling family of the Pergamene kingdom, known for their patronage of arts, sciences, and the city of Pergamon. Philadelphia was founded during this dynasty.

Basilica: Originally a Greek word meaning "place of royalty," referring to a public building or hall. In the context of early Christianity, it became a common architectural style for churches, often with a central nave and side aisles.

Christogram: A monogram or symbol representing Christ, such as the chi-rho or the eight-spoked wheel (IXΘ for Ιησούς Χρίστος Θεός).

Chrysostomoi: "Golden mouths," a term possibly referring to a prophetic office indicated by gold plates found on the mouths of Montanus and his prophetesses.

Collegia: Latin term for voluntary associations or vocational associations, widely present in Greco-Roman society and often referred to as "synagogue" (συναγωγή) in the Greek context.

Cryptoporticos: A covered passageway or gallery, often subterranean or semi-subterranean, found in Roman architecture.

Cybele: An ancient Anatolian mother goddess, widely worshiped in Asia Minor, depicted wearing a crown and flanked by lions.

Diakonos: A title for a "deacon" in early-Christian and pagan cultic associations.

Didache: An early-Christian treatise (late first/early second century) providing liturgical instructions and moral teachings.

Dipteral temple: An architectural style of temple with a double row of columns surrounding the inner sanctum (*cella*).

Dionysos: Greek god of wine, ecstatic ritual, and theatrical performance, prominent in Philadelphia, sometimes identified as "Kathegemon" (the leader).

Domus-synagoga: Refers to a Jewish gathering place located within a private house, particularly where dedicated physical structures were sparse.

Ecclesiology: The theological study of the nature, structure, and mission of the Christian church.

Epigraphy: The study of ancient inscriptions, crucial for understanding historical, religious, and social contexts.

Euergetism: A practice of public benefaction or patronage, where wealthy individuals donated resources for the public good, often for civic buildings or cultic activities.

Hierophantes: A "revealer of sacred objects" or an interpreter of sacred mysteries, a priestly title found in various cults, including the Dionysian.

Hiereus: A Greek term for "priest," often associated with those serving specific deities or cults.

Homereium: A structure or shrine dedicated to Homer, found in Smyrna, reflecting the city's claim as his birthplace.

Homotechnos (ομοτεχνος): Literally "same craft" or "fellow craftsman," used to describe those who shared the same trade, often members of a guild.

Hyperetes: An "attendant" or "servant," used in Luke 1:2 ("attendants of the word"), creating a polemical parallel with cult attendants of Artemis.

Ichthys (ΙΧΘΥΣ): An acrostic for "Jesus Christ, God's Son, Savior," often represented by a fish symbol, used as a monogram for Ιησους Χριστος Θεος (ΙΧΘ).

Iconoclast controversy: A dispute in the Byzantine Empire (eighth TO ninth centuries) over the use and veneration of religious images (icons).

Isopsephism: A numerological practice where letters in a word or phrase are assigned numerical values, and sums are compared for symbolic meaning (e.g., "Lord" and "Faith" both summing to eight hundred in Smyrna).

Jus gladii: Latin for "right of the sword," referring to the authority of a Roman official or city to enact capital punishment, held by Pergamon.

Kantharos: A type of ancient Greek drinking cup, often associated with Dionysian rituals.

Kouretes: Young men serving as guardians of Leto (Artemis's mother) in the Artemis myth, whose annual re-enactment involved clanging spears against shields. Theophilos and Tyrannos in Ephesos may have held this role.

Kyrios (κυριος): Greek for "lord," a title claimed by some Roman emperors and a central confessional term for Jesus Christ.

L Source ("L"): A hypothetical unique source material used only by Luke in composing his Gospel, containing stories or hymns not found in Matthew or Mark.

Logos (ΛΟΓΟC): Greek for "word" or "reason." In Christian theology, it refers to Jesus Christ as the divine Word of God (John 1:1).

Martyries: Places commemorating Christian martyrs, often associated with their tombs or sites of martyrdom.

Medism: Adopting or sympathizing with Persian customs or attitudes, often viewed with suspicion in the Greco-Roman world.

Menorah: A seven-branched candelabrum, a symbol of Judaism.

Metanoia: Greek term for "repentance" or a "change of mind." Often used to indicate switching allegiances, whether religious, philosophical, or political.

Miaphysite: Describes a Christological doctrine asserting that in the person of Jesus Christ, the human and divine natures are united as one, without confusion, separation, or division.

Montanism (New Prophecy): A new religious movement emerging in Phrygia in the mid-second century, led by Montanus and two prophetesses (Priscilla and Maximilla), emphasizing ecstatic prophecy, moral rigor, and the imminent return of Christ.

Motus Dei: Latin for "movement of God," referring to God's missional initiative in the world.

Mystes: An "initiate" into a mystery religion or cult.

Neocaesarea: A name given to Philadelphia for a time, honoring Emperor Tiberius.

Neokoros: "Temple guardian" or "keeper." A prestigious civic title granted to cities that hosted an imperial cult temple, signifying imperial favor and religious prominence.

Neopoi: Temple administrators, particularly for the cult of Artemis in Ephesos. Theophilos may have achieved this position.

Nomen sacrum: "Sacred name." A contracted form of divine names (like God, Jesus, Christ) in early-Christian manuscripts and inscriptions, often with a horizontal line above the letters (e.g., $\overline{\Theta\Upsilon}$ for θεου).

Numismatics: The study of coins, medallions, and paper currency, providing historical, political, and religious insights.

Oikos: Greek for "house" or "household," often referring to early-Christian house churches or the broader network of a patron–client system.

Opus sectile: An ancient decorative technique that involves cutting and inlaying thin pieces of stone (or other materials) to form patterns or images.

Orarium: A scarf or stole worn by clergy in later Christian tradition.

Ortygia: A mythical location associated with the birth of Artemis, which Ephesos claimed as its own.

Pantokratoros (παντοκρατορος): Greek for "Almighty" or "All-powerful," a doxological epithet for God, used in both Jewish and early Christian contexts.

Patrogeron: A "patriarch" or "elder father," a position of high standing, possibly held by Theophilos in Ephesos.

Patera: A shallow dish or bowl used for pouring libations in ancient rituals.

Peripteral temple: A temple surrounded by a single row of columns.

Peristyle home: A house with a courtyard surrounded by columns, common in affluent Greco-Roman homes.

Phanero-Christianity: "Open" or "public" Christianity, referring to visible declarations of Christian identity in epitaphs or other public displays, particularly in rural Phrygia.

Philagathos: A "goodness-loving official."

Polemical parallelism: A literary or rhetorical device where a writer intentionally presents a narrative, idea, or image that mirrors another but does so to critique, challenge, or subvert the original.

Poimenon: A "shepherd," possibly a term for a Christian leader.

Presbyteros: An "elder" or "presbyter" in early Christian and cultic associations.

Prophylactic: Something that prevents or guards against disease or evil.

Proseuchen (προσευχην): A Greek word often meaning "prayer" but also used for a "place of prayer" or a Jewish gathering place, sometimes distinguished from "synagogue."

Protoevangelium: The "first gospel," typically referring to Gen 3:15, seen as the first prophecy of the Messiah.

Prytaneion: The seat of the *prytanis* (president of civic and religious affairs) in a Greek city, often housing an eternal flame and archives. Theophilos inscriptions were found here in Ephesos.

Q Source ("Q"): A hypothetical common source of sayings of Jesus used by both Matthew and Luke, distinct from Mark.

Quartodeciman controversy: A dispute in early Christianity regarding the date of observing Easter, specifically whether to celebrate it on the fourteenth day of the Jewish month Nisan (like Passover) regardless of the day of the week.

Regina inscription: An inscription found in the Sardis Synagogue, dedicated by a donor and his wife Regina, containing the terms "*pantokratoros*" and "ΘΥ," indicating a Christian contribution or use of the space.

Sebastoi, Cult of the: The cult of emperor worship in the Roman Empire.

Soter (σωτὴρ): Greek for "savior," a title claimed by Roman emperors, pagan gods (like Zeus and Asklepios), and centrally applied to Jesus Christ.

Spolia: Repurposed architectural elements (stones, columns, capitals) taken from older buildings and reused in new constructions, often pagan structures reused in Christian churches.

Staurogram: A Christian monogram formed by the Greek letters *tau* (t) and *rho* (p), forming a cross shape, used to represent the crucifixion of Christ.

Stoics: An ancient Greek school of philosophy emphasizing virtue, reason, and living in harmony with the natural world. Their use of allegory is relevant to how Jesus communicated in Revelation.

Synodos: Greek term for an "assembly" or "council," also used for cultic associations.

Tabula ansata: A rectangular tablet or plaque with two handles or wings on either side, used for inscriptions.

Temenos: The sacred precinct or consecrated area surrounding a Greek temple.

Theophilos: The addressee of Luke's Gospel and Acts, meaning "friend of God." He was a prominent Ephesian official, possibly a *Kouretes*, *neopoi*, or *hiereus*.

Theosebes: Greek term often mistranslated as "God-fearer," referring to Gentiles who were attracted to Jewish monotheism without fully converting.

Theotokos: Greek for "God-bearer," a title for Mary, affirmed at the Council of Ephesos (AD 431).

Thiasitides: Female members of a *thiasos* or cultic society.

Thiasitai: Male members of a *thiasos* or cultic society.

Thiasos: A Greek term for a cultic association or religious guild.

Tripteral temple: A temple with a triple row of columns surrounding the inner sanctum.

Tympanum: A type of framed drum, often associated with the worship of Cybele.

Tyche: The Greek goddess of fortune, chance, and destiny, often personifying the prosperity of a city.

Viticulture: The cultivation of grapevines, particularly for wine production, significant to the economy of Philadelphia.

Voluntary associations: See "Collegia."

Zeus Philios: "Zeus the Friend," a re-imagined benevolent form of Zeus, perceived as a protector and mediator, creating a polemical parallel with Jesus Christ.

Bibliography

Alexander, Loveday. "Paul and the Hellenistic Schools: The Evidence of Galen." In *Paul in His Hellenistic Context*, edited by Troels Engberg-Pedersen, 60–83. Minneapolis: Fortress, 1995.

Allen, Roland. *Missionary Methods: St. Paul's or Ours.* Chicago: Moody, 1959.

Álvarez-Pedrosa, Juan Antonio. "The Peacock's Arrival in Greece and Rome: How an Exotic Animal Became an Eschatological Symbol." *Anabasis. Studia Classica et Orientalia* 10 (2019) 326–41.

Amberg, A. K., and Michael T. Cooper. "Revisiting Contextualization: Missiological Parallelism as an Alternative." *Global Missiology* Vol. 23, No. 1 (2026).

The Ante-Nicene Fathers [*ANF*]. Edited by Alexander Roberts and James Donaldson. 1885–1887. 10 vols. 2nd Repr. Peabody, MA: Hendrickson, 1999.

Aristides, Aelius. *Orations.* Vol. 2. Translated by Charles A. Behr. LCL. Cambridge: Harvard University Press, 1981.

Arlund, Pam, and Warrick Farah. "Discussing and Catalyzing Movements: An Invitation to Research, Sacrifice, and Commitment." *Global Missiology* 19 (2022) 5–17. http://ojs.globalmissiology.org/index.php/english/article/view/2691/6622.

Arnold, Clinton. *Colossians.* Word Biblical Commentary 44A. Grand Rapids: Zondervan, 2025.

———. *The Colossian Syncretism: The Interface Between Christianity and Folk Belief at Colossae.* Grand Rapids: Baker, 1996.

Ascough, Richard S., et al. *Associations in the Greco-Roman World: A Sourcebook.* Waco: Baylor University Press, 2012.

———, trans. "Dedication of an Altar for a Synagogue of Barbers (I–II CE)." Associations in the Greco-Roman World. https://philipharland.com/greco-roman-associations/63-dedication-of-an-altar-for-a-synagogue-of-barbers/.

———. "Interactions Among Religious Groups in Sardis and Smyrna." In *Religious Rivalries and the Struggle for Success in Sardis and Smyrna*, edited by Richard S. Ascough, 5–13. Waterloo: Canadian Corporation for Studies in Religion, 2005.

Augustine. *City of God.* Vol. 7. Translated by William M. Green. LCL 417. Cambridge: Harvard University Press, 1972.

Bagnall, Roger S. *Everyday Writing in the Graeco-Roman East.* Berkeley: University of California Press, 2011.

———, et al., eds. *Graffiti from the Basilica in the Agora of Smyrna.* New York: Institute for the Study of the Ancient World, 2016.

Barna. "51% of Churchgoers Don't Know of the Great Commission." May 27, 2018. https://www.barna.com/research/half-churchgoers-not-heard-great-commission/.

———. "Competing Worldviews Influence Today's Christians. May 9, 2017. https://www.barna.com/research/competing-worldviews-influence-todays-christians/.

Barton, Tamsyn. "Augustus and Capricorn: Astrological Polyvalency and Imperial Rhetoric." *The Journal of Roman Studies* 85 (1995) 33–51.

Bauer, Walter. *Orthodoxy and Heresy in Earliest Christianity*. Philadelphia: Fortress, 1971.

Bayliss, Richard. "From Temple to Church: Converting Paganism to Christianity in Late Antiquity." *Minerva* (2005) 16–18.

———. *Provincial Cilicia and the Archaeology of Temple Conversion*. Oxford: BAR, 2004.

Bede, The Venerable. *The Ecclesiastical History of the English Nation*. Edited by Cecil Jane. Mobile, AL: RE, 1983.

Bentwich, Norman. "The Biography." In *Josephus: Complete Works*, 9617–9843. Delphi Classics, 1914.

Bird, Michael F. "Challenging Mike Winger on Paul, Artemis, and Women in the Church." Early Christian History with Michael Bird, Jan. 19, 2025. YouTube, 1:24:29. https://youtu.be/Q92W994iDfs.

———. *Jesus Among the Gods: Early Christology in the Greco-Roman World*. Waco: Baylor University Press, 2022. Kindle.

Bitner, Bradley J. "Acclaiming Artemis in Ephesus: Political Theologies in Acts 19." Pages 127–69 in *Ephesus*. Edited by James R. Harrison and L. L. Welborn. Vol. 3 of *The First Urban Churches*. Atlanta: SBL Press, 2018.

Blair, Anthony L., and Michael T. Cooper. "Do Not Make Disciples: Moving from an Obligatory to Organic Understanding of the Great Commission." Forthcoming.

Bonz, Marianne Palmer. "Beneath the Gaze of the Gods." In *Pergamon: Citadel of the Gods*, edited by Helmut Koester, 251–76. Harrisburg: Trinity, 1998.

———. "Differing Approaches to Religious Benefaction: The Late Third Century Acquisition of the Sardis Synagogue." *Harvard Theological Review* 86 (1993) 139–54.

Bosch, David J. *Transforming Mission: Paradigm Shifts in the Theology of Mission*. Maryknoll: Orbis, 1991.

Butler, Rex D. *The New Prophecy and "New Visions": Evidence of Montanism in The Passion of Perpetua and Felicitas*. Washington, DC: Catholic University of America Press, 2006.

Byron, John. "Paul and the Background of Slavery: The Status Quaestionis in New Testament Scholarship." *Currents in Biblical Research* 3 (2004) 1–31.

Cadoux, Cecil J. *Ancient Smyrna: A History of the City from the Earliest Times to 224 AD*. Oxford: Oxford University Press, 1938.

Cadwallader, Alan H. "Honouring the Repairer of the Baths: A New Inscription from Kolossai." *Antichthon* 46 (2012) 150–83.

Cadwallader, Alan H., and James R. Harrison. "Perspectives on the Lycus Valley: An Inscriptural, Archaeological, Numismatic, and Iconographic Approach." Pages 3–72 in *Colossae, Hierapolis, and Laodiciea*. Edited by James R. Harrison and L. L. Welborn. Vol. 5 of *The First Urban Churches*. Atlanta: SBL Press, 2019.

Calder, W. M. "Philadelphia and Montanus." *Bulletin of the John Rylands Library* 7 (1923) 309–53.

Caldwell, Larry W. *The Bible in Culture: Reading the Bible with All the World Using Ethnohermeneutics*. Littleton, CO: William Carey, 2025.

Callaghan, P. J. "On the Date of the Great Altar of Zeus at Pergamon." *Bulletin of the Institute of Classical Studies* 28 (1981) 115–21.

Carroll, Michael P. *The Cult of the Virgin Mary*. Princeton: Princeton University Press, 1986.

Cassius Dio. *Roman History*. Vol. 7. Translated by Earnest Cary and Herbert B. Foster. Cambridge: Harvard University Press, 1924.

Ceylan, Bruce. "Episkopeia in Asia Minor." In *Housing in Late Antiquity*, edited by L. Lavan et al., 169–94. Leiden: Brill, 2007.

Clement of Alexandria. *Paedagogus*. In *Clement of Alexandria: Complete Works*, translated by William Wilson, 218–457. Hastings: Delphi Classics, 2016.

Cicero. *Letters to Friends*. Vol. 1. Edited and translated by D. R. Shackleton Bailey. LCL 205. Cambridge: Harvard University Press, 2001.

Coles, Dave, and Stan Parks. "Movement Servants Needed!" *Mission Frontiers* 43 (2021) 37–41.

Collar, Anna. *Religious Networks in the Roman Empire: The Spread of New Ideas*. Cambridge: Cambridge University Press, 2013.

Collins, Adela Yarbro. "Pergamon in Early Christian Literature." In *Pergamon: Citadel of the Gods*, edited by Helmut Koester, 164–84. Harrisburg: Trinity, 1998.

Contreras, Russell. "15,000 Churches Could Close This Year Amid Religious Shift in U.S." Axios, Oct. 3, 2025. https://www.axios.com/2025/10/03/us-churches-close-religious-shift-christians.

Cooper, Loré Kaylor. "Learning from Persecuted Believers in the 21st Century." MA project, Kairos University, 2023.

Cooper, Michael T. *Ephesiology: A Study of the Ephesian Movement*. Littleton, CO: William Carey, 2020.

———. *A Faithful Witness: Lessons for Times of Political, Economic, and Societal Turmoil from the Third Century Church*. Littleton, CO: Ephesiology, 2021.

———. "John's Missiological Theology: The Contribution of the Fourth Gospel to the First Century Movement in Roman Asia." In *Motus Dei: The Movement of God and the Discipleship of Nations*, edited by Warrick Farah, 129–40. Littleton, CO: William Carey, 2021.

Cooper, Michael T., and David Garrison. "Church Planting Movements." Ephesiology, Oct. 23, 2021. YouTube, 41:10. https://youtu.be/CBJZKmYRBLI.

Cotter, Wendy. "The Collegia and Roman Law: State Restrictions on Voluntary Associations, 64 BCE–200 CE." In *Voluntary Associations in the Graeco-Roman World*, edited by John S. Kloppenborg and Stephen G. Wilson, 74–89. London: Routledge, 1996.

Creamer, Jennifer M., et al. "Who Is Theophilus? Discovering the Original Reader of Luke-Acts." *In Die Skriflig* 48 (2014) 1–7.

deSilva, David A. *Archaeology and the Ministry of Paul: A Visual Guide*. Grand Rapids: Baker, 2025.

Dever, Mark. "A Biblical Understanding and Practice of Missions." *The Great Commission Baptist Journal of Missions* 3 (2024) 1–6.

———. *Nine Marks of a Healthy Church*. 2nd ed. Wheaton: Crossway, 2013.

Didache. Pages 416–35 in *1 Clement. 2 Clement. Ignatius. Polycarp. Didache*. Vol. 1 of *The Apostolic Fathers*. Edited and translated by Bart D. Ehrman. LCL 24. Cambridge: Harvard University Press, 2003.

Diodorus Siculus. *Library of History*. Vol. 2. Translated by C. H. Oldfather. LCL 303. Cambridge: Harvard University Press, 1935.

Diogenes Laertius. *Lives of Eminent Philosophers*. Vol. 2. Translated by R. D. Hicks. LCL 185. Cambridge: Harvard Univesity Press, 1925.

Dittenberger, Wilhelm, ed. *Orientis Graeci inscriptiones selectae. Supplementum sylloges inscriptionum Graecarum*. Vol. 1. Leipzig: S. Hirzel, 1903.

Doig, Allan. *Liturgy and Architecture: From the Early Church to the Middle Ages*. New York: Routledge, 2016.

Douglas, A. E. "Roman *Cognomina*." *Greece & Rome* 5 (1958) 62–66.

Ehrman, Bart D. *The New Testament: A Historical Introduction to the Early Christian Writings*. New York: Oxford University Press, 2008.

———, ed. and trans. "Martyrdom of St. Polycarp, Bishop of Smyrna." In *The Apostolic Fathers*, 1:355–402. Cambridge: Harvard University Press, 2003.

Epiphanius. *The Panarion of Epiphanius of Salamis*. Leiden: Brill, 1994.

Epistle to Diognetus. Pages 130–61 in *Epistle of Barnabas. Papias and Quadratus. Epistle to Diognetus. The Shepherd of Hermas*. Vol. 2 of *The Apostolic Fathers*. Edited and translated by Bart D. Ehrman. LCL 25. Cambridge: Harvard University Press, 2003.

Eusebius of Caesarea. *The History of the Church from Christ to Constantine*. Translated by G. A. Williamson and edited by Andrew Louth. Rev. ed. New York: Penguin, 1989.

Evans, Jonathan, et al. "Religion and Spirituality in East Asian Societies." Pew Research Center, June 17, 2024. https://www.pewresearch.org/religion/2024/06/17/religion-and-spirituality-in-east-asian-societies/.

Evans, Richard. *A History of Pergamum: Beyond Hellenistic Kingship*. New York: Continuum, 2012.

Fairchild, Mark R. *Christian Origins in Ephesus and Asia Minor*. 2nd ed. Peabody: Hendrickson, 2017.

Fant, Clyde E., and Mitchell G. Reddish. *A Guide to Biblical Sites in Greece and Turkey*. New York: Oxford University Press, 2003.

Farah, Warrick, ed. "The Homophilous Unit Paradox: Church Planting Movements Within and Beyond the Oikos." *International Journal of Frontier Missiology* 40 (2023) 69–77.

———. *Motus Dei: The Movement of God to Disciple the Nations*. Littleton, CO: William Carey, 2021.

Feldman, Louis H. *Jew and Gentile in the Ancient World: Attitudes and Interactions from Alexander to Justinian*. Princeton: Princeton University Press, 1993.

Fine, Steven. "Synagogues as Foci of Multi-Religious and Ideological Confrontation? The Case of the Sardis Synagogue." In *Jerusalem and Other Holy Places as Foci of Multireligious and Ideological Confrontation*, edited by Pieter B. Hartog et al., 97–108. Leiden: Brill, 2021.

———. "Synagogues in the Greco-Roman World." In *Jewish Religious Architecture: From Biblical Israel to Modern Judaism*, edited by Steven Fine, 96–121. Leiden: Brill, 2019.

Fisher, Greg. *Rome, Persia, and Arabia: Shaping the Middle East from Pompey to Muhammad*. London: Routledge, 2020.

Flemming, Rebecca. "Galen and the Christians: Texts and Authority in the Second Century AD." In *Christianity in the Second Century: Themes and Developments*, edited by James Carleton Paget and Judith Lieu, 171–87. Cambridge: Cambridge University Press, 2017.

Foerster, Gideon. "Remains of a Synagogue at Corinth." In *Ancient Synagogues Revealed*, edited by Lee I. Levine, 185. Jerusalem: Israel Exploration Society, 1982.

Foss, Clive. "The Persians in Asia Minor and the End of Antiquity." *The English Historical Review* 90 (1975) 721–47.

Fox, Robin Lane. *Pagans and Christians*. New York: Penguin, 1986.

Freeman, Charles. "The Emperor's State of Grace." *History Today* 51 (2001) 19.

Friesen, Steven J. *Twice Neokoros: Ephesus, Asia and the Cult of the Flavian Imperial Family*. Leiden: Brill, 1986.

Galen. *Hygiene*. Vol. 1. Edited and translated by Ian Johnston. LCL 535. Cambridge: Harvard University Press, 2018.

Garipzanov, Ildar H. *Graphic Signs of Authority in Late Antiquity and the Early Middle Ages, 300–900*. Oxford: Oxford University Press, 2018.

Garrison, David. "10 FAQs: Church Planting Movements." *Mission Frontiers* 33 (2011) 9–11.

———. "Church Planting Movements Are Consistent with the Teachings and Practices of the New Testament: A Response to Jackson Wu." *Global Missiology* 1 (2014) 1–8. http://ojs.globalmissiology.org/index.php/english/article/view/1713/3800.

———. *Church Planting Movements: How God is Redeeming the World*. Monument, CO: WIGTake, 2012.

———. *Inside Church Planting Movements: What 25 Years of Assessments Reveals*. Monument, CO: WIGTake, 2025.

Gasque, Ward W. *Sir William Ramsay: Archaeologist and New Testament Scholar. A Survey of His Contribution to the Study of the New Testament*. Grand Rapids: Baker, 1966.

Gehring, Roger W. *House Church and Mission: The Importance of Household Structures in Early Christianity*. Peabody, MA: Hendrickson, 2004.

Gradel, Ittai. *Emperor Worship and Roman Religion*. Oxford: Oxford University Press, 2004.

Graham, Elizabeth. "Mission Archaeology." *Annual Review of Anthropology* 27 (1998) 25–62.

Graves, David E. "Local References in the Letter of Smyrna (Rv 2:8–11), Part 2: Historical Background." *Bible and Spade* 19 (2006) 23–29.

Gray, Stephen, and Franklin Dumond. *Legacy Churches*. Apple Valley: Churchsmart, 2009.

Graziadio, Giampaolo. "The Importance of Mouth Coverings in the Late Cypriot Burial Customs." In *Identity and Connectivity: Proceedings of the 16th Symposium on Mediterranean Archaeology*, edited by Luca Bombardieri et al., 345–51. Oxford: Archaeopress, 2013.

Greatrex, Geoffrey, and Samuel N. C. Lieu. *The Roman Eastern Frontier and the Persian Wars. Part II, AD 363–630: A Narrative Sourcebook*. London: Routledge, 2002.

Green, Joel. *The Gospel of Luke*. Grand Rapids: Eerdmans, 1997.

Hacker, Randy. *House Churches in Post-Communist Europe: Qualitative Interviews from Poland with a View to Informing Missiological Practice*. Eugene: Pickwick, 2023.

Hadas-Lebel, Mireille. *Philo of Alexandria: A Thinker in the Jewish Diaspora*. Leiden: Brill, 2012.

Hammer, Keir E., and Michele Murray. "Acquaintances, Supporters, and Competitors: Evidence of Inter-Connectedness and Rivalry Among the Religious Groups in Sardis." In *Religious Rivalries and the Struggle for Success in Sardis and Smyrna*, edited by Richard S. Ascough, 175–96. Waterloo: Canadian Corporation for Studies in Religion, 2016.

Harland, Philip A. *Associations, Synagogues, and Congregations: Claiming a Place in Ancient Mediterranean Society*. Minneapolis: Fortress, 2013.

———. "Banqueting Values in the Associations: Rhetoric and Reality." In *Meals in the Early Christian World: Social Formation, Experimentation, and Conflict at the Table*, edited by Dennis E. Smith and Hal E. Taussig, 73–85. New York: Palgrave, 2012.

———, trans. "Dedication of an Altar for a Synagogue of Small-wares Dealers (I-II CE)." Associations in the Greco-Roman World. https://philipharland.com/greco-roman-associations/dedication-for-a-synagogue-of-small-wares-dealers-i-ii-ce/.

———, trans. "Dedication of an Altar to Dionysos Kathegemon by a Company (II CE)." Associations in the Greco-Roman World." https://philipharland.com/greco-roman-associations/dedication-of-an-altar-to-dionysos-kathegemon-by-a-company-ii-ce/.

———, trans. "Dedication to Zeus and Hera as a Vow by a Society (82 CE)." Associations in the Greco-Roman World. https://philipharland.com/greco-roman-associations/dedication-to-zeus-and-hera-as-a-vow-by-a-society-82-ce/.

———, trans. "Divine Instructions for the Household Association of Dionysios (Late II–Early I BCE)." Associations in the Greco-Roman World. https://philipharland.com/greco-roman-associations/divine-instructions-for-the-household-association-of-dionysios/.

———. "Honoring the Emperor or Assailing the Beast: Participating in Civic Life Among Associations (Jewish, Christian, and Other) in Asia Minor and the Apocalypse of John." *Journal for the Study of the New Testament* 77 (2000) 99–121.

———, trans. "Honors by a Society for the Priestess with a Relief." Associations in the Greco-Roman World. https://philipharland.com/greco-roman-associations/honors-by-a-society-for-a-priestess-with-a-relief/.

———, trans. "Honors by Civic Institutions for a Hierophant of Dionysos Kathegemon (ca. 250 CE)." Associations in the Greco-Roman World. https://philipharland.com/greco-roman-associations/honors-by-civic-institutions-for-a-hierophant-of-dionysos-kathegemon-ii-ce/.

———, trans. "Honors by Physicians for the Chief-Physician of Emperor Trajan (102-114 CE)." Associations in the Greco-Roman World. https://philipharland.com/greco-roman-associations/165-honors-by-physicians-for-the-chief-physician-of-emperor-trajan/.

———, trans. "Honors for an Initiate of Dionysos Kathegemon (II CE)." Associations in the Greco-Roman World." https://philipharland.com/greco-roman-associations/honors-for-the-superintendent-of-the-initiates-of-dionysos-kathegemon-ii-ce/.

———, trans. "Regulations of an Association of Zeus Hypsistos (69–58 BCE)." Associations in the Greco-Roman World. https://philipharland.com/greco-roman-associations/295-regulations-of-an-association-of-zeus-hypsistos/.

Hauerwas, Stanley. *Matthew*. Grand Rapids: Brazos, 2006.

Hays, J. Daniel. *The Ichthus Christogram and Other Early Christian Symbols*. Grand Rapids: Kregel Academic, 2025.

Hefele, Charles Joseph. *A History of the Councils of the Church*. Vols. 1–5. Aeterna, 2014. Originally published in 1883 by T&T Clark.

Heine, Ronald E. *The Montanist Oracles and Testimonia*. Macon: Mercer University Press, 1989.

Hemer, Colin J. *The Letters to the Seven Churches of Asia: In Their Local Setting*. Grand Rapids: Eerdmans, 1986.

Herodotus. *The Persian Wars*. Vol. 1. Translated by A. D. Godley. LCL 117. Cambridge: Harvard University Press, 1920.

Hiebert, Paul G., et al. *Understanding Folk Religion: A Christian Response to Popular Beliefs and Practices*. Grand Rapids: Baker, 2000.

Hildebrandt, Frank. "The Emperor Claudius in Western Asia: Portraits, Statues, and Inscriptions." In *Sculpture in Roman Asia Minor*, edited by Maria Aurenhammer, 219–28. Vienna: Österreichisches Archäologisches Institut, 2013.

Hippocrates. *Places in Man. Glands. Fleshes. Prorrhetic 1–2. Physician. Use of Liquids. Ulcers. Haemorrhoids and Fistulas*. Edited and translated by Paul Potter. LCL 482. Cambridge: Harvard University Press, 1995.

Hunt, David. "Christianising the Roman Empire: The Evidence of the Code." In *The Theodosian Code: Studies in the Imperial Law of Antiquity*, edited by Jill Harries and Ian Wood, 143–58. London: Duckworth, 1993.

Hurtado, Larry W. *The Earliest Christian Artifacts: Manuscripts and Christian Origins*. Grand Rapids: Eerdmans, 2006.

Huttner, Ulrich. *Early Christianity in the Lycus Valley*. Leiden: Brill, 2013.

Iamblichus. *Life of Pythagorus, or Pythagoric Life: Accompanied by Fragments of the Ethical Writings of Certain Pythagorians in the Doric Dialect*. Translated by Thomas Taylor. Project Gutenberg. https://www.gutenberg.org/files/63300/63300-h/63300-h.htm.

Ignatius of Antioch. *1 Clement*. Pages 34–153 in *1 Clement. 2 Clement. Ignatius. Polycarp. Didache*. Vol. 1 of *The Apostolic Fathers*. Edited and translated by Bart D. Ehrman. LCL 24. Cambridge: Harvard University Press, 2003

———. *Letter to the Ephesians*. Pages 218–39 in *1 Clement. 2 Clement. Ignatius. Polycarp. Didache*. Vol. 1 of *The Apostolic Fathers*. Edited and translated by Bart D. Ehrman. LCL 24. Cambridge: Harvard University Press, 2003.

———. *To the Magnesians*. Pages 240–55 in *1 Clement. 2 Clement. Ignatius. Polycarp. Didache*. Vol. 1 of *The Apostolic Fathers*. Edited and translated by Bart D. Ehrman. LCL 24. Cambridge: Harvard University Press, 2003.

———. *To the Smyrnaeans*. Pages 294–309 in *1 Clement. 2 Clement. Ignatius. Polycarp. Didache*. Vol. 1 of *The Apostolic Fathers*. Edited and translated by Bart D. Ehrman. LCL 24. Cambridge: Harvard University Press, 2003.

Introvigne, Massimo. *Inside the Church of Almighty God: The Most Persecuted Religious Movement in China*. New York: Oxford University Press, 2020.

Irenaeus. *Five Books of St. Irenaeus, Bishop of Lyons: Against Heresies with the Fragments That Remain of His other Works*. Translated by John Keble. Oxford: James Parker, 1872.

Israelowich, Ido. *Society, Medicine and Religion in the Sacred Tales of Aelius Aristides*. Leiden: Brill, 2012.

Jenkins, Philip. *The Lost History of Christianity: The Thousand Year Golden Age of the Church in the Middle East, Africa, and Asia—and How It Died*. New York: HarperOne, 2008.

Jones, Bryce C. *Matthean and Lukan Special Material: A Brief Introduction with Texts in Greek and English*. Eugene: Wipf and Stock, 2011.

Jones, Prudence, and Nigel Pennick. *A History of Pagan Europe*. London: Routledge, 1995.

Josephus, Flavius. *The Works of Flavius Josephus, the Learned and Authentic Jewish Historian, and Celebrated Warrior*. Translated by William Whiston. London: Thomas Tegg, 1828.

Justin Martyr. *First and Second Apologies*. Translated by Leslie William Barnard. Ancient Christian Writers 56. New York: Paulist, 1997.

Kampmann, Ursula. "Homonoia Politics in Asia Minor: The Example of Pergamon." In *Pergamon: Citadel of the Gods*, edited by Helmut Koester, 373–93. Harrisburg: Trinity, 1998.

Kästner, Volker. "The Architecture of the Great Altar of Pergamon." In *Pergamon: Citadel of the Gods*, edited by Helmut Koester, 137–62. Harrisburg: Trinity, 1998.

Keener, Craig S. *Acts: An Exegetical Commentary*. 4 vols. Grand Rapids: Baker Academic, 2012.

———. *The IVP Bible Background Commentary: New Testament*. Downers Grove: InterVarsity, 2014.

Ketubbot. Sefaria. https://www.sefaria.org/Ketubot?tab=contents.

King, Rachel, and Mark McGranaghan. "The Archaeology and Materiality of Mission in Southern Africa: Introduction." *Journal of Southern African Studies* 44 (2018) 629–39.

Kloppenborg, John S., trans. "Aphrodito Village." Associations in the Greco-Roman World. https://philipharland.com/greco-roman-associations/regulations-of-an-association-of-fishermen-538-ce/.

———. *Christ's Associations: Connecting and Belonging in the Ancient City*. New Haven: Yale University Press, 2019.

———. "Collegia and Thiasoi: Issues in Function, Taxonomy, and Membership." In *Voluntary Associations in the Graeco-Roman World*, edited by John S. Kloppenborg and Stephen G. Wilson, 16–30. London: Routledge, 1996.

Knibbe, Dieter. *Der Staatsmarkt: Die Inschriften des Prytaneions: Die Kureteninschriften und sonstige religiöse Texte*. Vienna: Österreichische Akademie der Wissenschaften, 1981.

Knoll, Mark. "The Challenge of Contemporary Church History, the Dilemmas of Modern History, and Missiology to the Rescue," *Missiology* 24 (1996) 47–64.

Koester, Craig R. "The Message to Laodicea and the Problem of Its Local Context: A Study of the Imagery in Rev. 3:14–22." *New Testament Studies* 49 (2003) 407–24.

Kontogianni, Bella. "Skeleton of Ancient Woman Lying on Her Bronze Bed Found in Greece." Greek Reporter, May 8, 2022. https://greekreporter.com/2022/05/08/stunning-archaeological-finds-greece-dig-reveal-ties-to-apollo/.

Korner, Ralph. "Συναγωγή and Semi-Public Associations." In *Greco-Roman Associations, Deities, and Early Christianity*, edited by Bruce W. Longenecker, 225–46. Waco: Baylor University Press, 2022.

———. *The Origin and Meaning of Ekklesia in the Early Jesus Movement*. Leiden: Brill, 2017.

Kroll, John H. "The Greek Inscriptions of the Sardis Synagogue." *Harvard Theological Review* 94 (2001) 5–55.

Kuecker, Aaron. "Luke." In *T&T Clark Social Identity Commentary on the New Testament*, edited by J. Brian Tucker and Aaron Kuecker, 103–68. New York: T&T Clark, 2020.

Lafferty, Jerry Todd. "Developing Pastors and Teachers Within the Fivefold Framework of Ephesians 4:11 to Sustain Church Planting Movements." DMiss diss., Malaysia Baptist Theological Seminary, 2020.

Laing, Gordon J. *Survivals of Roman Religion*. New York: Longmans, Green and Co., 1931.

Larkin, William J., Jr. *Acts*. Downers Grove, IL: InterVarsity, 1995.

Levine, Amy-Jill, and Ben Witherington III. *The Gospel of Luke: The New Cambridge Bible Commentary*. New York: Cambridge University Press, 2018.

Levine, Lee I. *The Ancient Synagogue: The First Thousand Years*. New Haven: Yale University Press, 2008.

Lifeway Research. *Evangelism Explosion Study of American Christians' Openness to Talking About Faith: A Survey of 1,011 Americans*. Aug. 4, 2022. https://research.lifeway.com/wp-content/uploads/2022/08/Evangelism-Explosion-Survey-of-American-Christians-Report-8_4_22.pdf.

Long, Justin D. "1% of the World: A Macroanalysis of 1,369 Movements to Christ." *Mission Frontiers* 42 (2020) 37–42.

———. "How Movements Count." In *Motus Dei: The Movement of God to Disciple the Nations*, edited by Warrick Farah, 68–78. Littleton, CO: William Carey, 2021.

Louw, Johannes P., and Eugene A. Nida, eds. *Greek-English Lexicon of the New Testament Based on Semantic Domains*. New York: United Bible Societies, 1988.

Magness, Jodi. "The Date of the Sardis Synagogue in Light of the Numismatic Evidence." *American Journal of Archaeology* 109 (2005) 443–75.

Maguire, Henry. *Earth and Ocean: The Terrestrial World in Early Byzantine Art*. University Park: Pennsylvania State University Press, 1990.

Mason, Steve N. "Philosophiai: Graeco-Roman, Judean and Christian." In *Voluntary Associations in the Graeco-Roman World*, edited by John S. Kloppenborg and Stephen G. Wilson, 31–58. London: Routledge, 1996.

Massey, John David. "Theological Education and Southern Baptist Missions Strategy in the Twenty-First Century." *Southwestern Journal of Theology* 57 (2014) 5–16.

Matthews, A. "Person of Peace Methodology in Church Planting: A Critical Analysis." *Missiology: An International Review* 47 (2019) 187–99.

McDowell, Gavin, et al., eds. *Diversity and Rabbinization: Jewish Texts and Societies Between 400 and 1,000 CE*. Cambridge: Open Book.

McGinn, Sheila E. "The 'Montanist' Oracles and Prophetic Theology." *Studia Patristica* 31 (1997) 128–35.

McKnight, Scot. *A Light Among the Gentiles: Jewish Missionary Activity in the Second Temple Period*. Minneapolis: Fortress, 1991.

McKnight, Scot, and Cody Matchett. *Revelation for the Rest of Us: A Prophetic Call to Follow Jesus as a Dissident Disciple*. Grand Rapids: Zondervan, 2023.

Melito of Sardis. *On Pascha and Fragments*. Translated and edited by Stuart George Hall. Oxford Early Christian Texts. Oxford: Clarendon, 1979.

Meeks, Wayne. *The First Urban Christians: The Social World of the Apostle Paul*. New Haven: Yale University Press, 1983.

Metzger, Bruce. *A Textual Commentary on the Greek New Testament*. Stuttgart: United Bible Societies, 1971.

Mitchell, Stephen. "An Apostle to Ankara from the New Jerusalem." *Scripta Classica Israelica* 24 (2005) 207–23.

———. "The Cult of Theos Hypsistos Between Pagans, Jews, and Christians." In *Pagan Monotheism in Late Antiquity*, edited by Polymnia Athanassiadi and Michael Frede, 81–148. Oxford: Clarendon, 1999.

———. "Epigraphic Display and the Emergence of Christian Identity in the Epigraphy of Rural Asia Minor." In *Öffentlichkeit–Monument–Text*, edited by Werner Eck and Peter Funke, 275–98. Auctarium Series Nova 4. Berlin: Walter de Gruyter, 2014.

———. "Further Thoughts on the Cult of Theos Hypsistos." In *One God: Pagan Monotheism in the Roman Empire*, edited by Stephen Mitchell and Peter Van Nuffelen, 167–190. Cambridge: Cambridge University Press, 2010.

———. *The Rise of the Church*. Vol. 2 of *Anatolia: Land, Men, and Gods in Asia Minor*. Oxford: Clarendon, 1993.

Morris, Leon. *Luke: An Introduction and Commentary*. Grand Rapids: Eerdmans, 1997.

Murray, Michele. "Down the Road from Sardis: Adaptive Religious Structures and Religious Interactions in the Ancient City of Priene." In *Religious Rivalries and the Struggle for Success in Sardis and Smyrna*, edited by Richard S. Ascough, 197–210. Waterloo: Canadian Corporation for Studies in Religion, 2016.

Musurillo, Herbert. *The Acts of the Christian Martyrs: Introduction, Texts, and Translations*. Oxford: Oxford University Press, 1972.

Nagy, Gregory. "The Library of Pergamon as a Classical Model." In *Pergamon: Citadel of the Gods*, edited by Helmut Koester, 185–232. Harrisburg: Trinity, 1998.

The Nicene and Post-Nicene Fathers, Series 2 (*NPNF*[2]). Edited by Philip Schaff and Henry Wace. 1893. 14 vols. Repr., Peabody, MA: Hendrickson, 1999.

Noble, O. Alan. "Let the Cultural Christians Come unto Jesus." *Christianity Today*, April 2024. https://www.christianitytoday.com/2024/04/let-cultural-christians-come-unto-jesus-richard-dawkins/.

Noll, Mark. "The Challenge of Contemporary Church History, the Dilemmas of Modern History, and Missiology to the Rescue." *Missiology: An International Review* 24 (1996) 47–64.

Oden, Thomas C. *The African Memory of Mark: Reassessing Early Church Tradition*. Downers Grove, IL: InterVarsity, 2011.

Ogereau, Julien M. "Methodological Considerations in Using Epigraphic Evidence to Determine the Socioeconomic Context of the Early Christians." Pages 245–76 in *Methodological Foundations*. Edited by James R. Harrison and L. L. Welborn. Vol. 1 of *The First Urban Churches*. Atlanta: SBL Press, 2015.

Origen. *The Song of Songs: Commentary and Homilies*. Translated and annotated by R. P. Lawson. New York: Newman, 1957.

Osborne, Grant R. *Revelation*. Grand Rapids: Baker, 2002.

Osiek, Carolyn, and David L. Balch. *Families in the New Testament World: Households and House Churches*. Louisville: Westminster John Knox, 1997.

Ovid. *Metamorphoses*. Vol. 2. Translated by Frank Justus Miller. Revised by G. P. Goold. LCL 43. Cambridge: Harvard University Press, 1916.

The Packard Humanities Institute. "Searchable Greek Inscriptions." https://epigraphy.packhum.org.

Pao, David W. *Colossians and Philemon*. Grand Rapids: Zondervan, 2012.

Parker, Robert. *Religion in Roman Phrygia: From Polytheism to Christianity*. Oakland: University of California Press, 2023.

Perseus Digital Library. "Word Frequency for συναγωγη." https://www.perseus.tufts.edu/hopper/wordfreq?lookup=sunagwgh/&lang=greek&sort=max.

Petrantoni, Giuseppe. *Corpus of Nabataean Aramaic-Greek Inscriptions*. Venezia: Edizioni Ca' Foscari, 2021.

Philo of Alexandria. *On Drunkenness*. In The Complete Works of Philo, translated by Charles Duke Yonge, 541–93. Hastings, East Sussex: Delphi Classics, 2017.

———. *On the Embassy to Gaius*. Vol. 10 of *Philo*. Translated by F. H. Colson. LCL 379. Cambridge: Harvard University Press, 1962.

———. *The Works of Philo Judeus—The Contemporary of Josephus*, translated by Charles D. Yonge. 4 vols. London: H. G. Bohn, 1854–1890.

Philostratus, Eunapius. *Apollonius of Tyana*. Vol. 1. Edited and translated by Christopher P. Jones. LCL 16. Cambridge: Harvard University Press, 2005.

———. *Lives of the Sophists. Lives of Philosophers and Sophists*. Edited and translated by Graeme Miles and Han Baltussen. LCL 134. Cambridge: Harvard University Press, 2023.

Pleket, H. W., and R. S. Stroud, eds. *Supplementum Epigraphicum Graecum*. Vol. 33. Amsterdam: Gieben, 1983.

Pliny the Elder. *Natural History*. Vol. 2. Translated by H. Rackham. LCL 352. Cambridge: Harvard University Press, 1942.

Pliny the Younger. *Letters*. Vol. 2. Translated by Betty Radice. LCL 59. Cambridge: Harvard University Press, 1969.

Plutarch. *Pericles and Fabius Maximus. Nicias and Crassus*. Vol. 3 of *Lives*. Translated by Bernadotte Perrin. Cambridge: Harvard University Press, 1916.

Polycarp. *Letter of Polycarp*. Pages 332–404 in *1 Clement. 2 Clement. Ignatius. Polycarp. Didache*. Vol. 1 of *The Apostolic Fathers*. Edited and translated by Bart D. Ehrman. LCL 24. Cambridge: Harvard University Press, 2003.

Porphyry. *Life of Pythagorus*. The Tertullian Project. https://www.tertullian.org/fathers/porphyry_life_of_pythagoras_02_text.htm.

Powell, Mark Allen. *Fortress Introduction to the Gospels*. Minneapolis: Fortress, 2019.

Price, S. R. F. "Between Man and God: Sacrifice in the Roman Imperial Cult." *The Journal of Roman Studies* 70 (1980) 28–43.

Proctor, Travis W. *Demonic Bodies and the Dark Ecologies of Early Christian Culture*. New York: Oxford University Press, 2022.

Ramsay, William H. *The Bearing of Recent Discovery on the Trustworthiness of the New Testament*. London: Hodder and Stoughton, 1915.

———. *The Letters to the Seven Churches of Asia*. New York: Hodder and Stoughton, 1905.

Ramsay, William M. *The Historical Geography of Asia Minor*. London: John Murray, 1890.

———. *The Teachings of Paul in Terms of the Present Day*. London: Hodder and Stoughton, 1913.

Rasimus, Tuomas. "Revisiting the Ichthys: A Suggestion Concerning the Origins of Christological Fish Symbolism." In *Mystery and Secrecy in the Nag Hammadi Collection and Other Ancient Literature: Ideas and Practices*, 479–500. Leiden: Brill, 2012.

Rathmayr, Elisabeth. "The Significance of Sculptures with Associated Inscriptions in Private Houses in Ephesos, Pergamon and Beyond." In *Inscriptions in the Private Sphere in the Greco-Roman World*, edited by Rebecca Benefiel and Peter Keegan, 146–78. Leiden: Brill, 2015.

Rautman, Marcus. "The Color-Inlaid 'Champlevé' Reliefs of the Synagogue at Sardis." *Bulletin of the American Schools of Oriental Research* 383 (2020) 97–113.

Reed, Jonathan L. *What Archaeology Reveals About the First Christians*. New York: HarperCollins, 2007.

Rhodes, Matt. "Advancing Conversations About Proclamational and Movements Methodologies." *Global Missiology* 19 (2022) 18–30. http://ojs.globalmissiology.org/index.php/english/article/view/2692/6655.

Richardson, Peter. "Early Synagogues as Collegia in the Diaspora and Palestine." In *Voluntary Associations in the Graeco-Roman World*, edited by John S. Kloppenborg and Stephen G. Wilson, 90–109. London: Routledge, 1996.

Rogers, Gideon M. "Demetrios of Ephesos: Silversmith and *Neopoios*?" *Belleten* 50 (1986) 876—83. https://dergipark.org.tr/en/download/article-file/1937097.

Rogers, Guy MacLean. *The Mysteries of Artemis of Ephesos: Cult, Polis, and Change in the Graeco-Roman World*. New Haven: Yale University Press, 2012.

Ross, Robert. "The Archaeology of Mission: Afterword." *Journal of Southern African Studies* 44 (2018) 743–47.

Runesson, Anders. *The Origins of the Synagogue: A Socio-Historical Study*. Stockholm: Almqvist & Wiksell International, 2001.

Runesson, Anders, et al. *The Ancient Synagogue from Its Origins to 200 C.E.: A Source Book*. Leiden: Brill, 2008.

Rushdoony, Rousas J. *The Foundations of Social Order*. Philadelphia: Presbyterian and Reformed, 1968.

Salameen, Zeyad al-. "A New Dedicatory Nabataean Inscription Dated to AD 53." *Arabian Epigraphic Notes* 2 (2016) 151–60.

Sand, Shlomo. *The Invention of the Jewish People*. Translated by Yael Lotan. London: Verso, 2020.

Saradi-Mendelovici, Helen. "Christian Attitudes Toward Pagan Monuments in Late Antiquity and Their Legacy in Later Byzantine Centuries." *Dumbarton Oaks Papers* 44 (1990) 47–61.

Schnabel, Eckhard J. *Early Christian Mission: Paul and the Early Church*. Downers Grove, IL: InterVarsity, 2004.

Schowalter, Daniel N. "Seeking Shelter in Roman Corinth: Archaeology and the Placement of Paul's Communities." In *Corinth in Context: Comparative Studies on Religion and Society*, edited by Steven J. Friesen et al., 327–42. Leiden: Brill, 2010.

———. "The Zeus Philios and Trajan Temple: A Context of Imperial Honors." In *Pergamon: Citadel of the Gods*, edited by Helmut Koester, 233–49. Harrisburg: Trinity, 1998.

Seland, Torrey. "Philo and the Clubs and Associations of Alexandria." In *Voluntary Associations in the Graeco-Roman World*, edited by John S. Kloppenborg and Stephen G. Wilson, 110–27. London: Routledge, 1996.

Shilling, Brooke. "The Many-Eyed Archangels in Early Byzantine Art." In *The Eloquence of Art: Essays in Honour of Henry Maguire*, edited by Andrea Olsen Lam and Rossitza Schroeder, 350–65. London: Routledge, 2020.

Şimşek, Celal. "Archaeological Site of Laodikeia." In *10. Yilinda Laodikeia (2003–2013 Yillari)*, edited by Celal Şimşek, 7–32. Laodikeia Çalişmalari 3. Istanbul: Ege, 2014.

Small, Stuart G. P. "On Allegory in Homer." *The Classical Journal* 44 (1949) 423–30.

Smith, Steve. "The Oikos Hammer—You and Your Household." *Mission Frontiers* 40 (2018) 44–47.

Smith, Steve, and Ying Kai. *T4T: A Discipleship Re-Revolution*. Monument, CO: WIGTake, 2011.

Smith, William, ed. *A Dictionary of Greek and Roman Biography and Mythology*. London: Taylor and Walton, 1849.

Smither, Edward. *Mission in the Early Church*. Cambridge: James Clarke, 2014.

Stambaugh, John E., and David L. Balch. *The New Testament in Its Social Environment*. Philadelphia: Westminster, 1986.

Stegemann, Ekkehard W., and Wolfgang Stregemann. *The Jesus Movement: A Social History of Its First Century*. Translated by O. C. Dean Jr. Minneapolis: Fortress, 1999.

Stetzer, Ed. "What 9Marks Purists Should Know About Church Planting." *Church Matters: A Journal for Pastors* 2 (2023) 43–46. https://www.9marks.org/article/what-9marks-purists-should-know-about-church-planting-2/.

Stott, John R. W. *The Message of Galatians*. Downers Grove, IL: InterVarsity, 1968.

Strabo. *Geography*. Vol. 5. Translated by Horace Leonard Jones. LCL 211. Cambridge, MA: Harvard University Press, 1928.

Suetonius. *Lives of the Caesars*. 2 vols. Translated by J. C. Rolfe. LCL 31 and LCL 38. Cambridge: Harvard University Press, 1914.

Tabbernee, William. "Asia Minor and Cyprus." In *Early Christianity in Contexts: An Exploration Across Cultures and Continents*, edited by William Tabbernee, 261–320. Grand Rapids: Baker Academic, 2014.

———. *Fake Prophecy and Polluted Sacraments: Ecclesiastical and Imperial Reactions to Montanism*. Leiden: Brill, 2007.

———. *Montanist Inscriptions and Testimonia: Epigraphic Sources Illustrating the History of Montanism*. Macon: Mercer University Press, 1997.

———. "The Montanist Oracles Reexamined." In *Talking God in Society: Multidisciplinary (Re)constructions of Ancient (Con)texts. Festschrift for Peter Lampe*, edited by Ute E. Eisen and Heidrun E. Mader, 317–44. Göttingen: Vandenhoeck & Ruprecht, 2020.

Tacitus. *Annals*. Translated by John Jackson. LCL 322. Cambridge: Harvard University Press, 1937.

———. *Histories: Books 4–5. Annals: Books 1–3*. Translated by Clifford H. Moore and John Jackson. LCL 249. Cambridge: Harvard University Press, 1931.

Terry, Milton S., trans. *The Sibylline Oracles*. New York: Eaton and Mains, 1899.

Thür, Hilke. "Sacred Space for Dionysos in Ephesos and the House of C. Fl. Furius Aptus." In *Religion in Ephesos Reconsidered: Archaeology of Space, Structures, and Objects*, edited by Daniel N. Schowalter et al., 135–57. Leiden: Brill, 2020.

Toch, Michael. "Jewish Demographics and Economics at the Onset of the European Middle Ages." In *Diversity and Rabbinization: Jewish Texts and Societies Between 400 and 1000 CE*, edited by Gavin McDowell et al., 323–36. Cambridge: Open Book, 2021.

Toynbee, J. M. C. *Animals in Roman Life and Art*. Baltimore: Johns Hopkins University Press, 1973.

Trebilco, Paul. *Jewish Communities in Asia Minor*. Cambridge: Cambridge University Press, 1991.

———. "The Jewish Community in Ephesos and Its Interaction with Christ-Believers in the First Century CE and Beyond." Pages 93–126 in *Ephesos*. Edited by James R. Harrison and L. L. Welborn. Vol. 3 of *The First Urban Churches*. Atlanta: SBL Press, 2018.

Vagi, David. "Tiberius Claudius Drusus (d. AD 20), Son of Claudius and Urgulanilla." *American Journal of Numismatics* 22 (2010) 81–92.

Waida, Manabu. "Birds." In *The Encyclopedia of Religion*, edited by Lindsay Jones, 2:947–49. New York: Macmillian, 2005.

Walls, Andrew F. "Eusebius Tries Again: Reconceiving the Study of Christian History." *International Bulletin of Mission Research* 24 (2000) 105–11.

Walzer, Richard. *Galen on Jews and Christians*. London: Oxford University Press, 1949.

Weddle, David L. *Sacrifice in Judaism, Christianity, and Islam*. New York: New York University Press, 2017.

White, L. Michael. *Building God's House in the Roman World: Architectural Adaptation Among Pagans, Jews, and Christians*. Vol. 1 of *The Social Origins of Christian Architecture*. Valley Forge, PA: Trinity International, 1990.

———. *Texts and Monuments for the Christian Domus Ecclesiae in Its Environment*. Vol. 2 of *The Social Origins of Christian Architecture*. Valley Forge, PA: Trinity International, 1997.

Wilken, Robert Louis. *The Spirit of Early Christian Thought: Seeking the Face of God*. New Haven: Yale University Press, 2003.

Wilson, Mark. "The Ancient Synagogues of Asia Minor and Greece." In *Jewish Religious Architecture: From Biblical Israel to Modern Judaism*, edited by Steven Fine, 122–33. Leiden: Brill, 2019.

———. *Biblical Turkey: A Guide to the Jewish and Christian Sites of Asia Minor*. Istanbul: Ege, 2020.

———. "Did the Laodiceans Drink Lukewarm Water? A Hydrological Inquiry into the Temperature Metaphor of Revelation 3:15–16." *Lycus Journal* 8 (2023) 72–87.

Wilson, Stephen G. "Voluntary Associations: An Overview." In *Voluntary Associations in the Graeco-Roman World*, edited by John S. Kloppenborg and Stephen G. Wilson, 1–15. London: Routledge, 1996.

Witherington, Ben, III. *The Letters to Philemon, the Colossians, and the Ephesians: A Socio-Rhetorical Commentary on the Captivity Epistles*. Grand Rapids: Eerdmans, 2007.

Wright, N. T. *The New Testament and the People of God*. Minneapolis: Fortress, 1992.

———. *Paul: A Biography*. New York: HarperOne, 2018.

Wright, N. T., and Michael F. Bird. *The New Testament in Its World: An Introduction to the History, Literature, and Theology of the First Christians*. Grand Rapids: Zondervan, 2019.

Wu, Jackson. "The Influence of Culture on the Evolution of Mission Methods: Using 'Church Planting Movements' as a Case Study." *Global Missiology* 1 (2014) 1–11. http://ojs.globalmissiology.org/index.php/english/article/view/1712/3797.

Vasilkov, Ya. "The Peacock as the Bird of Paradise: A Comparative Study." *Etnografia* 2 (2023) 74–92.

Yamauchi, Edwin M. *New Testament Cities in Western Asia Minor*. Eugene: Wipf and Stock, 1980.

Yegül, Fikret, and Diane Favro. *Roman Architecture and Urbanism: From the Origins to Late Antiquity*. Cambridge: Cambridge University Press, 2019.

Zimmermann, Norbert. "Archaeological Evidence for Private Worship and Domestic Religion in Terrace House 2 at Ephesos." In *Religion in Ephesos Reconsidered: Archaeology of Space, Structures, and Objects*, edited by Daniel N. Schowalter et al., 211–29. Leiden: Brill, 2020.

www.ingramcontent.com/pod-product-compliance
Lightning Source LLC
LaVergne TN
LVHW050615100826
845148LV00011B/1603
9798385235780